HOW RUSSIA REALLY WORKS

CULTURE AND SOCIETY AFTER SOCIALISM

A SERIES EDITED BY
Bruce Grant
Nancy Ries

How Russia Really Works

The Informal Practices That Shaped Post-Soviet Politics and Business

Alena V. Ledeneva

Cornell University Press
Ithaca and London

First published 2006 by Cornell University Press

Printed in the United States of America

Library of Congress Cataloging-in-Publication Data

Ledeneva, Alena V., 1964–
    How Russia really works : the informal practices that shaped post-Soviet politics and business / Alena V. Ledeneva.
        p. cm.—(Culture and society after socialism)
    Includes bibliographical references and index.
    ISBN-13: 978-0-8014-4346-6 (cloth : alk. paper)
    ISBN-10: 0-8014-4346-6 (cloth : alk. paper)
    ISBN-13: 978-0-8014-7352-4 (pbk. : alk. paper)
    ISBN-10: 0-8014-7352-7 (pbk. : alk. paper)
    1. Political corruption—Russia (Federation)   2. Political cul-
ture—Russia (Federation)   3. Corporations—Corrupt practices—Russia (Federation)   4. Corporate culture—Russia (Federation)   5. Social networks—Russia (Federation)   6. Business
networks—Russia (Federation)   7. Russia (Federation)—Politics
and government—1991- .   8. Russia (Federation)—Economic
conditions—1991- .   I. Title.   II. Series.
JN6695.A55C639 2006
320.947—dc22

2006023279

Cornell University Press strives to use environmentally responsible suppliers and materials to the fullest extent possible in the publishing of its books. Such materials include vegetable-based, low-VOC inks and acid-free papers that are recycled, totally chlorine-free, or partly composed of nonwood fibers. For further information, visit our website at www.cornellpress.cornell.edu.

Cloth printing   10 9 8 7 6 5 4 3 2 1
Paperback printing   10 9 8 7 6 5 4 3 2

To my grandmother
Vera Stepanovna Mikhailova

Contents

Appendixes

Illustrations

Tables

Acknowledgments

Above all, I am indebted to my respondents, who shared their insights and experience in a generous and articulate way. Without their expertise in how politics and the economy work in Russia this book could not have been written.

I am especially grateful to the British Academy for supporting my research with a sequence of research grants that enabled me to conduct necessary fieldwork over the years and to collect data for this book. I am grateful to Archie Brown, Caroline Humphrey, Rasma Karklins, David Lane, William Miller, and Teodor Shanin, who supported my ideas and my applications.

I thank Tim Colton and other colleagues at the Davis Center for the Senior Fellowship Award in the fall semester of 2005 that allowed me to complete this project within the stimulating surroundings of the Center for Government and International Studies at Harvard University. I am also grateful to my colleagues at the School of Slavonic and East European Studies, University College, London, who took over while I was on sabbatical.

I thank Susan Rose-Ackerman and Janos Kornai, who gave me time and support in 2001–2 within the "Honesty and Trust" research project at Hungary's Institute for Advanced Study, the Collegium, Budapest.

A number of people helped with various aspects of this project throughout the years. I am particularly grateful to Karen Birdsall, who helped me in various ways and stayed involved with this project from the beginning to the end. My close friends Ellen Dahrendorf, Irina Davydova, Vladimir Gelman, Valerii Kriukov, Roberto Mendoza, Bill Tompson, and Vadim Volkov contributed to this project.

My research assistants helped to dig out documents, put together charts, and trace visual materials: Yuko Adachi, Nina Fahy, Josie Furness, Anthony Lauren, Yulia Shirokova, and Inessa Tarusina. They also helped with transcribing interviews, finding sources, and preparing various drafts. My MA students in the Informal Practices classes motivated me to work on the clarity and structure of my argument.

I must mention "inspirational people" who influenced me intellectually and personally at various stages of this research: Sheila Fitzpatrick, Geoffrey Hosking, Anatolii Landsman, Inna Ryvkina, Charles Tilly, and my own daughter, Maria Ledeneva. Special thanks go to Tony Giddens, without whom this project would not have been possible.

Discussions with Rodric Braithwaite, Charles Grant, Phil Hanson, Tim Lankester, Robert Pynsent, Steven Sampson, and George Schöpflin were invaluable.

I also thank my editors, Nancy Ries and Bruce Grant, who have been so enthusiastic about the project and have given me detailed feedback. John Ackerman, Peter Wissoker, and Candace Akins at Cornell University Press, and copy editor Jamie Fuller, have been fantastic to work with.

For permission to reproduce visual materials I am grateful to Marat Guelman of the *Gallery of Marat Guelman*, S. U. Lantsova and G. P. Gilev of *Telemir*, Ruslan Kurepin of *Caricatura.ru*, Tatiana Malysheva and Olga Teplova of *Ekspert*, and Aleksei P'ianov of *Krokodil*. Some of the ideas in the book were tested in my previous publications. Unwritten rules were first tackled in a pamphlet published by the Centre for European Reform (www.cer.org.uk). The discussion of the genealogy of krugovaya poruka appeared in my contribution to the Proceedings of the British Academy volume 123, *Trust and Democratic Transition in Post-Communist Europe*, 2004, edited by Ivana Markova. The historical sections of chapter 4 are reproduced by permission of the British Academy. Chapter 6 is a revised version of "Underground Financing in Russia," in *Creating Social Trust in Post-Socialist Transition*, 2004, edited by Janos Kornai, Bo Rothstein, and Susan Rose-Ackerman; by permission of Palgrave-Macmillan.

Finally, I would like to acknowledge the impact of my Siberian family. My mother taught me never to give up and to stand up to a challenge, which was certainly tested by this project. My grandmother, Vera Stepanovna Mikhailova, has set a personal example of hard work with an exceptional degree of grace and dignity. I dedicate this book to her.

How Russia Really Works

Introduction

The Soviet system was not a planned economy. It was meant to be, but those living within its borders found that they had to counteract its over-centralization and its ideological limitations through intricate schemes of informal exchange, regional and industrial lobbying, and a variety of practices for cheating the system.[1] In much the same way, the post-Soviet system rarely operates according to its proclaimed principles of market democracy. Just as before, informal practices must regularly be used to compensate for its defects. These practices are essential if the system is to continue functioning, but they are also the enactment of know-how that enables competent players to manage and manipulate the system to their own advantage. The politics and economy of the 1990s remained dependent on the functioning of informal practices that were widespread, recognized, and reported upon in every region of Russia.

In my previous book, *Russia's Economy of Favours*, I argue that *blat* (the use of personal networks for obtaining goods and services in short supply and for circumventing formal procedures) is "losing its central significance in the conditions of the post-Soviet world."[2] In hindsight it is perhaps more accurate to say that changes in the political and economic foundations of the state-centralized economy have resulted in the monetization of blat and the reorientation of the use of personal networks toward a new type of shortage—a shortage of money. These changes have also generated a whole new range of informal practices; and in this book I identify the practices that emerged from, or adapted to, post-Soviet conditions. These include practices of *black PR* in politics, *kompromat* in the media, *krugovaia poruka* in professional circles, and a variety of scheming practices in business and law enforcement. Each evolved to compensate for the defects of the post-Soviet order and helped to reconfigure spheres once dominated by Soviet-era informal practices. I argue that just as blat was an essential type of know-how of Soviet socialism, these postsocialist informal practices represent the know-how" of post-Soviet Russia. As such, they are important indicators of Russia's political and economic development.

In post-Soviet Russia, ways of "beating the system" formerly associated with blat now amount to at least $2.8 billion a year in bribes paid by private citizens,[3] according to data provided by INDEM.[4] "Household" corruption (as opposed to business-related corruption), however, constitutes only 10 percent of the overall corruption market. About 90 percent of bribes in Russia are paid by businessmen for export licensing and quotas, state budget transactions, tax transfers, customs duties, privatization deals, and servicing debts to the federal budget.[5] One respondent with a diplomatic background explained the catch of privatization as follows:

> [In the 1990s] changes have taken place in various degrees in all sectors but their fundamental pattern is Sovietness—the state's capacity to distribute and to ration. The state used to ration everything plus to add a little something for *nomenklatura* such as *dachas*. Today, the stakes have gone up: larger possibilities associated with larger risks, but also distributed according to the same logic of authorization from above. Exceptions are rare. At the same time, the Soviet legacy of rationing should not be overestimated. There are even bigger problems with a new generation of businessmen who started business in their twenties in the late 1980s [often in criminalized form—AL]. They are about thirty now [in the 1990s] and they have no idea what the order is about—Soviet generations have much better sense of rules even if they violate them. [3.16]*

By exploring the role of informal practices, I illuminate the lesser-known side of the political institutions and economic realities in the first post-Soviet decade and their contradictions. For example, informal practices associated with barter, financial scheming, and alternative contract enforcement advance business but also rely on antimarket-type alliances; they are

*Bracketed numbers following quotations refer to the list of respondents in appendix 5.

competitive yet also undermine competition. Informal practices rapidly adapt to legal changes and make use of legal institutions, but they also create obstacles to the rule of law. While they primarily benefit certain groups, they also cater to the wider needs of the economy and are implicitly endorsed by the state. In other words, these informal practices are both an impediment to and a resource for the Russian economy, the Russian government, and the Russian people.

Although some practices, such as double bookkeeping and bribery, seem to have been in the Russian repertoire for a long time, they have been transformed in relation to market challenges, and there are both change and continuity in the ways they are employed today. On the one hand, grounded in Russian custom, informal practices maintain and introduce into economic life forms of reciprocity inhibiting the development of markets. On the other hand, these practices adapt to present-day economic concerns and become oriented toward problems of an economy undergoing market reforms. What is characteristic about these informal practices is their double-edged relationship to the "market" and "democracy": they are supportive but also subversive; they accommodate change but also represent resistance to change; they are beneficial for certain groups but also cater to the needs of the political regime and are implicitly endorsed by state; and they are divisive in their implications, serving and sustaining insiders at the expense of outsiders.

To operate in the post-Soviet economy one must sustain Soviet "informal" expertise but apply it to newly emerging financial institutions, electoral technologies, and shifting legal frameworks. Somewhat paradoxically, such expertise—the "navigational skills" between formal and informal sets of norms—is both the reason for and the consequence of the inefficiency of market institutions in Russia.

Terms and Concepts

In this book I define informal practices narrowly in order to distinguish them from social norms, customs, traditions, and other informal patterns of behavior that do not fit into the formal order of things. I analyze only those informal practices that infringe on, penetrate, and exploit formal organizations or make use of personal networks in order to achieve goals outside the personal domain. Such practices involve the manipulation of both formal rules and informal codes. I view informal practices in the context of the institutional frameworks in which they operate, defined by formal rules and informal norms existing in society, and suggest that it is insufficient to understand the workings of formal institutions or even to acquire insights into informal norms and codes. It is essential to analyze the interaction between the two and the implications that such interaction may have for the "rules of the game" in politics, the economy, and society. In scrutinizing informal practices I look for characteristics of formal institutions that underpin the informal economy and informal politics and for characteristics of informal practices that underpin the workings of formal institutions. My analysis illustrates that the rules of the game in the 1990s cannot operate consistently without players being compelled to engage in informal practices.

Assuming that most fundamental post-Soviet changes would be grasped in language, I identify informal practices that have been especially widespread by looking for the new "language games" in the vernacular and colloquial ways of describing the new order of things.[6] Some of these language games are of post-Soviet origin, such as *black piar*; some have Soviet roots, as in the case of *kompromat*; and some can even be traced centuries back, as in the case of *krugovaia poruka*. The informal practices that made it to the table of contents are also determined by the test of time. This project, it turned out, was impossible to accomplish by conducting in-depth interviews on "informal practices in the 1990s." It took me eight years of observation and analysis, four research grants—each of them covering at least three field trips—and a persistent effort to test my ideas about how things work with every Russian I met.

I started with economic aspects of the informal order of things and followed up with practices that spread out in politics. Initially, I looked into patterns of barter "chains"; tax evasion and financial schemes; and other aspects of nontransparency, such as creative accountancy, intricacies of industrial privatization, and issues of corporate governance. Some of these practices passed the test of time but are not included in the book because other excellent work has been produced on them in the meantime. I refer to the published work as I go along. Among the unpublished, I want to mention Eva Busse's excellent PhD dissertation on the unwritten rules of taxation and Yuko Adachi's fascinating PhD dissertation on informal practices in corporate governance.[7]

Finally, I discussed my terminology and ideas with my respondents. The test of time was applied to my respondents' judgments as well. As I have been collecting data gradually, I have had the luxury of getting back to some of my respondents to see if their views have changed in the meantime. I have also done a lot of routine cross-checking of evidence with other respondents. Cross-checks are informative and often help to start or to organize discussion with an interviewee around the subject of interest. It is unrealistic to expect an overall consensus on informal practices, but when I observed consensus among several respondents and found their views confirmed by other research and written reports, I felt safe in using the evidence. It also helped to imagine whether Russian readers would recognize the practices I described and whether my respondents would agree with my interpretations. Often, however, it was I who agreed with interpretations of my respondents and relied on their knowledge and expertise in my analysis.

Method, Data, and Fieldwork

A few words about my respondents and data are necessary here. In *Russia's Economy of Favours*, I argue that blat became the "reverse side of the over-controlling center" in Soviet Russia, relying on varieties of expertise about "how to get things done" shared by the majority of the population. (Ledeneva 1998, 3). By contrast, the current book focuses on a body of know-how that is largely unavailable to the public as a whole but is communicated by closed circles of professional elites or shared by individuals who understand one another. This book can be seen as an effort to give voice to the players in response to the challenge of a one-time Kremlin insider, Igor Malashenko:

> I would suggest that the outsiders get more in contact with the players, not the experts. We are not experts. We do not write, as experts do, by bullet-points . . . convenient for swallowing and digesting. We tell more complex stories, and because we are part of them, some things we can talk about, but some we can't. Sometimes I will acknowledge my influence, sometimes I won't. I won't lie without urgent need, but I surely won't tell the whole truth either. Of course it is much more difficult with me .than with an academic expert, but I dare say that we, the players, possess more adequate information about what's going on in Russia. What is going on in Russia cannot be packed into one simple formula.[8]

In accordance with such an approach, I have chosen research methodology and data in order to collect such stories and to offer a framework that accommodates their complexity while viewing them from a comparative and theoretically informed perspective. I conducted sixty-two in-depth interviews with fifty respondents, representative of: (1) elites, narrowly defined as those few going to the World Economic Forum in Davos, and the somewhat broader cross-section of attendees at the Russian Forums in London; (2) practitioners in possession of know-how relevant to the post-Soviet economy, from various economic sectors and levels of responsibility, including a few of the lesser-known shadow "oligarchs"; (3) those involved in the technical side of the know-how, such as accountants, auditors, legal experts, and law enforcement officers; and (4) journalists working for investigative agencies and engaged in a similar effort to report on "how things really work."

When I use direct quotations from the interviews, I refer to a respondent with a code in square brackets. The code contains the number of the chapter in which her or his comments appear most, followed by the number of the respondent in the list of respondents in appendix 5. For example, code [3.16] refers to respondent 3.16, whose remarks deal mainly with the subject matter of chapter 3. The list also includes dates and details of field trips, although sometimes I had to change details appearing in the list in order make my sources anonymous. I conducted most of the interviews used in this book between 1997 and 2003 in Moscow, St. Petersburg, the Urals, and Siberia. Although each region is more or less equally represented, the data are impossible to analyze for regional variation. The findings of this study are mainly applicable to the large cities. I asked different respondents different questions, depending on their expertise and the theme of the fieldwork, which makes it hard to generalize from their answers. The questions appear in appendix 6. Access to other databases and survey results allowed me to verify the findings of my qualitative study.[9]

Timing was crucial for this study. Just as the 1990s proved to be a window of opportunity for earlier research into Soviet-era practices of blat, it follows that the best time to reflect on the informal practices of the Boris Yeltsin era may come now, the period that has succeeded it. Many practices are being transformed under President Vladimir Putin's rule, which makes their role in the 1990s even more identifiable and their tendencies more pronounced. It was not easy to gain access to the respondents in this study, let alone ask them to speak on sensitive subjects. Where I managed to conduct thorough in-depth interviews, I discovered that just as with the study of blat, it was easier for respondents to answer questions about the past, however recent; and about others rather than their own experiences; and to assume that what they were describing was a widely accepted practice or the way in which the "system" works.[10]

This book aims to provide ethnography of gray areas emerging from the overlap of Russian politics, media, business, organized crime, and law enforcement agencies. Although I do not analyze the Russian state, the best-known Russian oligarchs, or criminal gangs directly (a great deal of research has been produced on the subject!), I believe this book sheds light on the nature and logic of their interaction and the atmosphere it creates at the level of the players. These aspects are mostly hidden from the eye, and I consider myself lucky to have collected a substantial number of recorded interviews touching upon them. These interviews might not be enough to generalize from and to work out how the relationship between the formal and the informal is structured, but they certainly help us to understand the respondents' perceptions of it.

The interdisciplinary nature of this work should appeal to those seeking innovative approaches to the analysis of politics, economy, and society in general and to those who, like myself, question Russia's alleged "uniqueness." Unlike researchers who study informal practices in Russia and are not interested in conceptualizing the role of such practices in wider contexts. I argue that informal practices constitute generic responses to structural pressures in all societies, can be found universally, and serve as indicators of economic and political regimes.

Structure of the Book

In chapter 1, I outline the political and economic situation in Russia in the 1990s, illustrate Russia's lack of transparency, and argue that the rules of the game in politics and the economy cannot be understood without reference to "unwritten rules." I suggest that the best way to grasp unwritten rules is to study informal practices, and discuss the advantages and limitations of my concept of informal practices. I identify the constraints of the post-Soviet institutional framework and show how they shape informal practices.

In chapter 2, I focus on the informal practices associated with the major political development of the post-Soviet period—competitive elections—which became notoriously associated with manipulative technologies, widely referred to as "black PR" (*chernyi piar*). The political consultants engage in black and gray PR by manipulating the legal system and by pushing the limits of the law for the advantage of their clients. In this chapter, I provide an analysis of the legal loopholes they exploit, review their techniques of manipulation, and discuss the implications of their actions for the development of Russian democracy.

PR practices often make use of compromising information—*kompromat*—to attack political opponents and business competitors. The explosion of *kompromat* in the 1990s, however, originated not only in PR technologies but also in the privatization of security services and the emergence of an independent press.[11] In chapter 3, I discuss the role of *kompromat* in the workings of security services, information agencies, the media, and law enforcement agencies, which often produce and distribute these compromising materials. The discussion focuses on the prominence of informal practices associated with *kompromat* in Russia, as opposed to "lustration" campaigns (legal process of exposing collaborators with the secret police in previous regimes) across Central and Eastern Europe, and points to the continuity of political power in Russia.

If *kompromat* is used publicly in PR practices, that is, in its media- and elections-targeted form, its hidden forms are associated with the ties of *krugovaia poruka* (joint responsibility) among professional elites. In chapter 4, I identify the phenomenon of *krugovaia poruka* as predicated upon a form of circular control that ensures conformity and solidarity; reduces individuals to being part of a circle, community, or network; and thus diverts their course of action. I discuss the origins of the pattern of *krugovaia poruka* and reveal its extraordinary adaptability and perseverance in the Russian political and economic landscape. The ties of *krugovaia poruka* limit changes in the nature of the political regime in post-Soviet Russia that are perhaps not as fundamental as liberal reformers would have liked to believe.

The next three chapters supply evidence of informal practices associated with barter, financial scheming, and alternative contract enforcement that are part of the host of scheming practices in business, corporate governance, selective law enforcement, and alternative contract resolution. These practices serve as important indicators of the workings of the Russian economy. I argue that they have channeled change and facilitated reforms as well as created a poor investment climate.

In chapter 5, I discuss informal practices associated with nonmonetary exchanges in industry and small business during the 1990s and illustrate the emergence of parallel currencies caused by defects in the formal frameworks. Aspects of financial scheming and double accounting in large industrial enterprises and small and medium-sized business are discussed in chapter 6. In chapter 7, I consider informal practices of alternative enforcement brought into existence by the distrust of state institutions and by the state's inability to give protection to the newly emerged market institutions. Just like *tolkachi* in Soviet times, post-Soviet *tolkachi* constitute an impor-

tant element in the workings of formal institutions, carry the burden of reforms, and make the development of business possible.

The evidence collected in the book strongly suggests that informal practices during the 1990s were not only subversive but also supportive of the
Russian reforms, and it illustrates the centrality of the role of specialists
such as auditors, accountants, and legal experts in accommodating political
change and facing the risks of the post-Soviet market transformation. The
conclusion sums up this paradoxical role of informal practices in the Russian transformation of the 1990s; points to their embeddedness in the
workings of formal rules as well as in informal norms; emphasizes their reliance on the implicit endorsement by the state; and assesses possible ways
they may change in the twenty-first century.

Chapter One

Why Are Informal Practices Still Prevalent in Russia?

Is Russia Transparent?

There is a certain mythology that Russia is a land of irregularities and para-doxes, to a large extent impenetrable to outsiders. At the level of cliché, the "Russian soul" and "Russian chaos" claim some implicit explanatory power. References to Russian history ("traumatic past"), geography ("size matters" and the "natural resource curse"), and the national psyche ("kleptomania") frequently appear in this type of discussion. A common assumption behind these ideas is that Russia is somehow different from other, more transparent economies. A similar conclusion could be drawn from post-1998 analyses of the macroeconomic reforms—also known as "too much shock, too little therapy"—introduced in Russia during the 1990s. These analyses suggest that reforms did not work as expected, owing to Russia's lack of trans-parency resulting both from defects in the institutional framework and from agencies that emerged to compensate for these defects.[1] Corruption has often been identified as a major, self-perpetuating source of problems. It seems impossible to combat corruption in a society where, supposedly, no agency or institution is free from it. As a result, it has become an accepted view that Russia's economy is nontransparent—that is, it is an economy in which the rules of the game are not easily recognized or understood.

Many reforms have been launched to address issues of taxation, corpo-rate governance, land ownership, banking, the judiciary, and civil service.[2] Putin's first term was associated with positive trends in Russia's GDP growth, capital flight, and levels of foreign investment.[3] Russia was finally removed from the blacklist of the Financial Action Task Force on Money Laundering (FATF) in 2002, a sign that it has made a positive impact in curbing money laundering abuses.[4] In the same year, the European Union (EU) announced its intention to recognize Russia as a market economy and to pass legislation allowing it to benefit from associated trade advantages, particularly those regarding antidumping procedures. The EU also restated its support for Russia's early accession to the World Trade Organization and welcomed the determination shown by Russia's leaders to continue pursuing the economic reforms that have been initiated.[5] Yet certain features of Russia's economic and political life still impede international business, foreign investment, and the country's integration into the world community.

Although organized crime seems to be on the retreat, poor corporate governance, selective law enforcement, and corruption pose serious obstacles to democratization and economic development.[6] Most Central and East European countries have achieved progress in these areas, particularly in the context of the EU accession process, but Russia and other former Soviet countries are still struggling with a range of challenges. These include corruption (Karklins 2005; Rose-Ackerman 1999; Komai and Rose-Ackerman 2004), state capture (Hellman and Kaufman 2001), the pervasiveness of the shadow economy (Schneider and Enste 2005), and an underdeveloped private sector and incomplete institutional transformation (Gaddy and Ickes 2002). The words of former prime minister Viktor Chernomyrdin—"We hoped for the best, but it turned out as it always does" (*khoteli kak luchshe, a poluchilos' kak vsegda*)—neatly sum up the problem of reforms initiated but not implemented, or implemented with unintended outcomes.[7] Chernomyrdin's statement refers to Russia's entrapment in its own ways and conveys a sense of irony. It has become something of an aphorism, not only because it makes sense for the country as a whole but also because it alludes to routine practices of the elites—from local bosses to transnational networks—that continue to benefit from such an order of things (Gel'man, Ryzhekov, and Brie 2000, 16–60, 146–180; Wedel 1998).

The examples in this book—from PR practices to alternative enforcement—demonstrate that informal practices are important because of their ability to compensate for defects in the formal order while simultaneously undermining it. This seeming contradiction serves to explain why things in Russia are never quite as bad or as good as they seem. Thus, reducing or evading taxes through the common practice of "double accountancy" may at first appear detrimental to the economy, but it must also be noted that "hidden" profits or "saved" taxes were one of the rare sources of enterprise investment at the beginning of the post-Soviet period (Ledeneva and Seabright 2000). Any attempt to assess the real impact of informal practices on the economy is faced with such nuances. It may be suggested, for instance, that capital flight during the 1990s also functioned as an avenue for foreign investment. The dual role of Cyprus as the most popular offshore zone for Russian business and one of the country's top five foreign investors—matching the levels of France and the United Kingdom—would seem to sustain this assumption.[8]

Russia's political landscape also provided abundant examples of informal practices throughout the 1990s. The state's role in these years as an active shareholder in many large corporations is a key starting point. The extent to which insider deals prevailed at privatization auctions and were used by the state as a means for asset disposal is well documented (Freeland 2000; Hoffman 2002). The hostile corporate takeovers that proliferated on the economic and political scene during that decade and the use of selective state capacity in settling such conflicts have been well detailed (Volkov 2004). The "information wars" of the 1990s, waged daily on the pages of the Russian press, employed *kompromat* in character assassination, blackmail, and the manipulation of public opinion (Mukhin 2000). During the same period, the electoral bids of local, regional, and federal candidates were advanced through the skilled use of "political technologies" and black PR.

This is not to say that there is no place for legal procedures or that the requisite components of the rule of law are absent in Russia—there are courts, legislation, and enforcement mechanisms. Rather, the ability of the rule of law to function coherently has been subverted by a powerful set of practices that have evolved organically into the post-Soviet milieu. The persistence of such practices should not reinforce stereotypes about Russians' innate inability to submit to law. Instead, the continuation of informal practices in the face of efforts to root them out is a challenge to reconsider how these practices really operate and the way they interact with the formal order.

Each agent active in the battles of the 1990s exhibited some expertise in the unwritten rules and ability to capitalize on a certain know-how. Arguably, this kind of expertise is behind the so-called nontransparency of the rules of the game in the Russian economy. The reproduction cycle of this nontransparency is organized in the following way.

- *The rules of the game are nontransparent and frequently change because the existing legal framework does not function coherently.* Some of the key building blocks of a transparent market system such as a land code, anticorruption legislation, and a functioning banking system are not in place, and basic market institutions do not work as they should—there are limits to open competition, protection of property rights, and transparency of corporate governance. The incoherence of formal rules compels almost all Russians, willingly or unwillingly, to violate them and to play by rules introduced and negotiated outside formal institutions.

- *Anybody can be framed and found guilty of some violation of the formal rules because the economy operates in such a way that everyone is bound to disregard at least some of these rules.* For example, nearly everybody is compelled to earn in the informal economy in order to survive—a practice that is punishable, or could be made so. Businesses are taxed at a rate that forces them to evade taxes in order to do well. Practices such as embezzlement of state property or tax evasion become pervasive. The fairly ubiquitous character of such practices makes it impossible to punish everyone.[9] Thus punishment becomes a resource in short supply.

- *Because of the pervasiveness of rule violation, punishment is bound to occur selectively on the basis of criteria developed outside the legal domain.* While everybody is under the threat of punishment, the actual punishment is "suspended" but can be enforced at any time. The principle of "suspended punishment," whereby a certain freedom and flexibility did exist but could be restricted at any moment, worked well in the Soviet system. It became routine practice for the authorities to switch to the written code only "when necessary." A similar tendency became evident in the 1990s, notably for the same reasons: the formal rules were impossible to follow and it was not feasible to prosecute everyone.

- *"Unwritten rules" compensate for defects in the rules of the game and form the basis for selective punishment.* The violation of unwritten rules can result in the enforcement of written ones, which paradoxically makes it just as, if not more, important to observe the unwritten rules as the written ones.[10] This perpetuates the reliance of the Russian economy on the nontransparent rules of the game.

Given the dependence of the Russian economy on unwritten rules, even the best attempts to restructure the rules of the game by changing the formal rules can have only a limited effect. This is partly because efforts from the top are difficult to sustain, and partly because any change in the formal rules introduces, and is perceived as, yet another constraint to be dealt with informally. This often results in readjustment and reconfiguration of informal practices around the new constraints, rather than a decline in significance of unwritten rules as a source of nontransparency.

In the 1990s, the burden of reforms was shouldered by those players who had mastered the unwritten rules by developing both expertise in the rules of the game and the ability to break them with impunity. I argue that without understanding how deeply such skills and knowledge are embedded in the formal rules, legal loopholes, and social norms contradicting formal rules, it is impossible to prevent an endless string of frustrations over the course of reforms in Russia. I also argue that in order to understand this pervasiveness, it is insufficient to analyze formal and informal constraints. One must have adequate conceptual tools in order to tackle the unwritten rules and to identify the gray areas associated with them. Before I present my empirical findings, let me introduce the concept of informal practices and explain its origins.

From Unwritten Rules to Informal Practices

This project started with an effort to identify some of the know-how that replaced blat in the 1990s and to conceptualize them as "unwritten rules" (Ledeneva 2001b). The difficulties in the use of this common Russian idiomatic expression standing for rules of breaking the rules, however, led me to think that "informal practices" is in fact the best category to address the elusive domain of political and economic know-how, even when compared with other available options such as informal institutions or informal networks.[11]

Although unwritten rules sounded like an informal institution of a kind, it turned out to be a trap conceptually and a dead end empirically.[12] One reason is the ambiguity of the word "rule." Pierre Bourdieu suggests that people have in mind at least one of two meanings:

> It's impossible to tell exactly whether what is understood by rules is a principle of the judicial or quasi-juridical kind, more or less consciously produced and mastered by agents, or a set of objective regularities imposed on all those who join a game. When people talk of a rule of the game, it's one or other of these two meanings they have in mind. But they may also be thinking of a third meaning, that of the

model or principle constructed by the scientist to explain the game.
(1990, 60)

Following Bourdieu, who spoke of "strategies," or of the "social uses" of kinship, rather than of "rules" of kinship, I refrain from the terminology of rules.

In Wittgenstein's terms, the third meaning in Bourdieu's quote can be expressed in a mathematical formula that most people do not need to know in order to continue the sequence of numbers: 2, 4, 6, 8. He distinguishes between the rule and "rule following," or "ability to go on," whereby participants may follow the rule without being able to articulate it. Although participants do not doubt the existence of unwritten rules, what they refer to as unwritten rules might not follow any of the categories of rules acknowledged from the observer's point of view (quasi-judicial rule, regularity, model).[13] "Unwritten rules" prescribe not so much patterns of rule *following* as patterns of rule *breaking*. They are patterns of navigating between the rules or playing one set of norms against another. They are strategies driven by what Bourdieu calls the practical sense (*sens practique*), the "feel for the game, as the practical mastery of the logic or the immanent necessity of a game—a mastery acquired by experience of the game, and one which works outside conscious control and discourse" (1990, 61). Besides, unwritten rules are impossible to pin down because they are a moving target: they change as soon as too many players learn them in order to sustain their exclusive nature.

The closest one can get to defining them is by illustrating their workings through identifying strategies or regular patterns of "navigating" between formal rules and informal norms. For example, take practices of false reporting that are fairly universal around the world, both historically and geographically. In the planned economy, the practical sense of managers determined the extent of their false reporting. They kept the authorities satisfied but the plan targets low in order to secure bonuses for employees for overfulfilling production plans. Today the comparable practice of not declaring one's profit is a main technique for hiding income and reducing tax liability. Curiously, some corporate scandals of recent years have involved both practices of profit overreporting (Enron in the United States) and profit underreporting (Yukos in Russia), depending on formal rules and informal norms navigated in this way. One could suggest that these scandals broke out because the agents in question lost their sense of proportion—the practical sense that guides the protagonists of more accepted informal practices.

Once I faced the difficulty of identifying post-Soviet unwritten rules, I recalled that in the context of blat, too, unwritten rules were impossible to operationalize as a set of rules, regularities, or models in empirical research. In my study of blat, inquiring about practices was the best way to approach those intuitively clear but unidentifiable principles of blat exchange. Rather than following a consistent set of blat rules, blat exchanges were based on shared expectations about formal rules of the centralized distribution system and on mutual understandings about informal norms of friendship or other relationships.

Thus, I could approach the unwritten rules of blat only by investigating more or less regular strategies of navigating between these formal rules and informal norms: blat strategies of navigating between rules of access to the state centralized system and norms of sociability. The rules of access depended on a particular commodity, service, or procedure and on formal instructions about their distribution or provision. The norms of sociability were set within networks and relationships and varied depending on the time, space, or circumstances of exchange. In these terms, blat practices originated in a conflict between formal rules and informal constraints that was resolved by individual players with a practical sense of what needed to be done in a given situation.

In terms of the unwritten rules of blat, we can speak of high expectations of mutual help shared by friends or acquaintances, resulting in the use of personal networks to approach those in charge of the distribution of goods and services in short supply: "It is not what you have, it is who you know," or "Do not have a hundred rubles, have a hundred friends." Within blat transactions themselves, however, the unwritten rules about who, how, and how much can be asked are not clearly set or universally applied: "Keep within limits"; "Do not expect gratitude but be grateful yourself" are simply guidelines formulated by expert practitioners of blat and can be violated in situations of acute pressure of formal rules or informal obligations. For example, formal pressures of army conscription and informal norms of giving the best to a child produce an extraordinary range of informal practices undertaken by mothers of conscripts-to-be from facilitating admission to universities indirectly (by paying tutors) or directly (by bribes), which constitute a legal way out of military service, to bribing doctors for false diagnoses and engaging in various services to the military to obtain a desired exemption. Not only do formal rules and institutions suffer from these practices (quality of and morale in the army), but the informal norms set within families—that lies and bribes are wrong—are bent as well.

Importantly, some favors are never given, whereas others are given sparingly or once in a lifetime. Also, some friends are "helped" more than others and not necessarily on the basis of need. To understand these restrictions and allowances, to know where and how they apply, and to measure the value of blat favors would be, in my opinion, the way to find out the unwritten rules of blat and to categorize *it* as an informal institution. The problem is that such rules about blat are impossible to research empirically or to generalize about theoretically. It made me realize that although informal institutions may originate in informal practices, it would be misleading to equate the two.

Helmke and Levitsky (2004) define informal institutions as socially shared rules, usually unwritten, that are created, communicated, and enforced outside officially sanctioned channels. Moreover, they reduce informal institutions to political rules of the game and relate them to the modern period when codification of law is nearly universal. Under this definition, only a limited number of blat transactions qualify to be considered as informal institutions.[14] Informal practices analyzed in this book—such as black and gray PR, *kompromat,* and *krugovaia poruka*—are much more "political games" than blat, but even so, their implications are much wider than the realm of politics. In my view, understanding the workings of informal politics or informal economy cuts across disciplinary boundaries. In this sense, informal practices require an interdisciplinary analysis.

Conceptualizing Informal Practices

In real life, some informal codes—for example, the mafia code of honor, the code of the criminal underworld (*poniatiia*), or informal requests received on the telephone from the Kremlin (*telefonnoe pravo*)—seem more efficiently enforced than any formal rule. Some formal rules are written but not enforced, such as obsolete but not annulled Soviet laws or decrees signed but not implemented. But in academic analysis, one has to distinguish between the formal and the informal in terms of ideal types: formal rules and informal norms. The ideal types of formal rules include juridical or quasi-juridical rules that are consciously produced and enforced by mechanisms created for purposes of such enforcement. The ideal types of informal norms include customs, codes, and ethics that are by-products of various forms of social organization (for example, family, personal network, neighborhood, community, club membership). My concept of informal practices takes into account the conflicting, fluid, and complex nature of interaction between formal rules and informal norms. But I use it rather narrowly.

Ordinarily the term "informal" refers to almost anything that is not formal. As Helmke and Levitsky put it in their discussion of informal institutions, the term appears in the context of "a dizzying array of phenomena, including personal networks, clientelism, corruption, clans and mafias, civil society, traditional culture, and a variety of legislative, judicial, and bureaucratic norms" (2004). Even more confusing, not only does the term "informal" mean different things in different contexts, but it is used equally frequently in its positive, neutral, and negative senses: when referring to informal codes of friendship, to informal norms of a London club, and to the use of informal contacts to achieve goals in formal context (say, in insider dealing or mediating "cash for question" and "cash for votes" in parliaments). Another example: the term "informal economy" can embrace both activities taking place outside the formal economy (and regulated by social norms such as exchange of do-it-yourself activities between neighbors or cash payments to a child-care giver or a cleaner) and those penetrating the formal economy (which often involves misuse of public resources, diverting or embezzling them for personal use, and which implies aggressive competence in formal rules). It appears that some informal activities are more informal than others. In other words, some rely on established and consensual norms, whereas others activities are viewed as opportunistic and improper in the sense that they are in some conflict with the formal rules. It is therefore unfortunate that the term "informal" refers not only to activities supporting existing norms, traditions, and customs that complement or substitute formal rules—thus constituting an important part of the institutional framework—but also to the activities resulting from a conflict of these norms, traditions, and customs with formal rules. In addition, one can also think of many examples where so-called informal activities do not clash with formal rules but use them manipulatively—that is, violate not the letter of the law but its spirit, or, even worse, are aimed at creating the kinds of formal rules that serve certain informal interests.

This overloading of the term "informal" has led scholars to invent other terms such as "state capture," "stealing the state," or "economy of favors," which refer to the institutional capture and hidden privatization of public institutions (Hellman and Kaufmann 2001; Solnick 1999; Ledeneva 1998). These not only make attractive titles but also reflect some dissatisfaction with already existing concepts and binary oppositions of the "formal-informal" type, which do not grasp the complexities on the ground. Ethnographic analyses aimed at "unmaking Soviet life" and revealing paradoxes occurring on the margins of public and the private property and "entrepreneurial governmentality" reflect on such complexities in detail (Humphrey 2002; Verdery 2003; Yurchak 2005). In political analyses, authors speak about hybrid economy, democracies with adjectives, political instrumentalization of disorder, organized disorganization, and competitive authoritarianism (Carothers 2002; Chabal and Daloz 1999; Levitsky 2001; Levitsky and Way 2002). Despite the attraction of introducing a new term, I believe there is value in conceptualization of an existing, and widely used, term, if only to clarify its meaning for purposes of empirical research.

Ideas that I found most helpful for conceptualizing "informal practices" come from two totally different attempts to grasp the complexity of social reality, from Douglass North and Pierre Bourdieu. North has revolutionized the understanding of institutional frameworks by attaching an equally important status to informal constraints. In his famous definition of institutions as the "rules of the game in a society or, more formally, humanly devised constraints that shape human interaction," North distinguishes between formal and informal types of constraints as components of institutions (1990, 3).[15]

> They [institutions] are perfectly analogous to the rules of the game in a competitive team sport. That is, they consist of formal written rules as well as typically unwritten codes of conduct that underlie and supplement formal rules, such as not deliberately injuring a key player on the opposing team. And as this analogy would imply, the rules and informal codes are sometimes violated and punishment is enacted. Taken together, the formal and informal rules and the type and effectiveness of enforcement shape the whole character of the game. (North 1990, 4)

Interestingly, the sports metaphor was also used by Bourdieu to explain his notions of the "logic of practice" and the "feel for the game." Even if they are describing the same game, the focus of the two writers is different. North is interested in rules, the structure behind the game; Bourdieu is interested in players and the logic behind their strategies. North argues that

> The purpose of the rules is to define the way the game is played. But the objective of the team within that set of rules is to win the game— by a combination of skills, strategy and coordination; by fair and sometimes by foul means. Modeling the strategies and skills of the team as it develops is a separate process from modeling the creation, evolution, and consequences of the rules. Separating the analysis of

the underlying rules from the strategy of the players is a necessary prerequisite to building a theory of institutions. (1990, 4–5)[16]

This separation is essential not only for building a theory of institutions but also for theorizing practices. Bourdieu argues that the theory must include

what sports players call a feel for the game, as the practical mastery of the logic or of the immanent necessity of a game—a mastery acquired by experience of the game, the one which works outside conscious control and discourse. (1990, 61)

The distinction between rules and players defines not only the choice of terminology but also data and method: *practices* with their focus on the players' strategies shaped by the rules versus *institutions* as rules of the game as such. And it is this distinction, and the focus on players' ability to manipulate the rules, that set "informal practices" conceptually apart from "informal institutions."[17]

My take on "informal practices" in this book differs from other available analyses in a number of ways. Unlike those interested in rules, I explicitly focus on players. It is players who are left to deal with conflicts between formal rules and informal norms on the ground and who get the blame for benefiting from their strategies. Players engage in manipulative ways of mixing formal rules and informal norms and develop mastery in navigating between the two. In a narrow sense, the concept of informal practices is an addition to the ideal types of formal rules and informal norms that reflects the relationship between the two. For example, it accommodates strategies that follow the letter of law but not its spirit or strategies that use informal norms in order to justify breaking formal rules. In a wider sense, its ambition is to challenge the approach represented by oppositions: formal/informal, transparent/nontransparent, official/unofficial, written/unwritten, codified/noncodified, legal/illegal, public/private. Just as Bourdieu redefines the notion of strategy—"one can refuse to see in strategy the product of an unconscious program without making it the product of a conscious, rational calculation" (1990, 62)—I redefine informal practices as an outcome of players' creative handling of formal rules and informal norms—players' improvisation on the enabling aspects of these constraints. Although players are individual actors, their individual strategies of navigating between formal rules and informal norms feed into or amalgamate into patterns of behavior of groups or professions. For example, strategies of gray PR and the use of legal loopholes identified by respondents were considered common for most PR specialists, and every type of practicioner had its own know-how built around a similar logic. The concept of informal practices allowed me to identify these strategies to understand how players manage to get things done under existing constraints.

The concept of informal practices is convenient because it is genuinely de-centered, that is, grounded equally in formal rules and informal norms. None of these categories is residually defined or given priority. Both formal rules and informal norms shaping informal practices are historically grounded and present themselves to the players in the form of preexisting constraints. Unlike those who theorize the types of interaction between formal rules and informal norms, I choose an empirical focus on players' strategies of integrating the two.[18] I attempt to grasp the logic of players' strategies and to generalize from what I find rather than to construe types analytically. Access to experienced players enabled me to adopt such an approach, reliant on the ability (both mine and that of my respondents) to articulate players' mastery of constraints of the given institutional framework.

By analyzing patterns of players' mastery (and manipulation) of both formal and informal constraints, I have discovered that informal practices can be both supportive and subversive of formal rules and informal norms, thus lacking consistency in their impact. I refer to such contradictory implications of informal practices as their "paradoxical role." Such a perspective complements, rather than contradicts, those accounts that refer to informal institutions as "parasitic" and assume that informal institutions are dependent on formal institutions and subversive to them.[19] What remains less noticed in these accounts is that by engaging in informal practices, players not only subvert formal rules and informal norms but also help to reproduce them. When formal rules are in conflict with informal norms, not only do informal practices exploit these rules and norms, but formal institutions and informal relationships, conducive to the rules and norms, also depend on these practices for their existence and functioning. Just as practices of blat and *tolkachi* were both subversive and supportive of the Soviet system, some similarly paradoxical practices serve the post-Soviet economy and politics.

I view informal practices as an integral part of the Russian transformation of the 1990s and identify their subversive and supportive aspects. At the same time, I argue that informal practices are not exclusively characteristic of post-Soviet or transitional contexts. Informal practices exist in every society but do not necessarily play similar roles. I point to similar practices in other political or economic regimes and make some comparisons in the book.

Practices stemming from and caused by sham democracies and misapplied economic models have been explored by many authors (Gel'man, Ryzhenkov, and Brie 2002; Merkel and Croissant 2000; Rose 1999; Stark 1994; Stiglitz 2002; Wilson 2005). It has been shown in empirical research, as well as argued theoretically, that to limit the subversive impact of informal practices it is not sufficient just to change the formal rules. In attempting to grasp the extent to which the workings of political and economic institutions are dependent on informal practices, I detect characteristics of both formal and informal constraints that "enable" such informal practices. In a detailed account of Russia's formal rules and informal norms and informal practices bridging the gap between these constraints, I emphasize that it is insufficient to reform formal rules without a focused effort to influence informal norms at the same time.

To sum up, I define informal practices as regular sets of players' strategies that infringe on, manipulate, or exploit formal rules and that make use of informal norms and personal obligations for pursuing goals outside the personal domain. Such strategies involve bending of both formal rules and informal norms or navigating between these constraints by following some and breaking others where appropriate. They also involve a creative interpretation of these constraints, a discovery of their enabling aspects, and an improvisation on this basis.

Why Are Informal Practices Prevalent?

Informal practices exist in all societies but predominate (and even become indispensable) where formal rules and informal norms are not synchronized, and where the rules of the game are consequently incoherent.[20] In other words, if one cannot follow both formal rules and informal norms consistently, it is widely manifested in patterns of recourse to informal practices bridging the gap between them and often manipulating both for the advantage of the players.[21] It might be tempting to assume that formal rules are fundamentally good, clear, enforceable, and universally applied, but this has not always been the case in Russia. Similarly, one should also avoid assumptions about informal norms. Given the mixed nature of constraints, informal practices have a paradoxical—alternately positive and negative—impact.

Reliance upon informal practices is an outcome of the inefficiency of formal rules and their enforcement on the one hand and customary disrespect for formal rules and distrust of formal institutions on the other. Correspondingly, we should consider two fundamental sets of factors to explain why informal practices are so prevalent in Russia. One set derives from the future-oriented formal rules—that is, the legislation designed to improve the political and economic order in Russia, and the loopholes in its formulation and enforcement. The other is related to the nature of informal norms as well as legacies of the past that continue to shape today's practices. Let us consider these factors, starting with the nature of formal constraints and the problems of Russia's legal framework in the 1990s.[22]

In this period there was an extreme inconsistency in various types of legislation, such as laws (*zakony*), decrees (*ukazy*), resolutions (*postanovleniia*), and instructions (*rasporiazheniia*). Yeltsin's presidential decrees often contradicted Duma legislation and were sometimes used as instruments to sidestep obstructionist moves by the parliament. When the World Bank interviewed members of the business community in the summer of 1999, about one-third of the respondents said their firms had been harmed by the president's decrees—laws that were seen as beneficial to oligarchs or individuals closely linked to the government. Decisions taken at the subfederal level often openly contradicted federal law yet went unchallenged. In February 2001, First Deputy Prosecutor-General Iurii Biriukov reported that over the previous six months, his office had uncovered 3,273 pieces of legislation adopted by the regional governments that contradicted federal laws, and he stated that these governments continued to draft laws as they wished.[23] The inadequate synchronization of federal and local legislation was also reported on a regional level. The First Deputy Prosecutor of the Republic of Sakha (Yakutiia), Nikolai Takhvatulin, said that from 1999 to 2000 the republic's prosecutors had appealed to republic-level officials ninety times about 43 different laws and that 35 decrees violated regional legislation. As a result, some 34 laws and 22 decrees were changed.[24]

According to the Russian Ministry of Justice, regional laws became more highly attuned to the Constitution between July 2000, at which time every fifth law was still reportedly unconstitutional, and May 2001, when only 5 to 6 percent continued to be so (Smith 2003, 27–28).[25] This was partly due to actions taken by the constitutional court, which in July 2000 ruled several republics' constitutions unconstitutional (Smith 2001, 114). Matthew Hyde (2001) describes Putin's successes in pushing legislation on regional reform through parliament "a major victory." Further changes to the tax code reduced the financial independence of the regions by increasing their share of federal taxes. However, these measures were not consistently implemented in the regions, partially because many regionally enacted laws proved more efficient (Sharlet 2001, 218–25). The continued existence in Moscow of the

Soviet-style residence permit (*propiska*) violated federal law, despite the decision of the country's constitutional court to ban such practices in 1996.

Shatit'ko (2003) emphasizes the self-serving nature of so-called administrative barriers, and Kliamkin (2002) calculates their number at twenty-five thousand, including state standards such as construction, fire, and sanitary-epidemiologic norms. More than 80 percent of commodities are subject to state certification before they are put on sale. This was the way things were done in the state-centralized economy, and little has changed since. The certification procedures are impossible to follow, and the state standards often contradict one another or are mutually exclusive (because they are produced by different ministries). Moreover, not everyone can acquire the published standards. For example, the State Committee of Standardization sells its published volume of norms and procedures for 230,000 rubles (more than $7,000). Most entrepreneurs cannot afford such a sum, opting instead to pay for inevitable violations once caught (Kliamkin 2002; Pastukhov 2002).

Thus defects in formal constraints are associated not only with formal rules but also with their application and enforcement. Federal payments to the judicial system by the end of the 1990s barely covered the salaries of court officers, which in turn increased their susceptibility to corruption. In 1998, twenty-eight courts in the city of Tomsk were compelled to suspend operations because regional authorities refused to pay their heating bills (Solomon 2002, 118). A dire lack of funds for the courts led to their "sponsorship" by private enterprises and governments on the regional and local level, severely compromising Yeltsin's attempts to ensure their independence. For example, a 1994 presidential decree permitted local courts to accept contributions made to local and regional budgets by private entities to be used for court funding (Hahn 2001, 3). "Judges were more independent by the turn of the century than they have been in Soviet times but were still at the mercy of poor pay and organization. They were, under Yeltsin, now mostly appointed for unlimited terms (after a three-year probationary period) and could only be removed by a committee of their peers, a Judicial Qualification Committee (JQC) when the procurator requested it. Additionally, court administrations had been separated from the Ministry of Justice and put in court departments under the control of chief judges" (Solomon 2002, 118).

I would summarize issues related to enforcement in the 1990s as follows:

- Some of these issues are related to generally weak enforcement infrastructure. The Russian government has failed in its responsibility to collect tax revenues, to maintain a social safety net, to enforce laws and agreements, to ensure the physical safety of its citizens, and to provide the necessary conditions for a transition to a market economy. Formal institutions, including the judiciary, are widely seen as corrupt and self-serving, incapable of fulfilling their obligations to the citizenry and unworthy of popular respect.

- The inefficiency of the government in providing services to the private sector has facilitated the emergence of alternative institutions that operate with more efficiency, often by using methods that are not fully legitimate. Various security departments and private protection firms, often consisting of former employees of the state's coercive ministries, have assumed the function of enforcing laws and contract relations in the private sector of economy.

- There is a strong regional dimension to the problem of enforcement (Gel'man et al. 2002). Existing laws are applied unevenly and arbitrarily in different areas of the country. Regional governors dominate local prosecutors, courts, militia, and units of the security services (such as the FSB), effectively fracturing the coherence of these organs of federal power (and often representing the interests of a particular financial-industrial group). The impossibility of resolving disputes through formal procedures means that many problems get solved outside the legal domain and by unlawful means.

- As a result, the law becomes ammunition in the fighting of business wars and in regional-federal battles.[26] There are plenty of instances where attempts to enforce the legal order have been motivated not by the logic of law but by commercial, political, or personal interests.[27] It is fairly typical for legal sanctions to be imposed in the pursuit of an informal request. In such cases, the particular act of law enforcement is just one link in a complex scheme of backstage commercial or political operations, as happens rather often with insolvency cases.

The implementation of legislation depends on the context and particularly the degree of public support for law enforcement. Studies by scholars have shown a lack of public support of the state and low demand for law in Russia in the 1990s on the part of both individuals and organizations (Hendley 1997). Indeed, according to the results of a 1994 survey published in *A Decade of New Russia Barometer Trends,* 51 percent of the Russian public claimed to trust the church, and 41 percent trusted the army; only 17 percent trusted the court system. In 2000 and 2001 trust in the courts rose to 19 percent and 23 percent, respectively (Rose 2002, 21). In 2001, only 16 percent showed full or some confidence in the parliament and 11 percent in the political parties (Wyman 2000, 2002).[28] I see such figures as further indication that any reform of formal rules "from above" is likely to be a wasted effort, not because distrust of state is such a deeply ingrained historical feature or because patron-client relationships are so powerful, but because the public felt betrayed by the outcome of privatization over the course of the 1990s and placed all the blame on state institutions and bureaucrats, who found ways to prosper while abandoning the population at large. Either way, low expectations of state institutions led to the proliferation of informal practices and created an additional incentive for cheating the state and placing trust elsewhere. No society can operate on the basis of distrust and suspicion, however; thus there are compensating patterns of high trust elsewhere in Russian society, as illustrated in later chapters.

People's lack of respect for formal rules and their exploitative attitudes toward formal institutions resulted in an abundance of adjectives—such as semilegal, extralegal, quasi-legal, supralegal, or nonlegal—used to refer to the multiplicity of informal practices. The widespread use of this range of descriptive devices reflects the fact that some practices that are technically illegal might not be perceived as such and can be justified in particularistic terms or seen as necessary to compensate for defects in the formal system. For example, systems of double and sometimes triple accountancy may violate the law technically, but they are widely employed and are therefore not perceived as patently illegal.[29] Such logic is grasped in Scott's distinction of various shades of corruption: white, gray, and black (Scott 1972). The gap traditionally separating the letter from the spirit of the law in Russia is characteristic of its legal culture and serves to explain its indigenous practices of informality. Dichotomies found in the language, such as the following pairs, illustrate the gaps in formal rules and informal norms: *zakonnost'* (legality) and *spravedlivost'* (justice); *chestnost'* (honesty) and *poriadochnost'* (propriety); *svoboda* (freedom) and *volia* (free will); *pravda* (rightness) and *istina* (truth) (see appendix 1).[30] The discrepancy, say, between legality and justice is indicative of a gap between impersonal rules encapsulated in legal procedures and norms and customs reproduced and enforced socially. Alexander Iakovlev argues that law in Russia has never been associated with moral truth. "[The law] existed 'out there' but reality for most people was harsh and oppressive, unjust and cruel." With reference to Russian intellectual history, he remarks:

> That conscience and ethics are supposed to be the basic part of law-consciousness and that public morals are supposed to be the founda-

tions of law are taken for granted in Western legal culture. In the Russian cultural tradition a tragic contradiction existed between the law and conscience, between morals and the law. In a situation where the law is equated only with the power of a tyrannical state, where the law is not respected but only feared, the idea of fairness is contrasted to existing laws. (Iakovlev 1995, 12–14)

Legal behavior is generally assumed to be a norm, but in the context of the radical changes in the 1990s local knowledge was often essential for understanding what was "normal" instead. Ordinarily, laws are assumed to be made in a lawful way, but legislation may also serve specific interests, particularly in the context of state capture (Hellman et al. 2001).[31] Examples range from local legislation on privatization of garages in the center of St. Petersburg to legislation on product-sharing agreements for natural resources that often benefit a particular circle of people. The budget for elaboration of new legislation is so low (an estimate of $100 in some Duma committees) that it is inevitable that big businesses are invited to "help" with "independent" legal expertise by involving their own legal consultants in the process. This is a classic example of how the defects in formal institutions bring informal practices into being.[32] Because the law is used instrumentally by the state, it is replicated at all levels. Legal expertise is becoming a creative profession, full of wit and invention.

Informal practices are often justified as a rational response to perceived defects in formal rules and their enforcement, but they are also indicative of defects in informal norms, both producing and resulting from patterns of distrust of public institutions and disregard for formal rules. It is logical that Russian players engaged in strategies rewarded in the post-Soviet decade helped to carry the burden of Russia's overall transition and made personal fortunes. But it is also logical to blame these players for "abusing the rules of the game" and for manipulating the system to their advantage. It is the paradox of informal practices in the 1990s that they facilitated but also impeded the transition.

Given that informal practices are engaged in advancing but also undermining the workings of market and democracy, the field is too vast to cover. I start with identifying informal practices enveloping the electoral campaigning in the 1990s. Many assumed that if there were elections, democracy was working. Instead, imperfections of the emerging democratic institutions were often compensated for and manipulated by an increasing body of PR firms and electoral technologists.

Chapter Two

Chernyi Piar: Manipulative Campaigning and the Workings of Russian Democracy

Introducing Black *Piar*

If one has to decide on the most significant political change in Russia brought about by the end of communism, it is the fact of competitive elections. This change is fundamental not only because it reflects a breakthrough in the formal political framework codified in the Constitution and electoral legislation but also because it has reached the grassroots level: people's attitudes to and behavior during the elections have indeed transformed. Despite the variety of republican constitutions, regional political regimes, and patterns of electoral behavior across the eighty-nine federal subjects of Russia that have been well documented (Gel'man, Ryzhenkov, and Brie 2002; Nicholson 1999), competition became a universal and undisputed feature of Russian elections during the 1990s. At the same time, the key features of elections during this period—both political and pragmatic—are not always the ones people expect. One influential lobbyist offered the following overview of the Yeltsin period, when the strong controlling state lost its grip over the economy and society. Speaking in 1999, he captured the situation rather well:

> We face a situation where elections are decisive, not only in the sense of who is going to be the next president, but also which political and economic system Russia will have; where votes in the Duma are predetermined and no argument can alter the political standoff; where

the elites are extremely antagonistic among themselves; and where there is no middle class, the social structure is post-totalitarian, and there is no basis for real political parties (the only party is CPRF). This lack of structured political processes results in ongoing election campaigns. There is no other mechanism of protecting one's interests besides coming to power through election: fixed, not fixed—any victory will do. . . .

Under such conditions, to think that laws can work is unrealistic.[1] This is not an excuse—it's a reality. Needless to say, this creates the perfect environment for informal agreements [*dogovornye ot-nosheniia*]. When there are no universally applied rules, one is forced to just go and negotiate, bargain, and come to an agreement with a particular official. Both the official and I are keen to distance ourselves from these abnormal [elected] deputies and from these silly laws which either contradict each other or are impossible to follow. In situations of chaos, people are motivated to agree informally, to pay, or to use pressure because there is no other way to get things done. This is the situation. [3.15]

Such characteristics of the 1990s suggest that Russia has not followed the three-stage process of democratization—opening, breakthrough, and consolidation—into its third stage.[2] Rather, it has entered what Carothers characterizes as a political "gray zone" (2002, 7–8). Countries in the gray zone

have some attributes of democratic political life, including at least limited political space for oppositional parties and independent civil society, as well as regular elections and democratic consolidations. Yet they suffer from serious democratic deficits, often poor representation of citizens' interests, low levels of political participation beyond voting, frequent abuse of the law by government officials, elections of uncertain legitimacy, very low levels of public confidence in state institutions, and persistently poor institutional performance by the state. (2002, 9–10)

According to Carothers, of the one hundred or so countries that could be identified as transitional, fewer than twenty are clearly on the path to becoming successful well-functioning democracies. The majority of third-wave countries do not appear to be consolidating their early democratic promise. While some have regressed into explicit authoritarianism, most transitional countries (including Russia—AL) are "neither dictatorial, nor clearly headed for democracy" (2002, 9). The sheer number of prefixes and qualifiers that have been coined to describe the "democracies" that inhabit this gray zone is telling: semi, formal, electoral, façade, pseudo, weak, partial, illiberal, and virtual, to name only a few.[3]

Rather than inventing terms to describe transition and democracy, I analyze the colloquial ways of describing post-Soviet developments that characterize the gray zone of the post-Soviet political order. In this chapter I explain the workings of informal practices that not only compensate for the defects of political institutions, as illustrated by my respondent above but also exploit these institutions for the advantage of vested interests—thus accounting for the nontransparency of the political process. I argue in particular that practices of black and gray *piar* (a Russian transliteration of the abbreviation "PR" which has acquired its own connotations and circulation)[4] need to be examined, for they serve as an important indicator of the political regime that emerged in the 1990s. Viktor Shenderovich illustrates gray and black PR practices in the following satirical piece.

Black and Gray PR. Results Guaranteed.[5]

Good morning. I am from the firm "Reputation." Black and gray *piar*.
Black and gray . . . who?
Is this the election campaign headquarters?
Yes.
And who are you?
I do the cooking here.
Madam, call someone competent, only quickly.
Pavel Ignatevich, someone's come to see you!
Pavel Ignatevich enters.
Good morning. I am from the firm "Reputation." Black and gray PR. Results guaranteed.
Tell me more.
About black or gray PR?
Black. The very blackest type.
Oh, don't worry. Complete moral destruction of a rival assured. Creation of a black biography with evidence and documentation. Theft at school, schizophrenia, membership of the Jehovah's Witnesses, betrayal of our Motherland, child masturbation—anything you want.
How much?
Anywhere from a thousand up to one hundred thousand.
Up to one hundred thousand?

For one hundred thousand it will be on the evening news.

OK, but only if it's the main story!

As you like. It's possible to organize it so that there will be absolutely no other news on that day. But then that's two hundred thousand.

And what about all that together? Everything you mentioned—a sect, the masturbation, betrayal of the Motherland, but all together? So that he can't recover.

A million will be sufficient.

A million? You can't be serious.

You want him not to recover.

That's what I want. OK. One second. (*Into the receiver*). Hello! Serezha, do you know how much it costs to get rid of someone? Physically. It doesn't matter who—in general, man! I'll wait. (*To the visitor*). Now we'll compare prices. (*Into the receiver*). What? Thank you. (*He hangs up*). (*To the visitor*) You'll get nothing from me. For a million I can ruin him together with his election campaign headquarters and voters without the need for any PR.

You're disposing of me?

This is the market.

OK, eight hundred thousand.

You can't be serious.

And how much are you willing to pay?

All together?

Yes.

Including betrayal of the Motherland and masturbation?

Yes!

Three hundred!

You're joking.

Three hundred maximum.

I'll leave you now and go to your rival—and in five minutes you'll be the one accused of masturbation.

No!

Don't doubt me for a minute. Plus the green standard of Islam in your bedroom and the abuse of a minor during a public holiday.

No!

Tomorrow on the evening news. Be sure not to miss it.

OK, five hundred thousand.

Bestiality, house in the Bahamas, and relation to Chikatilo.[6]

Seven hundred thousand, and the deal is done.

I knew that we'd come to an agreement.

Only that should include everything: also Islam, bestiality and Chikatilo!
Hasn't he got enough already?
Just the right amount.

Like many other stories by Viktor Shenderovich, a screenwriter for the
satirical TV puppet show *Kukly,* which was popular in the 1990s for depict-
ing key politicians and reproducing their looks, mannerisms, and discourses, this one is as sad as it is funny. One simply cannot ignore the unprecedented development of the political consulting industry, as evidenced
by the proliferation of public relations firms, training programs, university
courses and degrees, literature, and an army of "craftsmen" specializing in
electoral technologies.[7] In calling themselves imagemakers, politologists,
PR men, political technologists, and political consultants, they introduce
new terms into the post-Soviet discourse. When asked to look back at the
history of Russian PR, Ekaterina Egorova of the PR Agency *Nikkolo M* remarked:

> Surprisingly, Russian PR appeared practically out of nowhere. Vari-
> ous professions that had already existed merged to give life to this
> new and alien phenomenon. It turned out that one had to communi-
> cate ideas to the people, to explain. Crucially, trust was requested
> from society. There had previously been few such practices in the
> USSR. Society, which had to be communicated with, requested "*tol-
> machi,*" who could translate from the official and political language
> into human. Soon afterwards such a translation was also in demand
> by businesses. (Egorova 2003)[8]

In a period of less than seven years during the 1990s, more than eighty institutions of higher-learning created departments to train these new specialists. PR degrees became popular, image-making courses filled up, text-
books were written, professional journals were established, and PR
professionals began to celebrate a Day of the Political Consultant (*Den'
politkonsul'tanta*) on February 24. Although the use of political PR essentially "professionalized" the election campaigns, it also became notoriously
associated with the use of manipulative campaigning during elections,
widely referred to as "black *piar.*"[9]

A recent dictionary of contemporary terminology defines *piar* as the release of "information in the mass media for publicity and imagemaking as
part of electoral technology" (*Kratkii slovar' sovremennykh poniatii i termi-*

nov, 2002, 410). The term "black *piar*" applies to the formation of a negative opinion of someone or something (*Tolkovyi slovar' sovremennogo
russkogo iazyka: Iazykovye izmeneniia kontsa XX stoletiia*, 2001, 569).

PR professionals have criticized the catchy phrase "black piar." Andrei
Biriukov, one of the public faces of the political PR agency Nikkolo M, remarked, "If we are talking about things like super-glueing leaflets with a
picture of a rival candidate onto someone's windscreen, then it's simply
'black technology,' rather than a form of public relations."[10] Some suggest
further that it is not even a technology but simply an illegal act. In its most
aggressive forms, black *piar* is associated with violation of both legal and
ethical norms, and should lead to criminal charges. In his book on informational and political technologies, Georgii Pocheptsov expressed a similar
opinion, claiming that "black *piar* is more of a journalistic term. . . . PR can
be either 'white' or nothing at all" (2003, 42).

Indeed, in the press, the dominant perspective used in covering the activities of political technologists is that of black PR. The head of the PR
agency Image-Contact, Aleksei Sitnikov, expressed his indignation:

> Ten years ago when the PR industry just started developing in Russia,
> we tried to do everything possible for the public to accept the idea
> and started talking about PR. Probably we overdid it—too much PR.
> Now a report in a newspaper about ordered killings can appear under
> the title "The next dirty *piar* campaign." . . . This is how our profes-
> sion is understood in society. Ordinary people relate it to shamanism
> or cheating. Businessmen and politicians see PR men as prostitutes.
> In this situation we will probably have to find another name and
> prove that what we are doing is not *piar* at all. This is already happen-
> ing. For example, many PR specialists started calling themselves spe-
> cialists in intergrated marketing and communication or specialists in
> development of relations with the public (*razvitie obshchestvennykh
> sviazei*), in fact simply using the direct translation of the term PR into
> Russian.[11]

The president of the PR Publicity holding, Gai Khanov, attacks the press
even more directly. He refers to black PR as "illegal methods, by which
media outlets or journalists accept bribes in exchange for publication of
materials, which are specifically intended to sway public opinion in favor of
or against a certain candidate."[12] This practice is also known as *zakazukha*
or *zakaznye stat'i* (prepaid publications). The cost of prepaid articles varies

significantly depending on the election, the candidate, and the media outlet. As one of my respondents, a qualified lawyer and an experienced participant in regional electoral campaigns, explained:

> Before the start of the election campaign we put together a list of
> journalists with whom we can work. On a regional level, it is regional
> television and newspapers. On the level of local government, exclud-
> ing large cities with their own television, television practically never
> takes part, while the printed leaflets and everything else is done on a
> very modest budget, as the local level is normally not interesting for
> big business. [2.5]

On a federal level, the situation is different. According to a published
source, a journalist would receive $1,000–$2,000 for an article of a positive
nature, but a compromising article would cost anything from $2,000–
$6,000, and the PR company would charge its client $8,000–$10,000.[13] In
my interviews, I frequently learned that it could cost $500–$3,000 for an
article to appear during the run-up to an election, depending on the article's size, source, and the name or the position of the journalist, whereas
PR charges were estimated at $8,000–$30,000. Custom-made (*shtuchnye*)
articles could cost as much as $30–$50,000, whereas a TV release to the
same effect would take the price up to the $20,000–$100,000 range [2.21].

By shifting the blame from bribe taker to bribe giver, Sergei Mikhailov,
the head of Mikhailov and Partners PR agency in Moscow, notes that "90
percent of Russian *piarshchiki* [PR men] bribe journalists and only 10 percent create informational incentives for the press to present their client in a
beneficial context, while in the U.S. the ratio is the reverse."[14]

Evgenii Minchenko, head of the analytical agency New Image, supports
the argument against the PR men, raising the question of their lack of professionalism and their own practices of accepting payment for black PR
technologies. In his book *How to Become and to Stay a Governor* (2001), he
states, "In our view, what is normally called 'dirty technologies' in a majority of cases comes from the lack of professionalism; the effectiveness [of
black technologists] is debatable. . . . Their talks with potential clients, regardless of the situation, are reduced to promises to apply the 'dirtiest technology' for corresponding payment" (11). Shenderovich has illustrated this
point in his satirical piece on black and gray PR, presented earlier.

Thus, responsibility for the omnipresence of black PR is shared between
those journalists interested in receiving "up to a month's pay for a single
article" and those technologists who pay the journalists to pursue their

goals, normally prepaid by their own clients.[15] "Thus, such journalism creates black PR, while black PR creates prepaid journalism [*zakaznoi zhurnalizm*]."[16]

As part of an anti-black PR action in early 2001, a St. Petersburg agency, Promaco PR, intentionally violated the Press Law by offering payment to twenty-one press outlets to publish commercial disinformation in an editorial format rather than as commercial advertising (introducing a nonexistent company that opened a nonexistent shop at a nonexistent address). A full story appeared in the article "The Russian press turned out to be for sale: 13 central press outlets have published misinformation for money" in *Kommersant*.[17] Thirteen out of twenty-one outlets published the covert advertising in the form of an article on the condition of prepayment, three recommended it for publication as advertising, four asked for additional information, and one published it for free (*Klient*). Invoices from the publications included the following euphemistic formulations:

Moskovskii Komsomolets, publication on February 17: 26,800 rubles for "advertising"

Rossiiskaia Gazeta, February 22: 57,320 rubles for "producing a media product for RG"

Novye Izvestiia, February 20: $800 for "publication in a newspaper"

Ekonomika i Zhizn', February 24: 18,360 rubles "for publication of an article with information about the shop Svetofor"

Vremia MN, February 17: $595 for "a publication in the newspaper"

Komsomol'skaia Pravda, February 17: 15,687 rubles for "informational material 1/8"[18]

Vremia Novostei, February 16: $525 for "publication of an informational article"

Nezavisimaia Gazeta, February 23: 14,340 rubles for "preparation of a publication on Svetofor"

Obshchaia Gazeta, February 16: 8,577 rubles for an "informational article 1/16"

Vecherniaia Moskva, February 19, 6,000: rubles for "services of the concern VM in publishing informational materials about the opening of Svetofor"

Tribuna, February 16: 3,859 rubles for "informational services at volume of 1/32 column"

Profil', February 19: $1,732 for "publication of advertising 1/4 column"

Argymenty i Fakty, February 21: 18,050 rubles for an "advertising publication on Svetofor"

In a press release, Promaco explained that it tried to do business in the Moscow media market by the rules outlined in the Press Law but realized that nobody else worked like that. Promaco claimed that prepaid journalism diminishes the trust of the population and creates "incentives that result in the media receiving less income from advertising and in companies opting for alternative [cheaper] ways of spending their PR budget."[19] Moreover, in the case of political PR, the damage has further implications for the public perception of liberal values, free media, and beliefs in principles of democracy.

To sum up the public debates on black PR, it is customary for the press to blame PR men, for the PR agencies to blame the press, and for citizens to blame both. Ordinarily, this kind of discourse ends up with a discussion of the "nonprofessional" (that is, "bribable," or "needy") behavior of individuals or groups, often along the lines of "Why do bad people do it?" This is similar to the old days, when certain immoral individuals were blamed for practices incompatible with the official ideology of the Soviet system. For a careful observer, however, the black PR discourse is symptomatic of a situation where certain defects of formal institutions (weakness of political parties, lack of independent media, disrespect for the law) create incentives for informal practices to spread. If one considers these practices systematically—that is, as indicators of formal systems—the issue that really should be discussed here is not why bad people do it but why good people do it.

It should be noted that the controversy around the term "black PR" is generic to the terms designating informal practices. Because it refers only to their dark side, the term is dismissed as wrong, speculative, coined by the press, and certainly unrelated to the respondents, or indeed the majority of professional players. By brushing off the term and stigmatizing it as a "journalistic construct," one avoids acknowledging the gray areas hiding behind it. Thus, the meaningful aspects of gray PR that are most essential for understanding the nature of black PR remain unexplored.

The Definition of Informal PR practices

It would be convenient to define black PR practices (such as the manipulation of results at polling stations, cutting the cables of a local TV station to block a competitor's campaign, organizing violent meetings in the streets and attributing them to one's opponent) as simply illegal. Yet in practice the term is used to include formally legal technologies, one of the most common examples being *dvoiniki* (double candidates). Candidates with the same or similar-sounding surname as a rival are often registered in order to confuse the voters on election day.[20] This trick has been used in the elections across the world and reinvented in Russia through the 1990s. Take, for example, a doctor from Riazan', Svetlana Moreva, who changed her surname in September 2003 to Svetlana Kprf, an acronym for the Communist Party of the Russian Federation (KPRF), and registered as a candidate in district 150 in Riazan' oblast'. Her electoral double, Sergei Kprf, registered in district 149. The president of the Association of Advertising Agencies, Vladimir Evstaf'ev, observed that these two candidates had no chance to be elected to the Duma, but their role was to divert votes from the Communist Party. He adds that the double candidates are normally independent candidates, who "did not sign or agree about anything," and that the law does not ban the use of doubles.[21] Likewise, entire political parties were set up along similar lines for the 2003 parliamentary elections, such as the Conservative Party of the Russian Federation (KPRF) and the Constitutional Party of the Russian Federation (KPRF). This is despite the fact that the main political parties—United Russia (ER), the Communist Party (KPRF), the Union of Right Forces (SPS), Iabloko (Russian democratic party), and the Liberal-Democrats (LDPR)—had agreed not to use "black technologies" in the elections.

Because the law is often not respected or enforced and legal loopholes are freely used, the criterion of legality is not sufficient for classifying the existing variety of practices. As Egorova (2003) put it, "There is the law and everything that does not contradict the law is legal. But this does not mean it is good and honest. This paradox is actively used by organizers of election campaigns. And these people are not exclusively PR men." Introducing an ethical dimension helps to illustrate this paradox in more detail (see table 2.1). There is little question about illegal and unethical forms of black PR as such, but as an idiom, "black PR" is applied to a wider range of practices, which makes it a helpful point of departure for looking into the gray areas as well. As mentioned above, black PR often refers to everything that is not white, thus conflating black (that is, illegal and unethical) forms of PR with gray ones, which can be either illegal but ethical or legal but unethical. There are further shades of gray, of course, and even these two types can hardly be equally "gray," but let me illustrate the multiplicity of gray areas with examples.

TABLE 2.1
Types of PR

	Legal	Illegal
Ethical	white PR[a]	gray PR
Unethical	gray PR	black PR

[a] An intelligent case of white PR can be found on the http://www.uznai-presidenta.ru (Get to Know the President) website, but I do not discuss white PR in this context. An impressive product of PR technologists is the study of the formation of Russia's new political and economic elites (Sitnikov et al. 2004).

Illegal but Ethical

Electoral law prescribes limits to the amount of money that can be spent during official electoral campaigns. However, this amount is so low that it is regularly exceeded as a matter of course. According to experts, "white," or legal, funding amounts to only a small percentage of the overall cost of electoral campaigns, which results in the use of various techniques to cover up "black" expenses with "white" finances.[22] The gap between official and unofficial funding can range from two to three times in local elections and from thirty to forty times in strategic regional elections.[23] One respondent estimated that in 1997–2000, the average total black cost of a regional election campaign involving a serious PR company from Moscow could reach from two to five million dollars (maximum $100,000,000 in the most complicated elections in oil regions) [2.21].

Although illegal, black finances can be used for ethical, or at least "not unethical," forms of campaigning, such as media coverage, organizational expenses, and political advertising (*nagliadka*), or can be used for bribing the electorate directly, which is both illegal and unethical (Kurtov and Kagan 2002, 108). One example came from then prime minister Putin's personal endorsement of the newly formed political party Unity (*Edinstvo*) in 1999. Putin was shown on TV embracing Sergei Shoigu, the minister for emergency situations and one of the leaders of Unity. He also was quoted in the media as saying: "As prime minister I have no right to support any party, but as a person I am going to vote for *Edin-*

stvo." Following this statement, a massive discussion was initiated in the press. The focus of the discussion was whether Putin had the right to make this statement and whether or not he had violated the law; the fact of the endorsement itself was taken for granted (a technique of controlled criticism envisaged by PR specialists). The average voter did not understand why the law should or should not allow Putin to express his sympathy for a political party, which seemed perfectly normal and ethical. Opposition to his having done so, formed on legal grounds and voiced in the media, worked in *Edinstvo*'s favor as well (Kagan and Kurtov 2002, 190).

There are further instances where black PR technologies are justified by the good, ethical, and democracy-supporting intentions of PR specialists. In an interview, Andrei Grachev, deputy director for public relations of the Zapoliarnyi office of Norilsk Nickel, tried to justify dubious means through the noble end of selecting the "right" candidate.

> Can PR men use black PR as a tool? For example, a surgeon uses a scalpel. Is this an inappropriate tool? It cuts and kills. Why do we not say that the surgeon's hands are bloody? Because he is saving human life. That's why there are no inappropriate tools or means [for electing the right candidate]. . . . An actual example: in the Krasnoiarsk legislative elections Viacheslav Nikonov defeated the popular [gangster] Pasha-Tsvetomusika.[24] For that many technologies were used, including those on the border of legality.[25]

The same logic was applied to Yeltsin's decision to launch an assault on his conservative enemies in parliament in 1993, as well as in his reelection campaign in 1996.[26] An eyewitness recalled,

> One could see in Davos in 1996 that Ziuganov was serious and that the risk to Yeltsin's electoral chances was real. Yeltsin did not come to Davos again. Ziuganov did sound sensible—like a leftist semi-red social democrat. We saw the reaction of the West: they will accept anybody. The situation prompted Chubais into action. Overnight, information (and *kompromat*) was collected and compiled so that in an impromptu press conference the next day, Chubais could illustrate the contrast between what Ziuganov said in his speeches in the Russian provinces and what he said in Davos. That certainly had an effect and resulted in the so-called Davos pact.[27] [3.16]

The ends of securing democratic development for Russia seem to have justified the means, which could be argued to be the only possible solution during this formative period. At the same time, these means put certain individuals and agencies above the law, thus violating the key principle of democracy—the rule of law—and possibly resulting in an escalation of the use of illegal but "justifiable" actions. The most sophisticated political technologies, however, do not require outright violation. The letter of the law can be followed formally while the spirit of it is broken.

Legal but Unethical

Among the legal but unethical practices of gray PR, the most frequent are the ones bending the law to the advantage of a certain candidate. For example, in regional elections, political consultants often come across cases of inconsistencies between regional and federal legislation. In an interview, Aleksandr Ivanchenko, the former chairman of the Central Election Commission (CEC) confirmed:

> We come across collisions like this very often, when regional laws contradict the Constitution. In St. Petersburg, elections of local deputies lacked the law on elections. . . . Right now the CEC is very much concerned with the situation in Udmurtiia, where the local elections are scheduled for April 4 [1999]. The election campaign is going on already, but there is no appropriate law for holding the elections.[28]

The actions of the CEC (*Tsentrizbirkom*)—itself an influential actor in any electoral campaign—always follow the law—that is, it can demand a synchronization of regional and federal legislation prior to the elections. At the same time, however, it can pursue hidden agendas: electoral committees at all levels are part of a complex web of interests and have their own positions toward candidates. They can be influenced and can exert influence themselves.[29] The CEC's capricious application of the law has done much to skew the playing field, with dozens of cases of candidates being selectively disqualified.[30] The CEC has refused to register candidates for trivial offenses and has often not given them a chance to resolve minor problems such as adding a signature or making a declaration of profession on a form. At the same time it has been extremely passive in considering cases involving the use of administrative resources during election campaigns.[31] In the context of the law being manipulated by the CEC, which is meant to monitor and arbitrate the legality of elections, the position of political technologists is not surprising. As Kurtov and Kagan have noted, when an inconsistency between federal and regional law is beneficial for their candidate, they would argue that the discrepancy is of no consequence to the elections, whereas in the opposite case they could initiate a scandal around this "appalling" fact (2002, 139).

Gray, Not Black

To sum up, the term "black PR" appears in various contexts, but it is commonly associated with negative information about a political competitor. As Aleksandr Lubenets, chairman of the Novosibirsk electoral fund put it, "I would say that this [black PR] is the creation, over a definite period of time, of a negative image of a subject using dubious, false information by means of various influences over the electorate."[32] From the perspective of informal practices, however, it is the gray areas that are particularly telling. I use a more inclusive term, "gray PR," to designate the body of practices used by political technologists who circumvent formal regulatory frameworks by exploiting legal loopholes and by using the law manipulatively (legal but unethical), or by engaging in illegal but not unethical practices in order to mastermind elections (illegal but ethical). It is these practices of gray PR that are essential for understanding the workings of informal politics and the technical aspects of "making" elections work.

In effect, political consultants perform the same function in politics as the present-day *tolkachi* do in the economy: they facilitate democratic or market changes in an environment where formal institutions are not yet fit to underpin such changes. Correspondingly, all large companies have their own PR agencies, as well as security departments, while smaller ones are serviced by independent agencies. Political consultants and PR firms should not, of course, be directly associated with informal practices, but their creative approach to the law, their expertise in finding and using legal loopholes, and their dependence on black cash are certainly conducive to the spread of informal practices stemming from the defects in the formal rules and procedures. Once invented as know-how, manipulative patterns are willingly or unwillingly reproduced and thus become established as "technologies." The effectiveness of these technologies depends on the existence of a gap between formal rules and informal codes—so-called practical or soft norms (Blundo and Sardan, 2001).[33]

ОТКРЫТОЕ ПИСЬМО
кандидату в депутаты Государственной Думы РФ
Виктору Леонидовичу

Уважаемый Виктор Леонидович!

Я с Вами давно и хорошо знакома. Прекрасно помню то холодное осеннее утро 1998 года, когда, выйдя из дома, я увидела Ваш предвыборный плакат. Вы сразу понравились мне как женщине. Я, можно сказать, даже влюбилась в Вас. Уверенное молодое лицо, преданный взгляд, искренняя улыбка, добрые вдумчивые глаза. Я помню Вас таким по Вашим листовкам пятилетней давности. Одна из них до сих пор хранится у меня.

На ней Вы преданно смотрите на портрет Юрия Болдырева. Человека, учеником и соратником которого Вы себя тогда называли. Человека, именем которого Вы клялись в своих предвыборных материалах. Человека, благодаря которому Вы тогда стали депутатом Законодательного собрания. Человека, которому Вы обещали сложить с себя депутатские полномочия, если не оправдаете его доверия. Вы даже подписали с ним договор об этом. И **Юрий Болдырев сделал все для Вашей победы в его избирательном округе.** По его просьбе мы проголосовали за Вас. Вы победили! Несколько дней спустя, Вы вышли из его фракции, заявив, что читаете себя свободным от любых обязательств.

Я даже не помню названия всех многочисленных фракций Законодательного Собрания, которые я узнавала после этого из каждого нового выпуска Вашей газеты «Виктория». Я получала ее постоянно все 4 года Вашей депутатской работы. Ведь Вы не забывали о нас, Ваших избирателях, потому что знали: в отличие от Юрия Болдырева, мы Вам еще пригодимся.

Став депутатом, Вы познакомились с Владимиром Анатольевичем Яковлевым. Вас даже приблизили к нему. Вы многое получили от Владимира Анатольевича. Вы стали его советником. У Вас появился кабинет не только в Мариинском дворце, но и в Смольном. **Вы гордились Вашей дружбой с Владимиром Анатольевичем.** В кругу своих близких он называл Вас своей надеждой. Дал вам карт-бланш на новые выборы. Я хорошо помню, как Владимир Анатольевич пожимал Вашу руку на листовках, как он агитировал в Вашу поддержку. Как, даже в нарушение закона, просил помочь Вам своих подчиненных. Вы твердо заверяли нас, своих избирателей, что всегда будете вместе с губернатором. Мы снова поверили Вам и избрали для того, чтобы защитить нашего губернатора. Теперь Вы пишете о том, что В.А.Яковлев мешал Вам заниматься законодательной работой, что из-за него в нашем городе не выплачиваются доплаты пенсионерам и детям из детских домов. Вам не стыдно, Виктор Леонидович?

Вскоре после выборов Вы перестали нуждаться во Владимире Анатольевиче. Не прошло и нескольких недель, как Вы увидели перед собой новые перспективы. Вам захотелось стать депутатом Государственной Думы. Так **Вы оказались в рядах его противников в городском парламенте.** Вскоре Вас заметили рядом с **предвыборным штабом В. И. Матвиенко.** Здесь Вы вновь были на коне. Готовясь к выборам в Думу, Вы были рядом с Валентиной Ивановной так же, как до этого с Владимиром Анатольевичем.

Виктор Леонидович, за время знакомства с Вами я поняла одно. **Вы привыкли использовать людей для того, чтобы подниматься по ступеням власти.** Правда, Вы недорого цените наши голоса: перед выборами Вы выдаете по 500 рублей или скудному продовольственному набору. Да, для многих пожилых людей и эти крохи — праздник. Поэтому Вы и используете наших стариков. Вы часто пишете о том, что за многое благодарны Вашим бабушке и дедушке. **Неужели это они научили Вас такому?**

Ваша политическая история — это история не одного предательства. Это цепь последовательно использованных Вами людей, в которых Вы переставали нуждаться. Сегодня Вы вместе с сильной и уверенной в себе женщиной — губернатором нашего города. Сколько времени Вам потребуется, чтобы предать нового патрона? И кого еще Вы хотите использовать, чтобы пройти в Думу?

Я снова вглядываюсь в Ваш плакат. И вижу, то, что замечаешь не сразу. Предавший не одного человека взгляд, свмоуверенное лицо, холодные, без капли человеческого тепла, глаза, надменная улыбка. Виктор Леонидович, мы с Вами давно и хорошо знакомы. Я уже дважды была использована Вами, когда Вы прорывались к власти. И очень не хочу быть использованной в третий раз.

Ваша бывшая избирательница Елена Фомина

Изготовитель ООО «Снайкс», 190031, Санкт-Петербург, ул. Гороховая, 33, лит. А. Заказ № 273 от 05.12.2003 г. Тираж 80 000 шт. Заказчик Фомина Елена Владимировна.

Figure 2.1. Sample of black piar: an open letter to the State Duma deputy candidate. The text is written as a personal letter to one of the candidates from a female supporter in the last elections. She nearly fell in love with him originally but became extremely disappointed later. This conspicuously smearing document refers to only a few facts that can be checked out (say, the candidate distributes 500 rubles and modest food packages to pensioners in an effort to "buy" votes) but rather portrays the candidate as a chameleon character who betrays his patrons, changes his political alliances, and manipulates relationships with colleagues to climb up the political ladder. The account of the candidate's unethical attitudes is framed by reference to his portrait on the electoral posters: confident young face, committed look, sincere smile, kind intelligent eyes in the previous elections, and the look of traitor with self-assured face, cold eyes, and arrogant smile now. The letter ends with the words "I have been used twice by you on your way to power. I absolutely don't want to be used for the third time" and a signature "Your former supporter Elena Fomina." Such propaganda is delivered to people's postboxes in the pre-run to the election.

Black and Gray PR in Electoral Technologies in Russia

One of most inclusive classifications of black PR technologies, based on material from the Russian press, has been suggested by Anatolii Gusakovskii.[34] Gusakovskii does not distinguish between black and gray PR, or between PR and the use of administrative resources. His argument is that black, or manipulative, technologies (or informational special operations) should be identified with electoral technologies that work. Gusakovskii thinks electoral technologies are pervasive in the sense that "no politician or political movement can do without at least some of these techniques." In other words, as other technologists also suggest, "There are no dirty technologies, there are effective and noneffective technologies."[35] In this sense, the term "black *piar*" is all-embracing, covering the use of dirty technologies, administrative resources, corrupt practices in elections, and lawful electoral technologies—which makes little sense for more rigorous academic analyses. What does make a lot of sense, however, is to ask which technologies are commonly applied around the world and which are not. In other words, one should distinguish between uniform features of technologies, which make them comparable despite differences in socioeconomic contexts, and unique features shaped by specific sociohistorical circumstances.

Gusakovskii suggests that manipulative techniques themselves are by no means unique to Russia. The roots of black—in his terminology, "diversionist"—technologies are linked to special security services around the world, though most of them have been reinvented and adapted to post-Soviet conditions by PR specialists. Dmitrii Staritskii (2003) suggests that the infamous political technologist Koshmarov was the one who reinvented manipulative technologies developed in America much earlier and adapted them for the St. Petersburg city Duma elections in 1990. By the mid-1990s the industry even came up with a term—"*koshmarit*' " (to give nightmares, or to scare)—stemming from the surname of the pioneer.

To understand specifics of PR practices in Russia one has to look at them in comparative perspective. Having followed the recent elections in the United Kingdom and the United States, for example, I conclude that electoral technologies commonly make use of black and gray PR techniques that transgress common values, norms, or moral codes.[36] Most black or gray PR operates through media outlets, and most black and gray PR technologies are applied as ammunition in the context of election campaigns, regardless of their location. Electoral discourse is similarly loaded with metaphors of fighting in all its forms: a war (competing with enemies), a

game (competing with friends), or a crisis (competing with nature or circumstances). Political marketing is widely used in electoral technologies
across the world, and the top "designers" in this field travel around the
world. It has been argued that political marketing has reversed the role of
political leadership: rather than offering an appealing program to rational
individuals, political programs are designed to satisfy inner preferences of
the electorate, which are established through market research and focus
groups. In particular, such research targets swing voters. It seems common
for black or gray PR practices to involve some element of secrecy and manipulation, but at the same time the use of such tactics also indicates that
political competition is real.

In table 2.2, I outline some generic features of PR practices and those
factors that make PR practices play a much more significant role in electoral process in Russia. All the factors in the right column—the weakness of
political parties, the lack of independent media, problems with the use of
administrative resources and manipulative technologies, concerns over legality of finances in the elections, and susceptibility of the population to
propaganda—help to explain why gray PR practices are effective and are
used ubiquitously, or, in other words, why good people do black and gray
PR. Some of these features are covered in academic literature (Gelman
2002; Wilson 2005), while others deserve to be considered in more detail
below.

The Susceptibility of the Population to Influence and Propaganda

Among other important factors—the media (Belin 2002), political uncertainty (Kahn 2002; McAuley 1997), ideological thinking (Bunce 1995;
Schopflin 2000, 70) and voting patterns (Rose and Munro 2002), political
parties (Colton and McFaul 2003; Sakwa 2003), and regional specifics
(Ross 2002)—poverty and social polarization are key features that account
for the vulnerability of the Russian electorate during the 1990s.[37] Andrei
Lebedev, the creator of a "virtual electoral technology—soap opera" and
editor of the newspaper *Lider*, points out how poverty influences the use of
black PR.

> If the voters can sell their vote for a bottle, it signifies how they assess
> the future. It is unfortunate that, as before, the majority of Russians
> have nothing to lose, and so don't expect anything: no one believes
> that anything will change after the elections. . . . Professionals
> arrange the turnout, which reminds one of a show, "mixing in drama,

TABLE 2.2
Similarities and differences of manipulative campaigning

Uniform features of PR practices in electoral democracies	Unique features of black and gray PR in Russia
Electoral technologies generically make use of black and gray PR techniques based on transgression of certain values, norms, or moral codes.	Specifics of formal institutions and informal norms and codes define the difference: PR technologists in Russia use the law more abusively and frequently and with more impunity. Law is viewed as yet another constraint to play with.
Black and gray PR are used as ammunition in the context of election campaigns viewed metaphorically as a war, a game, or a crisis.	There is less constraint on financing the ammunition in Russian elections: the resources are often illegally used (whether administrative resources or private funds) and not declared fully and serve the purposes of donors.
Black or gray PR often operates through media outlets.	Specifics of the media: media in the West have established images and produce a stronger effect on their readers, while in Russia the public does not trust print media and is no longer receptive to *kompromat* spillovers. Use of black PR fabricated on the request of clients is much more common due to widespread journalism "on demand." Independent and investigative journalism is rare and dangerous; journalists are not paid well to sustain the prestige of the media.
Use of political marketing, it can be argued, has reversed the role of political leadership: rather than offering an appealing program to rational individuals, political programs are designed to satisfy needs and preferences of the electorate, which are established through market research and focus groups.	Weakness of party politics: there are no stable party images in Russia because of the short party history and the specifics of the political party formation process. Due to the political instability of the 1990s, reputations of politicians in Russia are volatile: they are easy to create and easy to ruin.
Black and gray PR target swing votes.	Specifics of voting behavior: the impact of black PR is weaker in mature electoral democracies because of the settled patterns of voting behavior (family voting, economic voting). In Russia the whole population is made up of swing voters because of the legacy of personalized politics and the weakness of political parties.

TABLE 2.2—cont.

Uniform features of PR practices in electoral democracies	Unique features of black and gray PR in Russia
Black or gray PR can involve an element of secrecy and manipulation.	The scale of manipulation in Russia is greater (creating "clone" parties, use of neurolinguistic programming (NLP) techniques[a] on TV) because of the factors outlined above.
Use of black and gray PR indicates that political competition is real, which is conducive to democracy.	The limits of manipulation in Russia are set by open competition (PR firms working for political opponents), by resource constraints, and by secret alliances between the participants of the electoral process (presidential administration, financial interests, political figures) rather than by law or traditional norms.

[a] The roots of political advertising are often associated with neurolinguistic programming. See Dilts (1980).

tragedy, and the grateful spectators give out their votes to those who present bigger and more brilliant distractions."[38]

This account hints at the effects of the economic reforms of the 1990s: fraudulent privatization, poverty and social polarization, insecure property rights, and the lack of economic interest on the part of the majority of voters. As one of the major political technologists put it, "Voting people are not those who run businesses, voting people are those in need. Every material benefit that they can get with a discount or for free makes a difference for them." [2.3] (See figure 2.2.)

With the lack of democratic traditions, the political field in Russia in the 1990s was rather bipolar: on the one hand were the authorities with their administrative resources, and on the other was private capital with its interests that turned elections into a business in its own right. The "unrootedness" of civil society resulted from and often reproduced the features of the legal and political culture in Russia (Brown 2005) and the legacy of the Soviet political regime (Howard 2003; Slater and Wilson 2004). These circumstances forced electoral technologists to operate in gray areas by playing on differences between legal and ethical norms, thus following a new set of unwritten rules (Ledeneva 2001b, 9–15).

At the election campaign meeting:

- How much are the votes today?

- Are you buying or selling?

Figure 2.2. "Votes: Buying or Selling?" *Krokodil,* no. 10, 1998. By permission of editor in chief.

Use of Administrative Resource

In the context of elections, "administrative resource"[39] refers to the use (or abuse) of bureaucratic advantages and material resources associated with public institutions for purposes of electoral campaigns of one or more candidates (Gelman 2002; Allina-Pisano 2005). According to a veteran of many election campaigns, the use of administrative resource in the preparation for elections at this time included:

First of all, contracts with or open takeover of the media. The latter involves legal takeover, organizational takeover by which the authorities plant their people in the media organizations, prepare their own printing facilities, and engage their own journalists. Secondly, it is the use of official cars and telephones in campaigns, which is omnipresent, but almost impossible to prove in court. The use of one's own administrative position is obvious when employees are given instructions to do or not to do something, but this is never done in writing. Employees would not testify against their boss, and even with audio or video evidence a legal charge is not an option. More-over, the link between the candidate and the employees is normally mediated by a formal "trusted person" and many informal ones. The informal representatives are "known" to be associated with the candi-dates, but legally the candidate is not responsible for their "initia-tives." So if some citizen of the Russian Federation decided to hand out propaganda materials, the candidate did not know about it, has not asked or paid that citizen. This is a frequent line of argumenta-tion in the courts. For proving the use of telephones for the purposes of the elections, one has to record the conversations, which is illegal, and therefore cannot be used as evidence in court. Thus the legal norms about the use of administrative position do not work in the sense that they are violated on a regular basis, but they could be put to work in the interests of the authorities, i.e when the court is asked to apply them. [2.5]

The selective application of law is even more frequent in law enforcement agencies.

Selective Law Enforcement

Administrative resources are exercised through the use of the police, secu-rity agencies, or anticrime units. For example, an anonymous telephone call to the police can empower them to engage in subsequent investiga-tions, gain access to the premises of electoral campaign headquarters, raid offices of political technologists, and install or withdraw intelligence equip-ment (*proslushka*).[40]

PR firms working against an incumbent are under systematic pressure. During one election campaign I was detained by agents of the antinar-cotic department and subjected to a search at the local police station. In some regions, the apartment where we stayed would be bugged (*proslushivat'sia*)—this is also a pressuring technique. I cannot speak for all regions, but there are certainly a few where security and law en-forcement agencies are used to their full capacity. For example, during the same electoral campaign, they simply stopped our car in the street and detained us on the basis of "suspicion of transporting weapons." The law does have a provision for "detainment on the grounds of sus-picion for the purposes of clarification." The use of this provision pro-duces an enormous psychological effect on people. For me it is easier as I am a lawyer and have experienced similar pressure in the past. But I've seen the reaction of other people in the campaigning team under these circumstances—it's deep fear. I told them, "It's OK, mates," but still some people left the campaign after the incident claiming, "We don't need these problems." This is just an example of the pressure that I have experienced myself. In that campaign, after the intervention of federal authorities, after the elections, I got a formal apology for "a mistake," but the pressure they put on us was within the existing legal framework, nothing extralegal at all. [2.5]

Selective Law Nonenforcement

Just as often, strategic noninterventions, rather than pressure techniques, can be used. Apart from actual pressure by police or state security services, administrative influence can be employed in blocking their action. The same legal expert explains:

> For example, our lawyers identify certain violations of the law, but the law enforcement agencies sort of follow the unwritten order not to intervene. Besides, they always refer to the election law which says that the organs of state power and local authorities do not have the right to participate in the electoral process. We tell them, "Look, it's a violation." They say, "We don't have the right to intervene—settle it with the election committee." The election committee says, "This is not our competence, you should go to militia (UVD)." This completes the circle. Under these circumstances in practice, it is only on order of a certain official that some legal action can take place. This is what real administrative resource means. [2.5]

What these examples tell us in general terms is that impersonal systems of trust are replaced by particularistic patterns, allowing those in positions of power to make a decision about whether a law should or should not be enforced—that is, to mediate the workings of formal institutions in an informal way. As one of my respondents put it in 2000:

> The law is personalized. Even the constitution in Russia is Yeltsin's. Correspondingly, every governor has his own regional interpretation of federal legislation—every "regional tsar" shapes the mechanism of the state machine. That's why the role of personality in Russia is unique. [2.2]

Such "personalized" mediation in the workings of Russian legal system creates a deadlock of dependence of legal institutions, meant to operate according to universally applied principles, on particularistic interests in any given situation. Such a deadlock is hard to break because the "mediators" are not capable of giving up their informal leverage as it defines their actual power in the formal order: their ability to pull strings, to make the state institutions work, or to intervene in the course of formal procedures.

In addition, the decisions of mediators can be determined by principles of joint responsibility, or *krugovaia poruka*. As Liubarev (2001) points out, the use of administrative resources can be stopped only if electoral committees treat all candidates equally and objectively. But for this to happen, the electoral committees would first have to be free and independent from executive authorities. The law provides for this independence, but in practice electoral commissions are dependent on local authorities to such a large extent that in some cases they are simply controlled by them (2001, 29). The same has been said about the courts. One respondent explained, "Sure we have independent courts, but people who work there receive their housing (*zhil'e*), if not their salary, from the authorities. Which kind of housing, when, and where depends on these officials" [2.10].[41]

In using legal loopholes, black and gray PR practices serve candidates as defense mechanisms against the selective use of the electoral law and law enforcement by incumbents.

Enabling Aspects of Legal Constraints

Following the logic of the abuse of administrative resource by incumbents and the selective use of law by electoral commissions and courts in favor of certain candidates, political technologists use devices available to them and use the existing legal constraints creatively. For example, legal rules about organization of a meeting with the electorate by one candidate enable another candidate to take advantage of it. According to a respondent with experience in the 1990s' regional election campaigns, such incidents were a regular occurrence: "Say a candidate organizes a meeting in a kindergarten and starts telling his story. . . . Meanwhile a KPRF candidate passes out his own leaflets, does not disturb anybody, and may even ask questions. It is perfectly legal to ask questions, but of course doing so creates additional interest in the communist candidate and may even sway the opinion of those present" [2.5]. Other examples come from political technologists themselves. According to Kurtov and Kagan (2002, 246), meetings organized by other candidates can be used against them within the framework of so-called special projects. Special projects involve a variety of things.[42]

> If we know the schedule of meetings of other candidates, we need to minimize the effect of their meetings. Of course, we will try to send a couple of our people with a camera. In case they are not allowed in by security, they will start a scandal: "They won't let us in again," "Your candidate does not want to speak to the people." It is illegal to prevent the public from attending a meeting with the candidate. While at the meeting, they will be very polite and politically correct, but will ask the same question they asked before. An awkward one. It really annoys the candidate, when every meeting somebody stands up, smiles and says: "Last time you could not answer my question. Could you please tell us today, why do you need accounts in foreign banks?" Thirty times like this in a row. (Kurtov and Kagan 2002, 247–48)
>
> Or,
>
> We know for certain that tomorrow there will be an organized meeting of our opponent. There will be a podium, a mike, a crowd and a lot of posters in support of that candidate. The meeting is going to be televised. Under the circumstances we need a mobile group which would minimize the effect of this meeting. What do we do? Say, overnight we produce similar-sized posters, only theirs support Pupkin, and ours support Mumkin. As the meeting starts, our people will join in just walking and looking around. Their candidate arrives—light-camera-action! And then it turns out that the number of posters for Pupkin is the same as for Mumkin. Besides, a few people demand: "Give me my say, I want to support Pupkin, he's good." So they come out and start speaking—not for Pupkin, but for Mumkin. It is important that this special project is permitted by the law. Look, we have the right to attend the meeting and we have the right to propagate for our candidate in the street. (Kurtov and Kagan 2002, 247–48)

Centrality of Law

Somewhat paradoxically, the manipulative use of the law (both in terms of violating its spirit and its letter) in the organization of election campaigns makes the law central to the activities of PR firms and results in a special role for lawyers. In organizing electoral campaigns, PR firms require continuous input from lawyers. According to reports, lawyers make sure that the formal side of the electoral process is properly documented; for example, contracts for rental of premises for a meeting with the electorate are signed and paid for from official funds. If agitators are used, employment contracts are signed and salaries are paid from official funds. Legal expertise is essential for preparing any printed propaganda materials (these always have to have the print number, name of the person responsible for it, and the telephone number of the local printing press) in order to protect the campaign from possible reprimands by the CEC. The election campaigns of opponents require the same legal monitoring.

Lawyers are involved in preparing and placing formal complaints with the courts or the election campaign headquarters on a regular basis. "For example, there came information that now, at night, near the election campaign headquarters of our competitor, leaflets are unloaded from two trucks. We know that two trucks of leaflets are not at all fifty thousand copies, as they declared, but at least two million. So somebody has to run, to illuminate the site, to film everything" (Kurtov and Kagan 2002, 249). Lawyers play a crucial role in framing the event for the purposes of a formal complaint.

Monitoring the media is essential for all candidates in elections with a view to possibly preparing formal complaints. These are not necessarily used but can be placed strategically at a certain moment in the election campaign. Even if lodging a formal complaint does not bring tangible results, it distracts the opponent from his or her own election campaign, diverts the time and effort of the candidate and his staff, exerts psychological pressure, and reduces the effectiveness of the election campaign.

Needless to say, lawyers can be overzealous about compliance and can spoil the creative side of technologies. As Kurtov and Kagan put it, "A lawyer should be a sensible person and understand the mission correctly. The task of the lawyer is to help the electoral campaign to conduct the planned events, to adjust them to the legal framework rather than criticize and turn down everything when in doubt. . . . We explain to our lawyers that they have to find legal ways of implementing what we plan. Make it happen but make sure everything is legal!" (2002, 241).

The use of legal constraints creatively is an important feature of informal practices.[43] According to most of my respondents, creativity is the key. As Kurtov and Kagan (2002, 173–76) summed up, "A central skill in electoral campaigns is finding the special perspective, the flexibility and creativity for dealing with situations, for playing against the rules where necessary, but within the limits of what's possible."

To sum up, a short formula that embraces all the factors responsible for the spread of black and gray PR practices in Russia includes the susceptibility of the population to influence and propaganda, the manipulation of formal constraints by all participants in the political process, and the defects in democratic institutions.

What Do Gray PR Practices Tell Us about the Political Regime?

Analogous to other informal practices, gray and black PR practices play both supportive and subversive roles in relation to the political regime. Their supportive aspects compensate for the defects of formal institutions, for contradictory regulations, and for imperfections in legislation and law enforcement. Their subversive role is associated with the manipulation of these defects and legal loopholes. Thus, informal PR practices are conducive to democratic elections but also divert their course. According to my respondents, the elections can be used for other political and business purposes. For example, a new candidate in the gubernatorial elections can be introduced only to establish his or her image in order to gain support in the subsequent mayoral elections, or a businessman can use his election campaign purely in order to advertise his commercial product.

Practices of gray and black PR are also paradoxical in the sense that they serve competition as well as the needs of the political regime in terms of the "manageability" of democracy. They are beneficial for certain groups of political technologists but also cater to the weaknesses of political parties. Such practices can be viewed as a "weapon of the weak" in the context of competition with an incumbent who has access to the administrative resource. At the same time, the impact of gray and black PR in combination with the administrative resource can be enormous, especially when viewed in the context of creating so-called clone parties. Consider the potential of electoral technologies illustrated by the success of the 1999 campaign of Unity in the last three months before the elections. Figure 2.3 represents survey results for the main competing parties as a background to the unprecedented success of Unity, a party created just a few months before the elections.

Party	Leaders
NDR (Our Home Russia)	Chernomyrdin, Ryzkov, Aiatskov
RNRP (Russian People's Republic Party)	Lebed'

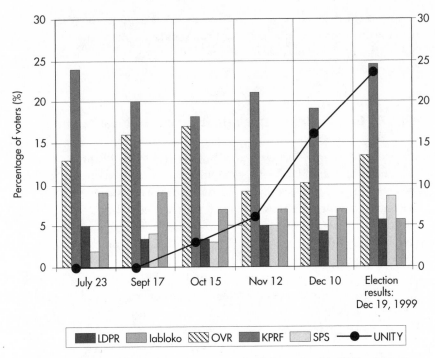

Figure 2.3. Results of public opinion surveys compared with the results of the 1999 parliamentary elections. Respondents were asked, "For which of the following parties [there was a list of parties to choose from] would you be most likely to vote if the elections were conducted over the upcoming weekend?"

LDPR (Liberal Democratic Party of Russia)   Zhirinovskii block

Iabloko (Russian democratic party)   Iavlinskii, Stepashin, Lukin

OVR (Motherland All Russia)   Primakov, Luzkov, Iakovlev

KPRF (Communist Party of the Russian Federation)   Ziuganov

SPS (Union of Right Forces)   Kirienko, Nemtsov, Khakamada

Unity (Edinstvo-Medved')   Shoigu, Karelin, Gurov

The well-documented weakness of party politics in Russia has certainly contributed to the effectiveness of electoral technologies in general and of gray and black PR practices in particular.

Characteristically, the public learns about the know-how of electoral technologies and gray and black PR practices after they have been used and have had an effect. Such secrecy makes them similar to the practices of *kompromat* and *krugovaia poruka,* considered in the next chapters, which normally can be grasped or interpreted adequately only after the fact. Needless to say, the timing of the disclosure of gray and black PR techniques and responses to such disclosures often depend on and are determined by the outcome of the elections.[44]

In the 1990s, practices of gray PR were indicative of the significant change in post-Soviet politics toward competitiveness, freedom of speech, and use of law in the new political contexts, but they were also indicative of the continuity of old ways of getting things done. The latter are grounded in features of Russian political culture and the Soviet ideological legacy, the frailty of individual rights, and the susceptibility of the population to propaganda. Gray and black PR practices also point to post-Soviet specifics of the media and informational field, characterized by the explosion of *kompromat* and the broker's role of security services in *kompromat* markets.

Most important, it is the scale and the manipulative patterns of following the letter of the law but violating its spirit that make PR practices in Russia different from electoral technologies used elsewhere. Understanding how legal constraints interact with social norms is especially important in identifying cases of gray PR (as seen in table 2.1), based on the violation of the spirit of the law (formal compliance, use of legal loopholes, avoidance of direct violation), and in attempts to regulate them. In an interview with *Rossiiskaia Gazeta* in October 2002, Aleksandr Veshniakov, chairman of the Central Election Commission, stated that the new electoral legislation (signed by the president on June 12, 2002) was intended to:

> put in place a systematic approach to shaping political power, which would cut off any accidental people with accidental connections and unclear financial inflows pumped into their election campaigns. . . . Raising the role of political practices in the electoral process, we also require transparency in all electoral tactics, along with removal from our laws of any nonspecific provisions that allow for sleazy electoral methods. Such provisions, together with political technologists, many of whom have no conscience or honor at all, make it possible to and are prepared to pervert the very concept of elections for the sake of making a profit.[45]

In the same interview he emphasized the importance of the new electoral legislation in stamping out dirty tricks:

Filth and falsehood should be opposed. We must learn from our mistakes, adjust and improve our election laws and comply with them, and impose rigorous sanctions on any perpetrators. . . . I believe that in a short time the legal framework for the electoral process will be set up and finely tuned, and it will start bearing tangible fruit. I mean it will be easier for us to counter black PR and other illegal forms of political campaigning.[46]

However, given that practices of gray and black PR by their very nature are informal practices that will continue to exist alongside the law rather than be directly regulated and curtailed by it, one has to assess their implications for the nature of formal institutions and the political regime at large. As has already been emphasized, the paradoxical role of informal practices points to the resistance to the administrative resource and to its predominance in electoral processes in Russia during the 1990s. The debate as to whether black PR should be stamped out through changes in legislation should take into account the fact that "abuse of the power of office, especially when it involves vote-tampering and removing candidates from the ballot, directly violates voters' rights. Negative campaigning, even in its most egregious forms such as libel, does not. It more likely violates the ruling elite's monopoly on tendentious campaign coverage."[47]

Naturally, the forms of political competition that existed in the 1990s have continued to change. Since 1999, the focus of competition, for example, first shifted to the regional elections. But even in the regions, the effectiveness of PR practices seems to have gradually diminished. As Pavel Klachkov suggested, the 2002 Krasnoiarsk regional elections signified the "end of Russian *piar*."[48] The electorate starts feeling cheated. Voters cannot understand the nature of it exactly, but they sense that what's going on is some kind of deception.[49] The technologies based on gray and black PR have become less effective, while elections themselves have become less trusted. It is therefore not surprising that when Putin revoked Yeltsin's 1996 decision to allow regional governors to be elected, it caused little protest in the regions. The nomination of regional governors by the president was intended to protect the governors from dependence on their pre-election supporters (see *krugovaia poruka* in chapter 4). There used to be "people with large sums of money who provide[d] for the elections and then [went] to the governor to solve various problems [*reshat' voprosy*] because they supported him before he became a governor" [5.40].

With fewer elections to work for, political PR agencies are on the decline and are switching to business PR and activities abroad. Overall, the decline of gray and black PR practices in politics could have been a good thing had it not also been indicative of an increasingly noncompetitive environment associated with Putin's rule (and the dependence of regional governors on those nominating them).[50] Only those PR agencies working with administrative resources have a chance to succeed, thus becoming tools of mass manipulation and propaganda. Although the decline of PR practices does not automatically imply that the security services will resume their Soviet functions of promoting the missionary ideology of the political regime, of controlling the opposition, and of organizing protests and special events, it is certainly indicative of the atmosphere of political intransigence.

Chapter Three

Kompromat: The Use of Compromising Information in Informal Politics

The Minister of Justice, Valentin Kovalev, was removed from his post in June 1997 after a Russian newspaper, *Sovershenno Sekretno*, published photographs from a video of Kovalev with prostitutes in a sauna controlled by the criminal group Solntsevskaia. The accompanying article was titled "The Minister Has No Clothes." In a subsequent interview with the newspaper, *Moskovskii Komsomolets*, Kovalev said, "Kompromat is vile. Once it starts, it knows no limits. Kompromat is always effective in Russia."[1]

Introducing *Kompromat*

The word *kompromat* has no direct equivalent in English. Its literal translation—"compromising material"—refers to discrediting information that can be collected, stored, traded, or used strategically across all domains: political, electoral, legal, professional, judicial, media, or business.[2] A recent dictionary of contemporary terminology defines *kompromat* as an abbreviated term for disparaging documents on a person subject to investigation, suspicion, or blackmail, derived from 1930s secret police jargon (*Kratkii slovar' sovremennykh poniatii i terminov* 2002, 254). In its contemporary context, the term is strongly associated with kompromat wars—intrigues exercised through the release of often unsubstantiated or unproven information (documents, materials)—which are damaging for all those involved.[3] Hungarian sociologist Akos Szilagyi (2000, 9) defines kompromat as the publication (or blackmail with the threat of publication) of information, documents, evidence, and revelations that are related to a genre of denunciation (*donos*), exposure/unmasking (*razoblachenie*), slander (*kleveta*), and allegations that can destroy or neutralize political opponents or business competitors. He notes that kompromat is associated with political indecency, and points to the double meaning of the suffix *mat,* which is an abbreviation of the Russian word *materialy* (materials) as well as a Russian word for "swear language."[4] In English, the essence of kompromat is best grasped by the phrase "blackmail files" that are gathered or fabricated for political or business purposes. For the purposes of this study, I use the term *kompromat* without translation.

In explaining the phenomenon of kompromat, it is tempting to provide details of kompromat stories to illustrate their wider impact on political life in Russia during the 1990s. Although the substance of these stories is often sensationalized, I do not consider kompromat too superficial for a scholarly study or too inconsequential for a serious analysis of post-Communist transformation. I argue that the kompromat boom of the 1990s should be viewed in a dual context: it was fueled not only by the change following the collapse of the Soviet Union but also by the patterns of continuity in Russian politics. Like black and gray PR, practices associated with kompromat can be organized into a typology. I provide examples to illustrate the types of information that constitute kompromat in the post-Soviet context and offer a way to organize its functions. As part of black and gray PR technologies, kompromat is involved as a weapon in fighting electoral wars and carries out corresponding functions. In informal negotiations and bargaining, it can be used less directly with varying degrees of leverage. In media markets, kompromat operates as a commodity to be bought, sold, and exchanged. I explore how these various functions help reflect the unique features of this complex phenomenon in Russia and discuss how kompromat might be compared to the phenomenon of scandal. Viewing informal practices as indicators of the workings of formal institutions, I emphasize those features of the Russian public, politics, and media in the 1990s that contributed to making the practices of kompromat operational and pervasive.

Typology of Kompromat

To understand the logics of this diverse phenomenon, it is helpful to identify four "ideal types" of kompromat. When we look at real-life cases

TABLE 3.1
Typology of *kompromat*

Ideal types of *kompromat*	Examples
Political	Abuse of office and power
	Discrediting connections
	Disclosure of secret information
	Political disloyalty
	Political incompetence
Economic	Misappropriation of budget funds
	Embezzlement
	Shady bank deals
	Improprieties in privatization process
	Offshore activity and capital flight
	Holding of foreign bank accounts
	Involvement in illegal financial schemes
	Cronyism and nepotism
	Inappropriate or illegal election campaign financing
	Preferential treatment in business deals and contracts
	Giving or accepting bribes
	Illegitimate income or fees received
Criminal	Ties to organized crime
	Contract killings and violence
	Spying and tapping
	Blackmail
Private	Property and possessions
	Extravagant spending habits
	Sexual behavior
	Sexual orientation
	Cultural or religious background or practices
	Beliefs and ideology
	Health and age
	Misdemeanors of family members

of kompromat used against rivals, it is clear that these four categories are primarily analytical: few cases can be defined as belonging exclusively to a single type, while a serious and sustained attack on a politician tends to make use of all types. The classifications in table 3.1 are distinguished by the nature of information contained in the kompromat.

The first type of kompromat consists of revelations about an individual's *political activities*, including abuse of office and power, relations with oligarchs, the disclosure of secret information, political incompetence, and political disloyalty. During the 2000 presidential campaign, political kompromat was used against Grigorii Iavlinskii, a presidential candidate expected to get about 6 percent of the vote. Kompromat linked Iavlinskii to Vladimir Gusinskii, Russia's then most prominent media mogul and enemy of the Kremlin. The main television channel, ORT, implied that Gusinskii had staged another candidate's withdrawal from the race in favor of Iavlinskii and was partly financing his campaign. ORT reminded viewers that Gusinskii was a citizen of Israel and that it was illegal for presidential candidates to accept money from foreign organizations or citizens.[5] ORT also played a Russian anti-Semitism card, alluding to Gusinskii's high-profile role in the World Jewish Congress and showing footage of him at a banquet with Hasidic leaders wearing yarmulkes.[6]

The second type of kompromat concerns a politician's disreputable, often illegal, *economic activities,* which could include any one or a number of the following: misappropriation of budget funds, embezzlement, shady bank deals, improprieties in the privatization process, offshore activity, capital flight, the holding of foreign bank accounts, involvement in illegal financial schemes, cronyism and nepotism, inappropriate or illegal election campaign financing, preferential treatment in business deals or contracts, and, most obvious, the giving and accepting of bribes.

One of the most high-profile cases of this type in the 1990s involved Boris Berezovskii, at the time Russia's most prominent and powerful tycoon. In 1997, Berezovskii was accused of creating and using Andava, a Swiss-based company, to transfer cash revenues abroad from Aeroflot, the Russian airline company that he effectively controlled. The newspaper *Moskovskii Komsomolets* claimed that Berezovskii had engineered the appointment of Yeltsin's son-in-law, Valerii Okulov, to the directorship of Aeroflot and that in return, Sergei Dubinin at the Russian Central Bank had granted a license to Andava to manage hard currency transfers from Russia.[7] In 1998, the magazine *Liudi* published what it alleged were fragments from a telephone conversation between Berezovskii, Dubinin, and Nikolai Glushkov (a commercial director of Aeroflot and ally of Berezovskii), in which Berezovskii pressured Dubinin to expedite the license for Andava. In February 1999, the authorities searched the offices of several companies connected to Aeroflot and worked with Swiss officials to gather evidence of embezzlement. A warrant for Berezovskii's arrest was issued on April 6, 1999, while he was in France but was repealed eight days later on April 14. Berezovskii returned to Russia on April 19, claiming that he had "never violated a law," and the case was not pursued.[8]

To understand this puzzling sequence of events, we need to look more closely at the personalities involved, the political climate at the time, and the exact timing of events. Berezovskii's arrest warrant was supposedly issued by Mikhail Katyshev, deputy prosecutor general, who also repealed the warrant eight days later on the grounds that in an interview Berezovskii had said he would return to Moscow voluntarily for questioning. However, during those eight days Katyshev's situation had changed. Immediately after issuing the arrest warrant, he was removed from his position as head of the prosecutor general's main investigations department by Iurii Chaika, the acting prosecutor general. Chaika had replaced Iurii Skuratov as prosecutor general after Skuratov's resignation on the grounds of ill health on February 1, 1999.[9] On this same day, the Federal Security Service (FSB) raided the offices of Sibneft', Russia's seventh-largest oil company, then believed to be controlled by Berezovskii, after claims in *Moskovskii Komsomolets* that Berezovskii's private security firm, Atoll, was conducting surveillance on members of Yeltsin's family and other top government officials.[10] Twenty other offices and private residences, including those of Atoll, were searched on the same day. After Skuratov's resignation, conflicting reports appeared in the media speculating on whether or not Skuratov had signed the order to search Sibneft, whether his resignation was in any way connected with this, and whether he had resigned voluntarily or been forced out. Chaika's move against Katyshev, who was seen as an ally of Skuratov, may well have suggested that Skuratov himself was behind the arrest warrant for Berezovskii. The initial discrediting accusations in *Moskovskii Komsomolets* are believed to have come from Okulov, who had turned against Berezovskii. Okulov is believed to have received support from Evgenii Primakov, the then Russian prime minister. *Moskovskii Komsomolets,* is a newspaper known for its willingness to discredit Berezovskii, and its loyalty to Iurii Luzhkov, the mayor of Moscow.[11]

The third type of kompromat involves *criminal activities,* including ties to organized crime, contract killings and violence, spying and tapping, and blackmail. Vladimir Iakovlev, the governor of St. Petersburg, has long been mentioned in connection with the work of organized criminal groups in the "criminal capital of Russia." Iakovlev was elected governor of St. Petersburg in June 1996, and during his first years in office, a number of high-profile murders occurred in that city.[12] However, it was not until the spring of 1999 that Iakovlev himself began to come under direct attack for his alleged involvement in a number of criminal cases, including the murders of Viktor Novoselov, the St. Petersburg lawmaker, and Galina Starovoitova, the State Duma deputy.[13] A flurry of "anticorruption" activity in St. Petersburg, resulting in the arrest of several individuals linked to Iakovlev, coincided with the run-up to the December 1999 Duma elections. Observers generally agree that such bursts of enthusiasm in combating corruption are linked to the electoral cycle. *Novye Izvestiia* published a transcript of what it claimed were phone conversations linking Iakovlev's administration to organized crime. The paper claimed that these tapes had been in Starovoitova's possession from the beginning of 1998. Of particular interest were Iakovlev's ties to the criminal group that controlled St. Petersburg's funeral business. As the investigation into Starovoitova's murder deepened, it emerged that a year before her death Iakovlev's image-maker, Aleksei Koshmarov, had threatened her press secretary, Ruslan Linkov.[14] Linkov was then targeted in the Iakovlev-controlled media as a possible suspect in the case.[15] It has been suggested that politicians linked to St. Petersburg (thus implicating Vladimir Putin) were eager to discredit Iakovlev before the elections, and they used information that had long been in their possession.

The fourth type of kompromat consists of revelations about *private life*, including details of illegitimate income or fees, property and possessions, extravagant spending habits, sexual behavior, sexual orientation, cultural or religious background, beliefs and ideology, health or age, and misdemeanors by family members. In the summer of 1999, Iurii Luzhkov, the mayor of Moscow, and Evgenii Primakov, Russia's former prime minister, formed a party, Fatherland–All Russia, to compete in the December 1999 parliamentary elections. The Kremlin instituted campaigns to discredit both men, allegedly orchestrated by Berezovskii. During his Sunday program on October 24, 1999, the TV star and Kremlin propagandist Sergei Dorenko claimed that Primakov was in poor health and might not be in a suitable physical condition for the presidency. He reminded viewers that Primakov was due to undergo surgery in Switzerland.[16] Immediately following the program, Primakov phoned in to the studios saying that he was sorry to disappoint his opponents, but he was feeling extremely well, and he challenged Dorenko to a televised swimming race.[17] Dorenko's claim was followed on October 30 by a profile of Primakov during the program *Vremia* that kept referring to his age (seventy), questioning why someone would be interested in becoming president at the beginning of his "eighth decade."[18] This profile also referred to Primakov as an "old-school Communist," emphasizing his long history within the Communist Party, and his "anti-Zionist" and "anti-imperialist" statements and writings.[19]

Some of the most effective kompromat relating to an individual's private life refers to behavior that, although not illegal, is associated with strong social prejudice. During the 2000 electoral campaign, it was claimed that the presidential candidate Grigorii Iavlinskii had undergone plastic surgery. The host of *Vremia* urged viewers:

> Look at his face. What's happened to the usual puffiness and the bags under his eyes? Doesn't it seem suspicious to you, dear viewers, that on the eve of the presidential campaign, candidate No. 3 suddenly seems to look a whole lot younger? Here's graphic confirmation that some people are using the services not only of Western moneybags but also of Western cosmetologists.[20]

Other reports showed members of a gay club, Blue Heart, endorsing Iavlinskii's candidacy. *Vremia* quoted one of the groups as saying, "Today, anyone who wants to can call us buggers and homos on the subway or in a store or wherever they please. We need support and protection. We see that this candidate will provide it." The event may well have been staged to undermine Iavlinskii, a further example of the use of gray and black PR (see chapter 2).

Few instances of kompromat can be confined exclusively to one of our "ideal types." The video of the minister of justice, Valentin Kovalev, cavorting with prostitutes in a sauna was all the more damaging because the sauna was believed to be controlled by the Solntsevo criminal group, and the tape was found in a safe of a banker, himself under a criminal investigation, who had likely collected kompromat in order to have his case closed. In another example, an appearance of Boris Nemtsov, the deputy prime minister, at a "very erotic" striptease show at a country retreat was in many ways a comment on his private life, it was also a comment on his links to Vladimir Potanin's Oneximbank, which owned the retreat.[21] Potanin, Gusinskii, and Berezovskii had previously launched competing bids when Sviaz'invest, the telecommunications giant, was being privatized, and Potanin (backed by Nemtsov) was successful. It was believed that this attack, along with others launched against Nemtsov, was organized in response to the Sviaz'invest outcome. They may also have been a warning sign to Chubais, Nemtsov's fellow deputy prime minister, whose publishing house was owned by Potanin, of what he could expect should he continue to favor Potanin.[22]

During the Kremlin's 1999 battle with Iurii Luzhkov, mayor of Moscow, kompromat of all types appeared in the media with serious defamatory potential.[23] In June 1999, Sergei Kirienko announced that he was considering the possibility of running for mayor of Moscow against Luzhkov. Soon afterwards he claimed that corruption and bribery lay at the heart of Luzhkov's "system of power," and he set up a hotline for Muscovites to report instances of corruption, with the results to be posted on a website.[24] Since Kirienko had little chance of victory, observers generally believed that he was being used by the Kremlin as a conduit for kompromat against the mayor.[25] Another theme repeatedly emphasized during the Kremlin's campaign against Luzhkov was that the Moscow city government had failed to curtail the growth of crime in the capital and had even turned a blind eye to it.[26] A federal television channel, RTR, broadcast a piece by the FSB suggesting that Moscow was an easy target for terrorist attacks. Vladimir Rushailo, the interior minister, openly called on Yeltsin to remove General Nikolai Kulikov, Moscow's chief of police, claiming that Kulikov had covered up the true rate of crime in Moscow and had failed to address the growing problem of drugs in the city.[27] Kulikov was subsequently removed against the mayor's wishes. Luzhkov and Fatherland-All Russia were also accused of colluding with Gusinskii and his Media-Most empire. ORT had repeatedly commented on Media-Most's financial difficulties, and it now alleged that the Moscow city authorities were depositing some of their budget funds into Most Bank to help Media-Most repay its debts in exchange for favorable coverage of Fatherland-All Russia during both the Duma and presidential campaigns.[28]

The source of much of the kompromat on Luzhkov during the end of the 1999 was *The Sergei Dorenko Show* on ORT.[29] The notorious Dorenko has been credited with the invention of the "dirtiest" kompromat discourse on Russian TV. Dorenko claimed that Luzhkov had spent Moscow city funds on purchasing and renovating a building in the Czech spa town of Karlovy Vary; that he had enriched his wife; that he had built a luxury residence outside Moscow; and that he had acquired property in Germany, Spain, and New York.[30] On October 10 1999, Dorenko claimed on his show that Luzhkov had presented a Spanish seaside town with a sculpture by a known sculptor, Zurab Tsereteli, as a sign of Moscow's friendship and received in return a kickback of $1.5 million in real estate from the mayor of that town. Opposition politicians in that town allegedly regarded Luzhkov, Gusinskii (who allegedly owned a villa there), and their cronies as the "Mafiosi of the East."[31] In the same program, Dorenko accused Luzhkov of hypocrisy for having taken credit for a hospital reconstruction project in Budennovsk in the Stavropol' region of Russia when in fact the hospital had been renovated by the firm Mabetex.[32] The program aired an interview with Bedzhet Pacolli, the director of Mabetex, supporting these accusations.[33] On November 7, Dorenko implicated Luzhkov in the murder of American businessman Paul Tatum, who had been vying for control of Moscow's Radisson Slavianskaia hotel with his Russian partners when he was assassinated on November 3, 1996. Dorenko aired an interview with Jeff Olsen, an acquaintance and "special consultant" of Tatum, who claimed that Tatum's dying words had been that Luzhkov was behind the murder.[34] On November 24 a lawsuit was filed against Luzhkov, charging him with covering up Tatum's murder. Luzhkov immediately accused ORT and Berezovskii of being behind the lawsuit.[35] On November 17, Luzhkov filed a suit against Dorenko and ORT, demanding 450 million rubles ($17 million) in compensation for damages to his reputation stemming from the charges levied against him. The sum requested was roughly equal to the amount of money Dorenko had accused Luzhkov of embezzling. According to Luzhkov's representative, Dorenko's allegations portrayed Luzhkov in an "extremely insulting manner," using a "grotesque form of indecent comparisons with notorious characters."[36] In response, Dorenko accused Luzhkov of involvement with Scientology, since his lawyer Galina Krylova had defended Scientologists in the past, and also linked Luzhkov to the Japanese cult Aum Shinrikyo.[37] On December 3, Luzhkov won a libel judgment of 100,000 rubles ($3,750) against Dorenko and 50,000 rubles against ORT.[38]

The examples above illustrate the core argument of this chapter: that informal practices associated with kompromat not only shaped events in the political arena during the 1990s through the manipulation of defects in the legal, media, and informational spheres but also reproduced long-lasting patterns of Russian informal politics. In other words, kompromat practices were a reflection of change and new opportunities, but at the same time they subvert the workings of democratic institutions and testify to the limited nature of the post-Soviet political reforms.

Suppliers of Post-Soviet Kompromat

The collapse of the Soviet Union resulted in the unemployment of many former security or special services employees. Between 1991 and 1993, the Yeltsin administration deliberately fragmented the former Soviet state security system, spreading its responsibilities across five separate successor agencies that were coordinated only to a very limited degree. Extensive budget cutbacks led to the dismissal of thousands of personnel; twenty thousand officers are thought to have left the security apparatus between September 1991 and June 1992, and many more opted to leave after the October 1993 assault on the White House (Volkov 2002, 485). At the same time, the post-Soviet period witnessed an explosion of private security services as part of the general privatization of law enforcement functions in Russia. The expansion of the private security and enforcement industry can be seen as an adaptive response by political figures and former Soviet security personnel to the rapidly changing demands of Russia's new market economy.

In 1992, legislation was passed that permitted private security agencies to protect the legal rights and interests of clients on a commercial basis (Volkov 2002, 486). Many of those who left the ranks of state security agencies, including those who were specifically trained in the art of gathering information, gravitated toward work in the private sector. Private protection agencies operating as private businesses coveted the experience and know-how of former state security officers and were able to pay wages far greater than those traditionally earned by employees of the state. It is estimated that some fifty thousand former officers of state security and law enforcement agencies had joined private security firms in the 1990s. At the end of 1999, Russia had 11,652 registered security agencies employing 196,266 licensed personnel (Volkov 487–89).

The security apparatuses of private firms performed a multitude of tasks, including that of supplying kompromat on rivals. Ex-employees of the special services sustained informal relations and had close connections with remaining state security employees, through whom they obtained much of their information. One respondent working with former KGB officers said: "At the moment, anything one wants to buy or order is leaked from the special services. They do not work for the courtroom, they work for money" [3.18]. Another commentator suggested, "Whether you are in need of kompromat or afraid of it, among your acquaintances seek out former or current employees of the special services—there is no other way."[39] Anger at their ruined careers along with what they viewed as betrayal from above also drove former special services employees to discredit those in power. The role of special service in a new context is illustrated in figure 3.1.

In Soviet times, the KGB had a monopoly over the sophisticated technology of surveillance. The fragmentation of the KGB in the early 1990s resulted in the dispersal of this technology. By 1995, the following organizations were permitted to tap phone lines: the FSB (Federal Security Service), the GUO (Main Administration for the Protection of the Russian Federation), the SBP (Presidential Security Service), the FPS (Federal Border Service), the SVR (Foreign Intelligence Service), the Tax Police, and the Customs Service.[40] At the same time a wave of illegally imported intelligence-gathering equipment was put on sale almost without restriction until 1999. During this period, se-

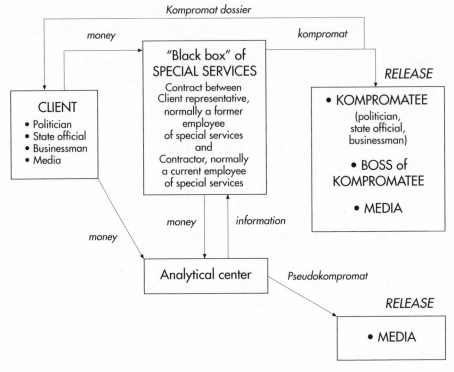

Figure 3.1. Kompromat cycle in Russia. From "Material'nye sekrety," Ekspert, December 20, 1999, 25. By permission of photoservice, Ekspert.

curity teams working both for private firms and on a freelance basis collected vast quantities of kompromat. Not only was the technology for obtaining information easily available, but former colleagues provided access to the classified databases of state organizations on the basis of mutual help, barter, or payment.

Security teams engage in various forms of surveillance—phone tapping, stakeouts, shadowing, and videotaping. The details of intelligence obtained by bugging, revealed in the article *A Brief History of "Proslushka,"* imply that the privatized security services have successfully reproduced their own employment opportunities in the post-Soviet context along with the familiar conspiratorial features of "Muscovite folkways" (Keenan 1986).[41] They maintain detailed kompromat files on partners, clients, competitors, politicians, and "bandits." These files might include personal details (address, telephone number, cell phone number, location and size of apartment, family members, relatives, cars), passports and official documents, bank details (including account numbers, copies of statements, and details of currency transfers), information on business activities and ties, background (education, training, Soviet-era affiliations), political tendencies (including affiliation with patriotic, nationalist or Communist groups), transcripts of phone conversations, details of contacts and acquaintances (especially with criminals or those in powerful positions), foreign citizenship, apartments and property abroad, business and real estate transactions, general correspondence, as well as rumors and stories of all sorts. Such information becomes useful when it is necessary to "clear up" an issue (*raz"iasnit' vopros*), bring about a desired outcome, or settle a dispute at a *strelka* (informal negotiation) without recourse to violence (Volkov 2002, 92).

Security teams not only collect kompromat on rivals but also monitor kompromat on their own employers, thus providing advance warning about potential discrediting allegations that could arise (Gambetta 2002, 6). Although one cannot be fully "protected" against kompromat (buying up kompromat on oneself is no guarantee since there may be copies elsewhere), one can gather "counter-kompromat" with which to threaten an opponent, or even preempt an opponent by being the first to release information and thus minimizing the impact. Valerii Streletskii, once a head of the Kremlin special security regiment, has emphasized an important disclosure function: the publication of kompromat protects one from being blackmailed by opponents (Streletskii 1998, 6).[42] In such cases the original source of kompromat becomes obscure, making it difficult to determine the purpose of its release. An article in *Novye Izvestiia* in May 2001 claimed that kompromat on the newly appointed Russian ambassador to the Ukraine, Viktor Chernomyrdin, was in fact released by his "friends" and was meant to "immunize the population against any genuinely incriminating material that could turn up." According to the newspaper, this showed that the authorities were "refusing to accept any negative information about members of the upper echelons, proclaiming a special kind of immunity against muckraking while virtually branding all complaints against state officials not sanctioned by the Kremlin as acts of political sabotage."[43] This is an old, familiar tactic that has become ever more prominent under Putin's administration.

Continuity should also be seen in the use of symbolic violence in the manipulation of the public. Where outbreaks of kompromat in the media appear in competitive electoral contexts, they are intended to exert familiar forms of symbolic violence aimed at the manipulation of public opinion. Although kompromat stories focus on particular individuals, their ultimate target is the electorate: voters' opinions and behavior on the day of the elections. In contrast to kompromat used in its bargaining capacity, which ideally should contain evidence sufficient for a conviction in a court of law, kompromat in the media can be based on suspicion or rumor. Egorova-Gantman (1999) emphasizes the significant role played by gossip and psychological tricks initiated by PR firms. Stereotypes or generally accepted types of "common knowledge"—for example, the proposition that customs officials are corrupt—do not require evidence in order to be convincing. As explained by a respondent working in PR business,

> The authenticity of information appearing in kompromat is not important in the sense that there is no need to prove or check things that are commonly known. For example, "Traffic police take bribes, customs officials take bigger bribes" [*gaishnik—vziatochnik, tamozhennik—strashnyi vziatochnik*]; or government minister X does not live on his salary (the business controlled by him thrives on guaranteed orders from his clients—whether new projects in Moscow, such as the third ring road, or the Lefortovo tunnel, which produce ludicrous profits). What is important is the *use* of information, the *attack*. Information only becomes kompromat when somebody wants it to work [*kogda eto komu-nibud' nuzhno*]. [2.4]

In this context, *Ekspert* reports on the phenomenon of "pseudo-kompromat" which appears on floating, anonymous, or individual Internet sites—for example, the site Organizovannaia vlastnaia gruppirovka (http://www.ovg.ru) sometimes associated with the political technologist Gleb Pavlovskii. This site has published long lists of suspicions about high-powered politicians such as Iurii Luzhkov and Vladimir Iakovlev. A contending site with a telling title, www.sovesti.net (literally translated as "no.conscience") has responded with a detailed if obscure biography of Evgenii Primakov as well as the results of some "operative investigation" on the businessman Aleksandr Mamut.[44]

According to *Ekspert* informants, professionals from the special services are not seriously concerned with such "competition" in view of the ephemeral and amateurish character of the information provided. In political games, however, the aim of kompromat is not to discover the truth but to find a way to discredit the target. Therefore if facts are unavailable, an invented kompromat is used instead, often with equal effect on the public. Such information may initially appear on a floating website and thus lend a degree of credibility before being taken up by the press. One should note the prominence of kompromat on the Internet, but a full analysis of Internet sites devoted to kompromat (such as www.compromat.ru) has yet to be made.

Given that about 90 percent of kompromat is perceived as fabricated [2.4], it is curious that those who disseminate it are rarely if ever prosecuted. A few reasons for this have been suggested. The Russian political scientist Sergei Kurginian argues that "the fight against kompromat only serves to excite people's interest, since everything forbidden inevitably becomes attractive. As a result, prices in the kompromat market increase, giving rise to yet more filthy fabrications" (Tsepliaev 2000). Another reason for the relative impunity is the fact that it is almost impossible to apprehend the authors of kompromat. "As a rule, they live not in Russia but abroad," says Maksim Grigor'ev, the manager of the consulting group Governmental PR. "To do this it is not necessary to go anywhere. You can easily set up a free page on one of the popular servers, say, in the United States. There you install kompromat—texts, photographs, documents. Then the information on the page can be sent by e-mail to the addresses of officials in the Kremlin, the government, the Duma, the mass media" (Tsepliaev 2000).

The impact of published kompromat on the Russian electorate is complex. On the one hand, the rise of kompromat indicates the increasing importance of the public sphere, of public opinion and the existence of free expression. On the other hand, as one respondent put it, "the freedom of gossip has been mistaken for freedom of speech," and kompromat based on rumor does not aid the cause of transparency or accountability [2.4]. The press is controlled by a small number of media magnates who use their papers to publish kompromat on opponents, which is hardly the same as independent journalism or reporting in the public interest. One respondent summed up bitterly: "The press is not accountable for the slander it spreads; it is divided into private estates and is used to serve private interests" [3.19]. The media situation is rather volatile because political parties are weak and their capacity for consistent and trustworthy influence on the informational field is rather limited (Ricker 1986; Halevy 1979). This feeds into people's negative attitudes toward those in authority and encourages the stereotype that politicians steal, behave badly in their personal lives, and do little for the country. Initially it was exciting to read about the reprehensible behavior of politicians who would have been beyond criticism in the past, but in recent years, as kompromat has saturated the media, the public has grown weary of it. Many interviewees have suggested that increasing regulation in the media is bringing the era of black PR to an end—"in the

1990s, anything was possible for money, but this is no longer the case" [2.4].[45]

Functions of Kompromat

Given the complexity of kompromat, it is very difficult indeed to make one's way through Russia's media minefield and to determine whether a particular bit of information is fake or not. Should it be interpreted as a profit-making commodity in the informational market? Is it part of the information war against political or business opponents or a strategy in the context of bargaining and exerting informal pressure in negotiations? It is easy to say that information is used instrumentally to serve a particular purpose, but it is difficult to identify exactly how this is done. In order to explore various roles played by kompromat, it is necessary to resort to expert advice and respondents' opinions while remaining aware that ambiguity is intrinsic to kompromat practices. Illustrated below are possible uses of kompromat: kompromat as a commodity for mass consumption, custom-made kompromat aimed at political or business opponents in "kompromat wars," and kompromat used for bargaining hidden from the public eye.

Kompromat as a Commodity

In contrast to the use of kompromat in Soviet times, post-Soviet "denunciation" practices take place in the context of an emerging market and political competition. Collecting, creating, or dealing in discrediting information becomes a way to be employed and have an income; it has become a business, regulated by the factors of supply and demand.

> Kompromat is a mass media phenomenon, based on the principles of propaganda. The skill of propaganda lays in the expertise of special services personnel. In the post-Soviet period there were about six or seven purges in the special services, which resulted in a lot of unemployed specialists with only one skill—that of informational violence: for example, pressure on the spouse of the candidate, exercised alongside violence that is very real, such as the kidnapping of a candidate's child (the child is returned to the streets five hours later, but during these hours a political advantage is taken). [2.2]

Szilagyi (2000, 16) suggests that in contemporary Russia there is a market for kompromat services, which exists parallel to the market for the services of contract killers and which is used by the kleptoratic, criminal, and corrupt clan structures that came to dominate the post-Soviet state, society, and mass media.[46] Indeed, in the 1990s kompromat dominated the Russian press, television, and Internet. There seemed to be no area of life that was immune to the revelations of kompromat. Some would argue that this was a welcome result of long-awaited freedom of speech. One of my respondents remarked, "I can't imagine a democratic society *without* kompromat" [3.11]. At the same time such apparent openness concealed the fact that kompromat constituted one of the most obscure features of political power in Russia, which downplayed the rule of law and the principle of fair competition, relying instead on nontransparent rules of the game in order to maintain the manageability of its subjects.

In order to comprehend the workings of the kompromat market, it is necessary to understand the specifics of supply and demand, as well as price dynamics, while viewing the role of that market in wider political and economic contexts. Several factors should be taken into consideration. There are the blind market forces pushing kompromat out into the open as well as a variety of conscious, intelligent, sophisticated strategies by individuals or groups seeking to "win" in competitive contexts. As one of my respondents put it, "One has to outplay the others, and sometimes even oneself by violating one's own rules" [3.17].

Kompromat serves the needs not only of former security services and their clients but also of intermediaries—the media and other institutions. Similar to other markets in Russia, the kompromat market is not an open affair regulated purely by market forces. As one respondent testified, "The entire press works on a prepaid basis [*po zakazu*]; the papers have special fees for kompromat. If the editor in chief works for somebody, certain materials will be blocked." [3.19] For an analysis of kompromat materials in the press, it is essential to establish facts about the political and financial dependency of media outlets. The site Freelance Bureau (www.flb.ru) has posted analyses of the main media outlets and the prices charged in 1999 for the publication of kompromat materials. Later on, the sources of funding and loyalties of each newspaper, along with the kompromat prices, were also examined in *Who Owns Russia,* a joint project of the television program *Namedni* (NTV) and the newspaper *Kommersant-Vlast'.*[47] Although the reliability of such information can be questioned, what follows provides an illustration of the data presented by the Freelance Bureau (see the full list in appendix 2).[48]

Argumenty i Fakty: The most popular weekly with a circulation in the millions. The most expensive for publication of kompromat, $18,000 per page. Regardless of the fee, the final decision to publish is taken by the editor in chief, who is financially independent and keeps no political alliances, a situation ensuring that any material can be published.

Izvestiia: Maintains the status of a serious and conservative newspaper. It belongs to Potanin's media holding, with a growing proportion of ownership held by Lukoil. All "sponsored" articles are framed with a discreet border.

Novaia Gazeta: From the mid-1990s supported and was supported by the National Reserve Bank, Iabloko, and more recently, Sibirskii Aliuminii. Its editor in chief is considered principled. Officially, *Novaia* charges $3,800 per page; kompromat costs $5,000, while urgent orders and guarantees of future editorial policy on the same matter amount to $8,000–10,000.

Thus, despite the apparent loss-making situation of the mass media in post-Soviet Russia, given the meager figures for circulation and subscription, the publication of kompromat generates substantial shadow profits, along with considerable political influence. Nevertheless, the proliferation of kompromat in the press remains a highly opaque phenomenon. Every "revelation" or "disclosure," including the study of kompromat publication costs cited above, is likely to be serving some unknown web of interests and strategies. The media are constantly subject to manipulation and use for agendas hidden from the public.

Given the amount of kompromat appearing in newspapers and on television, one might expect Russian reporters to be engaged in a great deal of investigative journalism, but this is not the case. As described above, information is normally obtained by security firms and the special services (*spetssluzhby*), who then pass it on for public dissemination. Indeed, it is dangerous for journalists to have opinions of their own or to pursue investigative reporting.[49] As one of my interviewees, himself a rare representative of that genre, put it rather cynically, "Journalism in Russia is not a mission of discovering facts; rather, it is a 'cash for information,' if not 'cash for publication,' service" [3.12]. Unlike some of its best Western counterparts, the Russian media do not perform a "watchdog" role, so essential for the working of markets and democracy. The implications for elections are significant. (The prominence of kompromat in the media, politics, and business was marked by an art exhibition. The posters in fig 3.2 illustrate some of kompromat functions.)

"The best way to increase your media outlet sales—to publish kompromat"

"Every active politician has opponents. The best way to get rid of them—kompromat"

Figure 3.2. Posters from exhibition "Kompromat," Moscow, December 17, 1996, at http://www.guelman.ru/eng/gallery/moscow/kompromat/. By permission of the Gallery of Marat Gelman.

Kompromat as a Weapon

Kompromat is closely associated with practices of black and gray PR used in electoral campaigns. Most electoral technologies present political opponents as "unelectable." As one of my respondents, a specialist in electoral technologies, explained,

> There is kompromat and kompromat. For example, a fact from the past, such as a criminal record, can be used. This might be unfair since the person has served the sentence, but a fact is a fact. For example, we used information of this kind in regional elections because we believe that if a person could rape a child, it tells people certain things about him, even if he has been through the correction process. However in the absence of facts or documents, anything will do, a lie, or even better, a half-truth. An elementary two-step procedure [*dvukhkhodovka*] is often used: put some inaccurate information on a floating website and then report it in the press. [2.2]

Run-ups to elections are known as "seasons of spillover of kompromat." Before elections kompromat is carefully collected on all political candidates and stored in an information archive covering all possible forms of illegal or morally reprehensible behavior—political, economic, social, criminal, or sexual. At its most "successful," the public disclosure of kompromat can destroy a competitor's business or bring an end to a political career, and even lead to imprisonment.[50]

Looking at kompromat in the context of political discourses of corruption, Szilagyi (2000) identifies the term as part of the language of violence. He argues that those using kompromat are motivated by a variety of considerations. They may have run out of political arguments (especially at times when political arguments do not work or insufficient for winning), or they are running out of time to shape public opinion by more acceptable means. The stakes may also be too high to risk relying on normal political or economic arguments. He sees kompromat as a tool, an instrument, a weapon, or a more "civilized" way to destroy a target (as opposed to contract killing). The unintended consequence of the extensive use of such weapon is symbolic violence against the public. By the end of the decade, kompromat had succeeded only selectively because the public grew exhausted from the informational avalanche of the "kompromat wars."

Kompromat terminology used by the various PR agencies is often hostile and confrontational. Ekaterina Egorova-Gantman and K. Pleshakov of Nikkolo-M defines kompromat as one of the key strategies of the "attack" on the image of a candidate (alongside critique of a program and negative advertising (1999, 204–27). PR specialists claim that effective kompromat should be target-oriented, in the sense that disclosure of information that would lead to the downfall of a politician might not have the same effect on a businessman or a criminal. It should be timed and well calculated: for example, revelations about a politician's money-laundering activities that might have caused a stir in previous years would not have the same effect in a society saturated with such stories. In other words, kompromat is both time- and context-bound.[51] Below I give a few examples from the regions.

In the 1995 elections for the regional governor of the Sverdlovsk Oblast', an attack appeared in the media on a former governor, Eduard Rossel, portraying him as a "candidate of criminals." It was claimed that Rossel was sponsored by the Uralmash criminal group[52] (which at that time did not yet have its rather more respectable designation, the Uralmash Economic Union). In response, Rossel's team used the technology of "confusion"— similar accusations were published against Rossel's main competitor (the incumbent Aleksei Strakhov) (Minchenko 2001, 21). The alliance of Rossel with Valerii Trushnikov became a decisive factor in Rossel's victory on the second ballot. Strakhov's campaign had gone over the top in its attack against Rossel, comparing him to Chechen leader Dudaev, attempting to present Rossel as a godfather of the Sverdlovsk mafia, and playing the "nationality card" (Rossel is German). All this turned out to be unsuccessful. Strakhov, in turn, was accused of offering, via his campaigners, shots of vodka in exchange for votes. Regardless of whether it really was Strakhov's campaigners or his competitors who employed this tactic, the media covered the story, which provoked a negative reaction among the electorate (Minchenko 2001, 25).

In the 1997 elections for the governor of the Irkutsk Oblast' all major PR teams were involved, resulting in the parade of political technologies. One of the candidates, a businessman, Ivan Shchadov, had been promoted intensely early on in the campaign, which prompted people to wonder where the money supporting him came from. At the same time, his opponents distributed leaflets with allegations of a past sentence for rape. Shchadov's elder son was also accused of participation in a gang-rape case, while his younger son was reported to have been responsible for a car accident that resulted in the death of a child. The leaflet was quite cleverly made to resemble a request to the office of the general prosecutor incorporating real names and signatures (see a similarly fake personal letter on figure 2.3). This combined attack on the candidate and his family had a dramatic effect, and Shchadov's approval ratings fell. The final two weeks of the elections witnessed an unprecedented kompromat war. On top of everything else, Shchadov was declared to be the representative of Moscow financial circles, and his physical resemblance to Chubais was used against him. The day before the elections, local television showed a ten-minute documentary ("The Coal Baron") about the adventures of Shchadov and his family. Simultaneously, another candidate, Sergei Levchenko, was attacked as a "new Communist" who did not pay wages to the workers but drove a Jeep himself. Further spicy gossip alleged Levchenko's departure from the army on the grounds of a sexual assault on a soldier who attempted suicide as a consequence. His attackers organized a noisy meeting called "Communists and Workers against Levchenko." Visits by Lebed' and Ziuganov to support their candidates did not help. On the contrary, Lebed's support for Shchadov backfired, giving substance to the story of "a rapist candidate and his supporter Lebed'" and receiving national publicity that damaged regional ratings even further.[53] The discrediting capacity of kompromat weaponry is devastating, particularly in skillful hands.

Kompromat as a Bargaining Strategy and as an Instrument for Informal Persuasion

One of the post-Soviet wisdoms, reflecting the high-risk environment, is "To keep *kompromat* on enemies is a pleasure. To keep *kompromat* on friends is a must" (Latynina 1999). Kompromat displays some of its discrediting potential when published, but it is its power in unpublished form that is used for bargaining and is most difficult to scrutinize. Unpublished kompromat files serve to threaten or exert pressure on opponents in classic blackmail scenarios where revelation or publication poses such a threat that opponents will alter their behavior in return for the nondisclosure.[54] Kompromat of this kind is difficult to trace, although it often surfaces in print at a later date. Chrystia Freeland quotes one oligarch describing the kompromat-centered nature of political power in Russia by admitting that Yeltsin's bodyguard and a chief of the Kremlin security force, Aleksander Korzhakov, had a very important function.

> People feared him and that fear, which is part of the Russian political tradition, in many ways anchored the vertical power structure of the state. Korzhakov collected dirt; he knew who every governor was sleeping with, who was paying him bribes and so forth. May be this was a stupid, pig-headed way to influence the regional authorities, but it worked. If some governor tried to do something against the Kremlin, Korzhakov would just say, "Look, I am just going to throw you in jail and only then will we start worrying about whether it was legal or not." (Freeland 2000, 226)

Schelling (1968), in his discussion of "the strategy of conflict," stresses the point that it "is not concerned with the efficient application of force, but with the exploitation of potential force" or "the employment of threats." Here, there is a common interest as well as conflict among participants, where "the best course of action for each player depends on what the other players do. . . . and on their expectations about each other's behavior." Thus, "winning" in the blackmail context, characterized by the impossibility of appeal to a higher authority for enforcement of the law, does not have a strictly competitive meaning. Success can be achieved by bargaining, mutual accommodation, or the avoidance of mutually damaging behavior. At this stage, kompromat strategies are not based on the actual *exposure* but on the *exploitation of the bargaining power of a threat of exposure*.

Unless it is a question of an ownership takeover or a pure case of conflict in which the interests of two parties are completely opposed, there is mutual dependence as well as opposition between the parties. To approach kompromat as a possible strategy in a conflict is to take the view that most conflict situations are essentially *bargaining* situations. To characterize the maneuvers and actions in conflict situations as a bargaining process is to emphasize that, in addition to a divergence of interest over variables in the dispute, there is a powerful common interest in reaching an outcome that is not enormously destructive for both sides. As a senior aide to one of the key media magnates of the 1990s explained,

> There are a lot of people with difficult characters working in TV. These people can say a lot of things about each other, often harsh and unpleasant things. Besides, they are all competitors in the business. However, they all understand that they live in a situation of mutual restraint [*vzaimnogo sderzhivaniia*], that is to say: if you live in a glass house, do not throw stones. It's an unwritten rule that continued to work even when some people did violate the informal agreements and misbehave within the TV market. The rules prevented the "poaching" of personnel and of programs as well as what was viewed as "piracy," the violation of antidumping and advertising agreements. Unlike our oligarchs, TV companies have never engaged in devastating [information] wars, despite the fact that managers of the channels were not on speaking terms with each other for years.[55] [3.15]

Despite the possible argument that it is better to have kompromat contaminate the press than to let it exercise its bargaining capacity in the dark corners of informal politics, it must be remembered that the publication of *kompromat* does not necessarily mean that it has not been used for bargaining purposes before, or would not be used that way in the future. In fact, the decision to publish, partially publish, or not to publish information is determined by the type of information one possesses, the status of one's rivals, and one's ultimate aims or intentions. Some players suggest that the decision may not be taken by those in possession of information:

> The elites keep things under control through the use of extralegal methods, embracing the courts and law enforcement agencies, the Arbitration Court, tax authorities, the police, or by means of mechanisms of informal pressure, involving threats to withhold election financing and to withdraw support for local social needs. The threat to release kompromat remains a restraining factor. The material does

exist but would not be released to the press without sanction from above. When the protagonists adhere to the existing order, everything works, although games may still be played with these documents. [3.19]

These considerations somewhat undermine the useful distinction between published and unpublished kompromat, introduced earlier, and between its corresponding bargaining and discrediting powers. Some information can be partially leaked to the press to signal the gravity of the threat. When published for a select audience, kompromat resembles an encoded correspondence performing the function of a warning, threatening, and giving clues with a purpose of neutralizing the opponent. When I asked a knowledgeable player how many real facts there were in the voluminous kompromat appearing in the media, he replied: "Very few."

Because our economy is an economy of bargaining and unwritten agreements, it is rarely the case that one of the parties in a conflict would be tempted to reveal real facts of corruption or other violations. Most commonly, one party tries to leak kompromat against another within a genre of shock-horror stories rather than concrete information. We do make facts public also but there are so few of them! For an outsider it is hard to understand why accusations contain so little hard evidence, but the explanation is trivial. When two sides are involved in the same deal, the one that has lost out is upset and inclined to discredit the other, but not with real facts that would implicate oneself just as much as the successful rival. Imagine that we play an illegal game, and you have won. I can hardly go and complain about it as I have violated the law just as you have done, only I have been unlucky and lost. Would I shout about it? [3.15]

A similar logic can explain why we know so little about the insider dealing around the loans-for-shares auctions. Although insider dealing was commonly alleged, evidence rarely surfaced. Admittedly, some facts are so obvious that direct evidence is not required. The same expert explained how the "forceful methods" (*silovye metody*) of kompromat work in the absence of documentary evidence, especially if one uses one's position in the media.

One can pressure officials by having them fired. Sometimes actual proof of a bribe might not even be required—facts speak for themselves. Once, someone literally "stole" our license. I then told the story to every boss I knew and backed it up with the known information about who got the license and when, which indirectly confirmed the fact of bribe-taking by that official. In the end he lost his job. This is what I call the "use of force"—a technique not available to just anyone. It helps if you work in the media, as people still have a fear of the media in Russia. In the regions, as soon as the governor starts pressuring our partners, we threaten to make it public. We actually had to do it a couple of times (once when our partner was put in jail for no reason), but usually we manage to come to an agreement since we do not really have any political interests in these regions. [3.15]

Needless to say, the price for obtaining kompromat for bargaining purposes is of a different type than the fee paid for planting material in the press and is likely to be determined on a case-by-case basis. It depends on the amount of information required, the degree of detail, the type of evidence needed, the degree of secrecy to be observed, and the urgency of the request—in other words, it is indeterminable out of context. Apart from the example of a threat of disclosure of corruption, referred to by my respondent above, kompromat in the bargaining context is more difficult to illustrate. According to a respondent working in law enforcement, the most powerful instances of kompromat today are undocumented. They would be known to a closed circle of insiders and could "cost one his life, even without a second thought" [3.12].

"There is no 100 percent protection for anyone against kompromat."[56] Given this general vulnerability, not just for a closed circle of insiders, it is interesting to see for whom this threat has to some degree become real. I have categorized individuals listed in the alphabetical menu on www.kompromat.ru, according to their occupations.[57] In October 2002, the list contained the following number of persons in these categories.

Nonelected officials in government and state positions (36)
Journalists, people involved with print media (21)
Businessmen, heads of firms and enterprises (15)
Bankers (14)
People involved in television media (13)
Religious and cultural figures (10)
Elected politicians (6)
Associates of prominent/influential people (4)
Intelligence/security figures (4)
Oligarchs (3)

Law enforcement officials (3)
Organized criminals (2)
Governors, regional leaders (2)
Lawyers (2)
Image makers (2)
Academics (1)

First, it may be surprising to find that the place of the elected politicians in the list is not as prominent as one would have expected, whereas civil servants constitute the top category. This could be explained by the fact that official positions are likely to increase the vulnerability of their holders while making them more likely to become candidates in future elections. Second, contrary to what has been stated by a media respondent above, a considerable amount of kompromat is available on people in the media, often aimed at tarnishing the reputations of those who have generated the initial kompromat provocations. Businessmen and bankers constitute the third group most vulnerable to kompromat.

Kompromat in the Public Sphere

Since most kompromat dramas unfold in public sphere, it is useful to clarify similarities and differences between kompromat and scandal (see table 3.2). In his book *Political Scandal,* John Thompson (2000, 13–14) defines scandal as actions or events involving certain kinds of transgressions that have become known to others and are sufficiently serious to elicit public discourse. If disclosed, kompromat can become a cause for a scandal but only if there are witnesses willing to disclose their identities and the public is truly "scandalized," which is an unlikely scenario in the context of widespread, overwhelmingly fake kompromat.

Further comparison between kompromat and scandal can be made. First, scandal ordinarily involves kompromat, whereas kompromat does not necessarily lead to a scandal. In other words, "scandal" is what happens after kompromat has been released, whereas "kompromat" is something you collect or create in order to be able to make scandals happen. Thus, an important distinction between kompromat and scandal derives from the fact that the purpose of kompromat has nothing to do with establishing the truth, even if its content is true.

The actual power of kompromat depends on the quality of information it contains. But even at its most explosive, an item of kompromat is often

TABLE 3.2
Kompromat as compared with scandal

Similarities	Differences
Both imply transgression of certain values, norms, or moral codes.	Kompromat can be a way of "framing" a person where no transgression has occurred.
Both involve an element of secrecy or concealment but also some witness testimony.	For a scandal, witnesses have to express their disapproval by publicly denouncing the actions or events in question.
Both may involve power games and interests behind the scene.	Kompromat can be fabricated at the request of clients, without witness testimony or reliable backup information.
Both presuppose some degree of public knowledge and some degree of public disapproval. This is true of kompromat when it is used as a weapon or commodity or after its use in bargaining or negotiations.	When kompromat is used as a bargaining strategy, no public knowledge is involved. Public disapproval might not occur where similar stories are frequent with consequent public exhaustion.
Both aim at the disclosure of actions and events that may damage the reputation of those responsible.	Reputations do not mean much in the context of omnipresent kompromat along with distrust of the media, law, and politicians.

just an excuse for punishment or a tool to harness the courts or public opinion against a rival, thus bringing about his or her political annihilation. The real motivation behind the instigation of punishment is likely to be the perception of the threat represented by a rival rather than any actual violation of rules or principles by the rival in question. Needless to say, scandals can also be unleashed as part of power games in political or business contexts, initiated on purpose and timed to do the most damage (the Clinton sex scandal has often been interpreted to this effect by his supporters). A key difference between kompromat and scandal is related to the actual impact caused by the release of information in different political, legal, and cultural contexts. Thompson outlines several theories of scandal and discusses the corresponding impact on society (Thompson 2000, 234–59). First, scandal can be seen as an ephemeral event, largely fabricated by the media, with little or no bearing on the material factors and processes that shape social and political life—Thompson calls this the "no-consequence theory." Second, scandals may have important consequences that are conservative—that is, they serve to consolidate the status quo. Third, scandal can have a damaging impact on public discourse and debate—the "trivialization theory." Here, the media's preoccupation with scandal tends to undermine the quality of public discourse and debate, focusing people's attention on relatively trivial matters while the important issues are pushed to the margins. Fourth, the "subversion theory" of scandal turns the trivialization theory on its head and questions the dominant norms of journalism in accordance with the assumptions of a more playful, "postmodern" approach to popular culture. "These texts, with their emphasis on sensationalism and excess, offensiveness and bad taste, are like rebellious children who refuse to play by the rules. They entertain their readers and viewers precisely because they reject dominant norms and conventions and, by floating them in an overt and even exaggerated fashion, subject them to a kind of subversive laughter" (242). Finally, Thompson suggests that scandals are struggles over symbolic power in which reputation and trust are at stake, where symbolic power is defined as a capacity to intervene in the course of events and shape their outcome as well as a capacity to influence the actions and beliefs of others by means of the production and transmission of symbolic forms (246).

All these approaches are applicable to kompromat when it is released into the public domain. But they provide little understanding of the role of kompromat in informal politics, where it infringes on the political process either through seemingly anonymous symbolic violence campaigns or by means of highly personalized blackmail.

To sum up the reasons that kompromat in Russia does not normally produce an impact similar to that of scandal in the West (whether political or Enron-type), the specifics of the public sphere should be noted. First of all, in Russia the media are directly or indirectly controlled, both financially and administratively. During the Soviet period the public sphere was strictly censored and controlled, and the use of kompromat for the purposes of shadow politics was restricted to authorized players: for example, Stalin was known to possess kompromat on all his subordinates. By the 1990s, kompromat had become available to a wider range of political and business actors, which resulted in kompromat wars fought in the media—this came closest to scandal but failed to produce a similar impact because of its manipulative and "sponsored" nature.[58]

Second, the public experienced a severe "informational shock" [3.20] as a result of the revelations of *glasnost'* and the kompromat wars of the 1990s. Kompromat appears in a context in which the sheer volume of released compromising materials produces an increasingly indifferent attitude in the media and among the public. Thus, the buildup of distrust in the media prevents kompromat from developing into a scandal.

Third, there is widespread distrust of official politics, certainly a significant factor. As one populist politician put it when asked why kompromat was so prominent in Russia,

> Kompromat? Because party politics does not work, kompromat is the method of applying informal pressure that works. There are so many myths about me, 90 percent of which are not true, including anti-Semitism . . . merely dirt in order to put me down." [3.21]

I would argue that apart from compensating for the defects of Russian official politics, kompromat also serves to reproduce certain practices of informal politics. There is a shared understanding that every puppet in the political "puppet theater" is vulnerable to kompromat and therefore subject to informal leverage whenever necessary. This results in governance based on "principle of suspended punishment" (Ledeneva 1998, 77). According to Vladimir Semago, "The law-enforcement agencies hold material on every deputy of the State Duma, including those working in surveillance.[59] They simply disclose it when needed."[60] Such a "need" arose when in September 1993 Kirsan Iliumzhinov, the president of Kalmykiia, spoke out in favor of reconciliation between the executive branch and legislature. The Yeltsin administration's response was to contact the Ministry of Finance with a list of Iliumzhinov's long-known but previously withheld transgressions, "shedding light on the origin of Iliumzhinov's private wealth and the capital under his control."[61] The threat was sufficient: Iliumzhinov decided to change Kalmykiia's republican constitution according to the federal advice and stated that "everything good" comes from the "center."[62] The principle of suspended punishment operates where there is a substantial gap between declared and actual norms. Since people are forced to violate defective laws almost ubiquitously, punishment becomes a resource in short supply to be distributed according to extralegal criteria. Everybody can be framed and punished. But in the meantime, they find themselves in a situation where the punishment is "suspended" until further notice. In order for this suspension to continue one has to comply with the unwritten rules of the informal order (which basically means following the informal advice of one's patrons and not questioning the informal rules of the system). It is such suspension that was referred to in the early 1980s when the distinguished chairman of a kolkhoz in Altai coined a catchy description of his post: "All kolkhoz chairmen are persons who are temporarily out of prison."[63] Following the same logic, Latynina stated that in the 1990s there was "no single Russian governor whom it would be impossible to jail" (1999). A somewhat shocking revelation to the same effect came independently from two generals serving in regional anticrime units in the 1990s.

> Organized crime would be easier to deal with if it didn't have protection (*krysha*) in governmental structures, if there was no corruption. We do in fact have all the information we need for a massive attack on criminal groupings: technical information, addresses, contacts, but they are protected from above. So all we can do is to collect kompromat and wait for a good moment. [3.40]

A banker who worked extensively with both federal and regional governmental structures in the 1990s summed up the key reason why the system of nontransparent rules and suspended punishment is still in operation.

> The state, the Duma, and the bureaucratic apparatus sustain the nontransparency of rules quite consciously because it increases the power of the apparatus. Given the lack of open competition, the risk of nontransparency is so significant that business has to achieve transparency through informal channels: by using the informal sources of information and by accumulating kompromat. [3.16]

Such dependence of the workings of Russian politics and media on informal practices prevents the occurrence of scandals. Unlike similar informal practices elsewhere, the scale of informal practices in Russia indicates a type of governance in which the functioning of formal institutions depends on them.

What Do Kompromat Practices Tell Us about Governance in Post-Soviet Russia?

The ubiquity of kompromat practices in the post-Soviet period demonstrates the specific unwillingness of the regime to address the question of kompromat and the general dependence of the current regime on the services of security sector. The experience of lustration in central Europe in the 1990s[64] provides an example of an alternative way of dealing with the Communist past (Halmai and Scheppele 1997; Miller 1998; Letki 2002; Williams

2000; Welsh 1996). Lustration is a legal process in the course of which knowledge about those who collaborated with the security services of the past regime, both paid and unpaid, is dealt with in order to prevent their involvement in politics or holding important positions. Lustration laws authorize governments and other organizations to engage in the mass screening of candidates for positions in a new government or to instigate legal proceedings against elites, state bureaucrats, or other servants in the former regime (Letki 2002). Czechoslovakia passed what became known as the Lustration Law on October 4, 1991, to legalize a process of screening individuals in positions of political or economic influence in order to determine whether they had previously had ties with the former state security services. Lustration is a commonly used version of the Czech "lustrace," which refers to politically motivated purging, or "cleansing" (Bren 1993). In Bulgaria, for example, former senior Communists were not allowed to occupy positions of governance in universities and research institutes (the law was annulled in 1995) (Welsh 1996). Supporters of lustration argued early on that those compromised by their collaboration with the former secret police might be vulnerable to blackmail by their former associates or employees. But this argument caused controversy and backfired. Opponents of lustration argued that once the Pandora's box had been opened, the process would result in unauthorized disclosures that could lead to political manipulation. While this was true on a small scale—most often in cases of politically motivated private screening—the proponents of lustration argued that although sometimes unfair or destructive, it was the least harmful alternative and the most legitimate way of addressing the Communist past in the process of transitional justice.[65]

Following the "revolutionary" upheavals in 1989, in Central and Eastern Europe the communist state security services were dissolved and new ones were created. However the extent to which the reorganization also resulted in the legal investigation and or replacement of the previous personnel has varied considerably. In Poland, special screening commissions investigated former security officers. In Bulgaria, senior officials of the so-called sixth department of the Interior Ministry, the state security service, were asked to retire. The absence of significant personnel turnover is most obvious in the Romanian case. In March 1990 a new secret service (SRI) was created in Romania. Many assert that it resembles its predecessor, the Securitate, in many aspects, including the composition of staff. According to different sources, between 17 and 80 per cent of the former Securitate

personnel have been rehired and no more than 20 to 30 former members were tried in court. No legal measures have been passed in Romania that required systematic investigation into the past Securitate
affiliations with public officials. (Welsh 1996, 415)

The Russian case is not even mentioned for comparison. In Russia, the rise
of kompromat in the 1990s has been symptomatic of the unwillingness
(and inability) of the new government to address the past or to attempt any
procedure of transitional justice.[66] Instead, the Russian secret police has
reinvented itself as the producer of kompromat, working almost as before
but through a wider variety of agencies while serving a wider circle of
clients, predominantly those with financial or political power. In the 1990s,
the population was left to witness the kompromat wars, unaware of the
phenomenon of lustration or of other legal ways of handling the legacy of
the secret police. It is tempting to suggest that outburst of kompromat
stood for "lustration Russian style"—an example of what happens to
blackmail files when legal procedures are unavailable or inefficient. In what
follows I offer a summary of implications of these two different ways of
dealing with the past (see table 3.3).

In contrast to Central Europe, where lustration laws were introduced
primarily to screen officials for their links with the secret police while simultaneously addressing the problem of vulnerability to blackmail, the
Russian political machine did not address its past in a similar way. Despite
the rhetoric of change, those in charge felt compelled to continue the practices of informal politics tried and tested by the previous regime. Political
authorities continued to navigate the gap between the façade of official discourse (whether Communist ideology or democratic principles and the
rule of law) and the unwritten rules set for a circle of insiders, and found
new applications for the principle of suspended punishment in order to
keep everybody under control. Kompromat files of an explosive nature
provided bargaining power in the application of informal pressure on political or business opponents. In certain circles, kompromat operated as a
system of mutual restraint and helped to sustain the bonds of mutual control (*krugovaia poruka*). When used as a weapon, kompromat offered a
devastating tool in the public sphere or was used as a pretext for prosecution whenever the political need arose. In other words, as well as serving its
manifest function of accountability and disclosure, kompromat acquired a
whole range of latent functions that served the purposes of informal politics, reproducing the atmosphere of suspended punishment, selective law
enforcement, and a manipulative use of the law.

TABLE 3.3
Kompromat as contrasted to lustration

Kompromat	Lustration
Any information suitable for blackmail (collaboration with the KGB is not discrediting)	Restricted to information on collaboration with secret police (collaboration is discrediting)
Types of kompromat: political, economic, criminal, private	Specific to each country, categories of collaboration indicating different degrees of involvement[a]
Extralegal tool	Politically motivated purging but part of a legal process
Affects "big fish"	Affects employment in public offices but not "big fish" capitalists
Kompromat market not controlled by single agency and kompromat is being produced at present	Secret police files retained by a legal authority; restricted to activity in the past
No legal redress, remedy only via the media	Legal redress procedures stipulated by lustration laws
Impact of kompromat on the political regime:	Impact of lustration on the political regime:
• Serves instrumental purposes of informal politics, rather than truth or justice	• Contributes to the process of transitional justice allowing society to address its past
• Exploits the past for purposes of the present, thus making it an integral part of existing regime	• Necessitates coming to terms with the past, thus eliminating its effects on the present
Negative consequences of kompromat:	Deficiencies of lustration:
• Affects citizen confidence in politicians, business, media, and the rule of law	• Affects citizen confidence in politicians (a politically motivated tool)
• Helps reproduce conditions where kompromat market and security agencies operate outside the law	• Only effective early on in the transition process
• Kompromat wars induce public fatigue	• Political infighting induces public fatigue

[a] For example, agents, informers, owners of "conspiratorial apartments" (cannot seek redress); "conscious collaborators" (can appeal to independent appeal commissions); and category C (includes everybody on StB lists, even prospective informants).

Time works against lustration, and it is unlikely that the issues of transitional justice will appear on Russia's future political agendas.[67] It is much more likely that together with the ongoing process of reprivatization, the use of kompromat and its release to the media will be brought under central control, sanctioned from above and returned to the service of state power, so that the "power vertical" (*vertikal' vlasti*) created by President Putin will enhance the "manageability" of Russia. As in the past, stability in Russia is preserved by means of an informal order, guaranteed by the mutual control exercised within informal networks or the ties of *krugovaia poruka*; instability may be introduced in order to keep powerful players off balance (the customary practice of "divide and rule"), while the gap between the formal and informal order of things allows a choice of legal and extralegal strategies, selectively applied in the interests of a circle of insiders. As the era of black PR and kompromat comes to an end—and most commentators believe that "there won't be another Dorenko"—it is essential, however, to understand the ongoing reproduction of the patterns and archetypes of informal politics that effectively undermine Russia's declared commitment to democracy and a free market.

The predominance of kompromat in the 1990s was the more-or-less inevitable outcome of long-awaited freedom of speech, but at the same time apparent openness concealed the fact that the informal leverage of kompromat constituted one of the most obscure features of political power in Russia. Principles of the rule of law and of fair competition were downplayed in favor of the operational mode of suspended punishment, and the use of nontransparent rules of the game in order to ensure the manageability of the country and its citizens. Kompromat practices were indicative of the specifics of the public sphere in Russia, where powerful political parties were absent, scandals did not reach out to the hearts of the public, reputations were fragile and hard to build, and the media themselves were compromised and unreliable. In contrast to the lustration option, the predominance of kompromat created a climate in which security services sustained their position while the principles of transparency, accountability, and disclosure were distorted. "Democracy" became associated with outbreaks of kompromat, the media were not independent, and the public was not likely to object to the political regime's curtailing media freedoms. Most of these tendencies persist despite efforts to reform the system.

Chapter Four

Krugovaia Poruka: Sustaining the Ties of Joint Responsibility

4,640 for krugovaia poruka
GOOGLE.RU SEARCH ON 27 JULY 2004

Various dictionaries translate *krugovaia poruka* into English as "solidarity," "surety," "collective responsibility," "circular control," or "cover-up." Krugovaia poruka describes a situation in which all the members of a particular group or circle are held jointly responsible for the actions and obligations of its individual members, and each individual member in turn can be held responsible for the actions and obligations of the group as a whole. Under the conditions of krugovaia poruka, the lives and fates of the members of a group are inextricably linked: if one member of the group is harmed, falls victim to misfortune, or is for some reason unable to fulfill his or her obligations, the burden shouldered by the remaining members of the group will be increased. Thus the remaining members stand up for one, whereas one is supposed to behave in a way beneficial to other members. Today, the phrase *krugovaia poruka* designates a pattern in behavior or relationship according to which a person is part of a bigger social unit (a group, network, family, or clan) rather than an isolated human being driven by self-interest. Such a social unit is "tied up" by joint responsibility and mutual obligations.

The institutional forms of krugovaia poruka emerged as a de facto administrative mechanism of circular control in the early communities of ancient Rus', and persisted in a codified form until 1903, when krugovaia poruka was abolished effective in 1907.[1] Nevertheless, it remained embedded in everyday practices and understandings during both the Soviet period and the post-Soviet era, when it came to designate "mutual cover-up in illicit affairs" (Ozhegov and Shvedova 1999). Understanding the transformations of krugovaia poruka provides a helpful insight into the political culture and genesis of social norms and instruments of informal politics in Russia.

In the long history of Russia, the role of krugovaia poruka in society has changed over and over again. From the annals of custom, it has gone through multiple stages of formalization, legalization, and abolition, resulting in its more recent reinvention as an informal institution that has survived the Russian Revolution and the collapse of the Soviet Union and has adjusted to the Russian style capitalism in the 1990s.

The Genealogy of Krugovaia Poruka

Krugovaia poruka is most commonly associated with the peasant communes of prerevolutionary Russia. Yet the practice appears to have roots extending back to the earliest periods of settlement in Slavic lands. The earliest recorded reference to krugovaia poruka is found in *Russkaia Pravda* (Russian Justice), the Russian legal code that was handed down by Iaroslav the Wise (who ruled from 1019 to 1054). *Russkaia Pravda* contains references to *vervi*—territorial divisions of a community whose inhabitants were collectively held responsible for any crimes committed by one of their members (Yaney 1973; Dal' [1881] 1996).

> The oldest form of surety—taking hostage—coexisted with collateral and was considered more reliable. As no sufficient policing services could be provided, the government asked all people to take part in the control and execution of administrative and juridical responsibilities. This was done by way of uniting the people into collectives. . . . This form of guarantee as a system of governmental control also became a system for enslaving people. To avoid its consequences, communities created krugovaia poruka, accepting responsibility for all their members. (Brokgauz and Efron 1898, 637–638)

According to Horace Dewey, the term *poruka* (surety or collective responsibility) rarely appears in pre-Mongol Russian texts. Formal *poruka* seems to have expanded enormously only after the Mongol invasion (Dewey 1988). Russian sources indicate that krugovaia poruka emerged at a time when independent clan-based tribes were the primary political and economic units. During this stage of historical life, clans, rather than individuals, were recognized as legal subjects and as such answered for the actions of their individual members. Krugovaia poruka was used, for example, to ensure that each clan or group of inhabitants paid the required tribute to the warrior groups that protected it. The clan as a whole was responsible for paying a certain amount of tribute, and each of its individual members was obliged to come up with a portion of the total tribute.

As disparate tribes came to be united into a defined territorial union under the Kievan princes, and later into a unified state and governmental apparatus, a process of differentiation occurred by which individuals became seen as legal subjects in their own right. Despite this shift, however, krugovaia poruka was maintained and periodically reintroduced by ruling elements because of its administrative usefulness. It provided an effective instrument for maintaining administrative and fiscal control with a minimum of exertion on the part of those at the top. According to George Yaney (1973), krugovaia poruka emerged as one of the basic elements of Russian political organization.

The use of krugovaia poruka in Russia can be divided into two broad categories: criminal and fiscal. Criminal krugovaia poruka was originally employed to collect fines (*peni*) from the inhabitants of an area in which a crime had been committed. It was also applied in cases of murder either when the murderer remained unknown or when the community refused to betray the murderer's identity and hand him or her over to the authorities. In Kievan Rus', this application of krugovaia poruka was known as *dikaia vira:* the entire community, or *verv,* would be forced to share the fines if the murderer was not handed over or turned in (Dal' [1881] 1996); Brokgauz and Efron 1895; Vvedenskii 1953).

In the fifteenth and sixteenth centuries, this practice became even more formalized. As the Muscovite state established judicial districts (*gubernye okrugi*), the inhabitants of each region were made responsible for the prevention and eradication of crime within their territories. If this responsibility was not upheld, both criminal and financial penalties could be imposed on the whole community according to krugovaia poruka. The practice was employed in the Muscovite state in several other contexts as well.[2]

By the seventeenth century, krugovaia poruka was used almost exclusively in fiscal affairs—primarily in relation to the collection of taxes. Historians differ on the emergence of krugovaia poruka within peasant tax affairs. While some scholars have argued that it has always been an inherent aspect of peasant tax dealings, others have claimed that the peasant communities' collective responsibility for taxes evolved only after certain conditions made it possible—namely, the consolidation of serfdom, the enslavement of peasants on the land, and the introduction of the poll tax (or head tax) under Peter the Great (Brzheskii 1897).

As the Muscovite and imperial Russian state evolved, tax collection was organized in such a way that the commune was the principal tax-collection unit. Tax assessments were levied upon communes on the basis of the amount of arable land they controlled, but the commune itself was granted the task of apportioning the tax burden among its local inhabitants. It was also responsible for collecting the taxes and remitting them to the state. The essence of krugovaia poruka in relation to tax affairs was simple in concept: the entire community was responsible for the timely collection of taxes. In the event that individual taxpayers were unable or unwilling to produce their payments, the unpaid sum would be spread among the remaining members of the community. For the state, krugovaia poruka was a crude but effective means of maintaining control over fiscal affairs in the countryside.

Although each community bore collective responsibility for the collection and submission of taxes, certain individuals within the community served as liaisons between the village and the authorities. As the "bearers of collective responsibility," village elders (*starosty*) and officers faced punishment if they failed to deliver on their obligations (Andrle 1994). These individuals, fearing recriminations from the state against their property or holdings, would use their local authority to enact the principle of krugovaia poruka within the community. Even in times during which krugovaia poruka was not explicitly sanctioned by law, its principles were employed in exacting tax payments from local residents (Brokgauz and Efron 1895).

Krugovaia poruka undermined the principle of equality in the face of the law in a number of ways. Because it required a community or a collective, rather than an individual, to be a responsible subject, the punishment within the community was distributed according to informal justice rather than the rule of law. Such layering within law enforcement sustained the niche in which so-called extralegal methods at a community level were allowed to function for the sake of the legal order. The state condoned the personalized power of the bearers of collective responsibility and their discretion in protecting members of the community from the universal system of punishment by introducing an informal particularistic one. Such informal justice did not apply equally to all, however. Thus the formal law was even more relative and actual punishment even more dependent on the person in charge and on the informal order in the community. As shown below, the legalization of krugovaia poruka only sealed the fundamental dependence of law enforcement in Russia on informal justice.

The Gap between the Law and Practice of Krugovaia Poruka

Krugovaia poruka continued to function throughout the eighteenth and nineteenth centuries, taking on an official character as a result of several manifestos and regulations relating to the status of peasants and the financial responsibilities of the countryside. A manifesto of May 16, 1811, declared that the timely collection of taxes was the responsibility of the community as a whole and granted the heads of each *volost'* (rural district) —both elected, and traditional (*starosty*)—certain rights to enforce the collection of taxes from residents. *Starosty* and elected leaders were permitted to appropriate the labor of delinquent taxpayers to pay off the village shortfall or to send such individuals away to workhouses to work off their debts. The same measures could be employed against village elders themselves, in fact, if a community remained in arrears to the state (Brokgauz and Efron 1895).

The Regulation on Monetary Collections of November 28, 1833 further extended the scope of krugovaia poruka within tax affairs. The law continued to recognize the village as primarily responsible for the timely collection of taxes, but a stipulation was added that the entire *volost'* would be held responsible according to krugovaia poruka if a particular village built up arrears that exceeded its annual tax assessment (Brokgauz and Efron 1895; Zheleznov et al. 1933).

As plans for the emancipation of the serfs progressed under Alexander II, one of the many questions that arose was the future of krugovaia poruka after peasant reforms. Upon emancipation, peasants would be responsible for redemption payments of 20 percent of the value of the land they received, in addition to all other existing taxes. It was important that landowners be guaranteed payments for the land they would be losing. Krugovaia poruka appeared the most feasible way to ensure this, and the institution was preserved in the emancipation reform of 1861 with some modifications. It was officially limited to individual villages and no longer extended up to the level of the *volost'* (Brokgauz and Efron 1895, 837).

The emancipation reform granted the village *obshchestvo* (society) almost complete independence in overseeing its own tax affairs (Zheleznov et al. 1933). Village elders and tax collectors continued to bear collective responsibility for the assessment and collection of taxes within the village. With the exception of a handful of minor measures—such as fines and temporary arrest—these individuals were not permitted to take coercive measures against delinquent taxpayers. The village assembly (*skhod*), however, had at its disposal a series of measures that could be enacted to collect taxes from those in arrears: taking compensation for arrears from income being made on the debtor's property, hiring out the debtor or one of his or her family members for additional work and adding the earnings to the communal treasury, designating a "guardian" for the debtor, selling off personal property belonging to the debtor (except for a house), selling off parts of the debtor's land that were not necessary for his or her livelihood, and revoking the debtor's right to farm communal lands (Brokgauz and Efron 1895; Burds 1991).

While the final three sanctions were to be used only in extreme cases—when the first three measures had proved unsuccessful—it is clear that krugovaia poruka was recognized by the state as the main instrument for *vyko-lachivanie,* the extorting or exacting of taxes and arrears from the peasantry (Schmidt 1937). The 1861 emancipation of the serfs armed the village *skhod* with an arsenal of measures for use in the battle for taxes and arrears. If the collections were still not completed in a timely manner, outside authorities such as the police and tax inspectorate could intervene and impose sanctions against the entire commune in order to retrieve funds to cover the arrears.

In practice, however, the collection of taxes and arrears and the use of krugovaia poruka occurred quite differently than in the procedures outlined on paper. The forcible redistribution of outstanding arrears among community members took place extremely rarely, according to official records (Brokgauz and Efron 1895). Instead, the *threat* of it often proved sufficient to motivate peasant communes to devise ways of meeting outside obligations. According to one account, coercive measures were often employed within the commune to ensure that the village met its tax obligations so as to avoid arbitrary actions by the state tax inspectorate. Such coercion reinforced distrust of the authorities and the tendency to solve problems informally, at the level of community. As one historian has noted, "The unifying element in all community affairs was opposition to behavior that would provoke the interference of state agents and the police" (Burds 1991, 82).

The community appears to have been effective in many instances, as official records from the time reveal. One of the sanctions that police and the tax inspectorate could impose was the forced sale of peasant property to raise funds to cover the tax arrears. Often such sales were conducted completely indiscriminately—that is, peasants who had paid their taxes were at just as much risk of having property sold as those who were in debt. Authorities would enter the village, conduct inventories of the contents of several households, and prepare the sale. Records suggest, however, that inventories (*opisi*) of possessions were conducted immeasurably more frequently than the sales themselves. In some regions, sales took place in only 10 to 15 percent of the cases in which inventories were carried out. Thus it appears that the police often resorted to inventories as a type of scare tactic to jolt the community into action. As soon as the frightened population came up with part of the arrears that were due, the case would not proceed any further (Brokgauz and Efron 1895).

To understand why krugovaia poruka so rarely resulted in the forcible redistribution of arrears, it is necessary to examine certain long-standing patterns and customs inherent to the peasant commune.[3] The practice of insider redistribution of land and tax burdens—the so-called *svalki-navalki* system—was carried out in some areas (particularly in poor-soil regions). This alleviated the tax burden upon poor families, or families with little labor power, by transferring parcels of land and the corresponding taxes to more prosperous families. In such a way, communities took upon themselves the responsibility of freeing their weakest members from the chronic burden of long-standing tax arrears and putting the village on a sounder economic footing (Brokgauz and Efron 1895).[4]

Evidence suggests that the borrowing of funds to cover tax payments was also a common practice—as our earlier description of customary practices in the commune would lead us to expect. Communal funds belonging to the *mir* (commune) were sometimes used to cover tax shortfalls, with the expectation that the debtors would pay back the treasury through donated labor or income from the next season's harvest. Private loans were also prevalent, with the wealthier members of the commune (*kulaks,* tavern owners, and shopkeepers) able to issue credit or lend cash to poorer peasants. As Burds (1991) has pointed out, personal contacts were essential in these village credit networks. This culture of mutual help and reciprocal obligations was so deeply embedded within peasant communes that its values and operating principles were understood intuitively by its members. Transactions were rarely cash for cash but involved rights to the use of communal lands or labor contracts for work to be performed at a future time (Burds 1991). Burds has concluded that many poorer peasants preferred being indebted to "village insiders" to facing the arbitrary nature of external interventions into the village, thus enhancing the long-standing tradition of informal problem solving when peasant communes were required to engage with outside authorities and institutions.

The krugovaia poruka legislation is therefore a classic example of the formal rules that not only implied the use of informal codes and practices but also required the existence of an informal order in the interests of both central authorities and local communities.

The Abolition of Krugovaia Poruka: Delegalization

By the end of the nineteenth century, it was increasingly obvious that krugovaia poruka was not functioning effectively as a tax collection mechanism for the state. Not only was it often subverted from within, but even in
those instances in which it was applied (through forced sales of property
and redistribution of the tax burden), it often resulted in the total collapse
of peasant livelihood. The tax burden was greater than the peasant population could bear, and the arrears had grown to unrealistic proportions. After
taking over as minister of finance, Sergei Witte saw the abolition of krugovaia poruka as one of his main objectives. Yet krugovaia poruka was such
an integral part of peasant life and economic existence, and such a fundamental pillar of imperial agrarian policy, that its elimination demanded a
great amount of time and preparation (Zheleznov et al. 1933).

In preparation for the elimination of krugovaia poruka, Witte convened
a special inquiry into the rural political situation. The commission solicited
reports from regional tax inspectors on the state of tax collection practices.
Many of the reports submitted to the commission brought about "a relent-
less blow to the idealization of the commune" by revealing the prevalence
of exploitation "masquerading as mutual aid" within peasant communities
(Simonova 1969). All the findings submitted by the inspectors supported
the same conclusion: that krugovaia poruka was not functioning in the way
that the emancipation reform of 1861 had intended. The reports underscored the fact that the tax procedures imposed upon peasant communes
after 1861 were rarely applied in their "true form"—that is, by apportioning taxes by head according to the census. Instead, a clear tendency had
emerged toward tax assessment based on income and wealth—reflecting
the growing economic diversification of the peasant population. The tax
mechanism had essentially broken down.

The commission found that coercive measures applied by the police or
tax inspectorate to exact taxes often produced no result. In many instances
(just as in the 1990s) arrears had built up to such an extent that they could
never feasibly be recovered.[5] Tax inspectors noted how peasant communes
could use the system of krugovaia poruka to their own advantage, as a type
of buffer against the arbitrary practices of the state. The Moscow province
report stated to the commission that the village *skhod*, which was granted
specific powers in the collection of taxes, would choose not to apply any
measures at all in cases in which the majority of peasants were in arrears.
(Simonova 1969). In other words, there was strength in numbers—the

greater the proportion of peasants deep in arrears, the lesser the likelihood of coercive measures from above. The *skhod* was thus rendered impotent in the face of widespread arrears, and forced redistributions of debts rarely occurred. Tax inspectors took this as an indication of the weakening of krugovaia poruka.

In the light of such findings, Witte reported to Tsar Nicholas II in 1898 that "the governor and the police can sometimes exact twice the tax and other times nothing at all. Krugovaia poruka, which was created alongside communal landholding and is tightly intertwined with it, holds peasants responsible not for themselves, but for everyone—and for this reason sometimes leads to complete irresponsibility" (Simonova 1969, 174). The findings from the special commission were not made public, but they did serve as the basis for Witte's presentation before the State Committee on the Abolition of Krugovaia Poruka. The conclusion reached by the body was that krugovaia poruka was no longer working to guarantee the delivery of taxes to the treasury (Simonova 1969). Furthermore, it was widely acknowledged that it had become a dangerous force within peasant communities that were undergoing a process of economic differentiation. Too frequently the law appeared to be used as a weapon in the hands of the rich peasants against the poor.

Several pieces of legislation weakened the scope of krugovaia poruka before it was finally eliminated. The law of June 23, 1899, exempted villages of fewer than sixty residents from the hold of krugovaia poruka. On March 12, 1903, a law was passed that established the individual head of household—not the commune—as the primary unit for tax assessment. Through a decree of October 5, 1906, krugovaia poruka was abolished throughout the empire as of January 1, 1907.

Krugovaia Poruka in Soviet and Post-Soviet Politics

A unique cultural artifact of krugovaia poruka in the Soviet period is a famous song "Bound by One Chain" (*Skovannye odnoi tsep'iu*) by the Nautilus Pompilius group, which astutely grasps the essence of the phenomenon in the 194 words-long satirized image of the Soviet society. Although somewhat lost in translation, the metaphors in the text reveal the main features and re-create the atmosphere of the Soviet political regime. The song was written at the very beginning of perestroika, when the Soviet memories were still fresh.[6]

> *Krugovaia poruka* sticks like glue
> I want friendship but feel pressure
> I look for eye contact but instead feel watched
> Where the position is more important than what we think
> Following the red sunrise is a pink sunset
> Bound by one chain,
> Tied by one aim (see full text in appendix 3)

The first verse depicts the sticky nature of krugovaia poruka ties, inevitable as the sunrise, and difficult to escape due to the surveillance of those keen on career-building, regardless of what they have to do to achieve it. The second verse points to alienation of the provinces, the worthlessness of human life, the doublethink, the suppression of individual freedoms and talent thus favoring mediocrity, and restrictions on privacy. The third stanza refers to the ideological beliefs without the faith in the political and economic foundations of the system, limitations of the welfare state, the impossibility of change, and the low levels of morality in a society based on vigilance and mutual control. The fourth verse is about the proclaimed but unrealized role of women, the inefficiency of economic stimuli, the impunity of state officials and the unmotivated political leadership during the stagnation period (with an allusion to Brezhnev and Chernenko, who took the office while gravely ill).

Each verse is enhanced by a refrain stating the key role of the ideological frame (one aim) and the "chains" of collective responsibility (one chain) for each of the featured characteristics and for the regime in general. It is implied in this text that everybody is caught in the chains of krugovaia poruka and that the principle is more or less universally applied. In the academic literature on the Soviet past we find more specific interpretations of krugovaia poruka.

With reference to the Stalinist period, Vladimir Kozlov (2000) conceptualizes krugovaia poruka as a defensive response of bureaucrats to practices of denunciation. The institutionalization of denunciation was a form of central control over the behavior of local authorities in the vast spaces of the USSR. A political regime in which the population had no means of democratic control over officials' actions used denunciation instead.

According to Kozlov (2000), krugovaia poruka became instrumental for the bureaucracy as a means of self-defense and a method of suppressing criticism. He identified a variety of practices by which bureaucrats protected themselves and their colleagues from criticism. Some of these, such as intercepting correspondence and using the military censor and postal workers for tracing denunciation letters, were considered "too devious." But other practices yielding similar results did not provoke distaste even from the central authorities, much less in the lower levels of the bureaucratic estate. For example, the common practice of returning a denunciation letter to local authorities was in essence little different from the interception of correspondence. In this case the denunciation most often fell into the hands of those against whom it was written, or of one of their friends or associates, none of whom had any interest in bringing things into the open.

For Soviet bureaucrats, violating the unwritten rules was in a way more serious than violating the written ones (Ledeneva 2001b, 12–13). In other words, the biggest risk lay not in breaking the laws themselves but in "losing a sense of proportion," or "feel for the game" (or *sens pratique,* practical sense), an understanding of what they could and could not get away with (Bourdieu 1989). Those bureaucrats who "kept within limits" and did play by krugovaia poruka rules were often saved from accountability by patrons at higher levels. Every "big boss" had his own people in local positions upon whom he depended, whom he trusted, and who were personally devoted to him.[7] If they had good relations with those higher up, the local bosses could avoid accountability for serious misbehavior and even crimes (Fitzpatrick and Gellately 1997; Hosking 2000). No wonder these traditional patterns rooted in Russia's political culture are so enduring.

One of the usual methods of saving "one's own man" from accountability was to punish him for internal disciplinary infractions, even in cases of criminal misconduct. Kozlov (2000) illustrates this point with an incident involving Beria, who removed an acquaintance from his post as NKVD commander of rear security forces on the Second Belorussian Front for misappropriation of captured material, sexual harassment, and other crimes and misdemeanors. Without bringing the case to trial, Beria prevented his acquaintance from sinning further—by removing him to another post on another front.

Party discipline intervened in law enforcement according to the familiar pattern of introducing a particularistic system of punishment—punishment through party channels (*po partiinoi linii*). These practices can also be found outside party contexts and are grasped by an old Russian expression *vziat' na poruki* (to take someone into community care), which means that the commune trusts in its member and takes responsibility for his or her activity (Sreznevskaia 1965, 1218). For example, if a worker broke some common rules or did something "incompatible with the behavior of a builder of communism," the work collective discussed his or her behavior and made a decision. In most cases the worker acknowledged guilt, asked for the pardon of the collective, and made a promise to behave as appropriate for a Soviet citizen, which enabled the work collective to view this person as trustworthy and to bail him or her out.

Irina Davydova (1999) claims that the protective side of krugovaia poruka (which she translates as "circular guarantee") could be identified in most work collectives in urban areas. Her evidence suggests that "the circular guarantee (now presented in moral terms) continued to be a principle of management for lower levels of the hierarchy." She also explains that work collectives in the USSR took responsibility for both benefits and sanctions bestowed on individuals (see also Hosking 2004, 53, on analogies with the village commune). Davydova documents:

> Many if not most goods—an apartment, a place in kindergarten for children, a sanatorium, health care, goods in short supply, etc.—were obtained through attachment to the collective. Small abuses of the law and public (or even private) behavior also were in the jurisdiction of so-called "comrades' courts" (*tovarishcheskie sudy*). So the *modus operandi* of the work collective included some elements of circular guarantee. (208–9)

Thus the use of krugovaia poruka by the Communist state and bureaucracy was replicated in various professional groups. In academia, a dissertation could not be published if it did not belong to a certain scientific "school" and preached a distinctive scientific paradigm.[8] Miners were another example of a group linked by krugovaia poruka. Once they became part of a closed circle, there was no way out. One could profit from it as an insider but risked losing one's position in society if one attempted to leave.

The second method of protecting krugovaia poruka insiders in the bureaucracies took the form of counterattack by discrediting denouncers. As Kozlov accurately notes,

> If the denouncer frequently relied on "a few words about myself" to strengthen his case, the reputation of the denunciation offered a mirror image of the same ploy. The denouncer, pointing to his services to the regime, tried to show that he was right because he was "one of our own" (*svoi*), while the bureaucrats tried to show that he was wrong because he was "an outsider" (*chuzhoi*). One distorted logic confronted another: it was the denouncer who was discredited rather than his or her information. (2000, 130)

Keeping such discrediting information (or kompromat) under control became a handy instrument in counteracting denunciations. The Soviet bureaucrats' system of corporate self-presentation included one very important pos-
tulate: that any "personal motive" on the part of a denouncer who appealed to
central authorities devalued his information, bringing it into question morally
and in many cases entirely obviating the necessity of seeking counterargu-
ments or offering a defense. This was especially the case with anonymous denunciations. Refusal to sign almost automatically evoked doubt about
whether the denouncer's motives were pure, leading to suspicion that there
was an element of personal interest in the results of the investigation.

Bureaucrats who observed the rules of the game and knew ways of manipulating the system could feel relatively safe and did not need to fear denunciations: the safety net of krugovaia poruka protected them. However,
under certain circumstances the described methods of bureaucratic self-
defense could malfunction. Kozlov (2000) distinguishes three types of circumstances that weakened the ties of krugovaia poruka in the Soviet period. First, during unstable or crisis situations, or periods of major reforms,
denunciations were provoked from above—the "chiefs" appealed directly
to the masses, calling on them to expose "enemies" and "saboteurs."

Second, in rare cases the denunciatory activities of the population of a
particular region, in combination with an influx of complaints and letters
to newspapers, reached such a magnitude that it became a political rather
than an administrative problem. This forced the central power to intervene
to reestablish "law and order," breaking up the circle of krugovaia poruka
and the web of personal ties. In this situation it was no longer safe to save
"one's own" people.

Third, certain problems in the bureaucratic krugovaia poruka did
sometimes occur as a result of a power struggle or an individual's attempt
to widen his sphere of influence. A wave of mutual denunciations and ex-
posures would then begin. The "disinterested denunciations" written
"from below" would become a dangerous weapon, whether they were truth
or slander. Intervention of the central authorities, undesirable under normal circumstances, would become the only exit from such local crises of
authority.

In all these cases the leaders of the regime were the arbiters in the conflicts
between the masses and the "apparatus," deriving their own power from this
conflict. Instead of democratizing the political regime, the leaders used denunciations as an instrument of control that maintained the equilibrium of
the entire system of relationships constituting Soviet society (Kozlov 2000).
Gerald Easter (2000) has shown how powerful regional elites were tied into

a complex network of interests that could facilitate but also contradict the interests of the center. The mechanisms of mutual protection and control operated tacitly but effectively and were revealed only when the elites were purged. In Stalin's time, the personnel policy often marked a deliberate effort by the center to decouple informal network ties from the formal structures of power. In the post-Soviet period, such networks have continued their existence.[9] One respondent, now a very successful businessman, explained his position in a region in the late Brezhnev period by referring to a circle of "friends" to which he belonged. The informal group included the first secretary of the regional party committee, the mayor of an important city, a KGB colonel, the police chief, and a representative (*svoi chelovek*) in the Central Committee in Moscow. These people were described as daily—high-intensity—contacts who helped one another do business, cared and protected one another, and, perhaps not surprisingly, represented all branches of power [5.30]. As Easter (2000, 46) emphasized, "the bosses of the provinces" (greater in size than most European states) possessed extraordinary and personalized power and embodied the authority of the party's central committee. They were similar to the tsarist regime's governors (*nachal'niki gubernii*), who served as the tsar's viceroys, representing the autocracy in the regions and sustaining cross-organizational networks in the military elites.

> The Soviet Russian state was a virtual labyrinth of bureaucratic structures, but it was a far cry from a rational-legal bureaucratic state. Beneath the formal façade of the monolithic party and the planned economy existed an informal world of cliques, factions, networks and *druzhina*.[10] Power and status within the state elite derived as much from the workings of these informal groupings as they did from the formal lines of command. . . . The Soviet Russian case was an early model of a process in which personalistic patterns of political authority and organization were adapted to new formal-legalistic structures within the institutional framework of hastily constructed post-colonial states. (Easter 2000, 173–74)

According to Easter, the reason that comparative theorists and area specialists were caught off guard by the collapse of the twentieth century's most feared state could in part be found in their lack of attention to this underworld of personalistic relations. It is logical to suggest that the impact of such relations in the post-Soviet transformation is also substantial. The traps of krugovaia poruka have been identified as a major obstacle by one of the authors of Ukrainian anticorruption legislation, who explained the workings of krugovaia poruka in the post-Soviet period as follows:

> [In the 1990s the mafia] is entering networks of control and backup (*krugovaia poruka*), the most harmful and ineradicable legacy of the past, which provides protection for people of their circle. . . . [D]eputies of the parliament are backed up by the administrative authorities. Administrative officials do not have the same legal immunity as deputies, but they are backed up by the security and police forces. Whenever cases are raised against high-up officials they are suspended or closed. Every administrator would back up his staff, because he knows if he does not do it, the day comes when he himself will have to rely on someone else's support. This mechanism follows the same pattern as professional expertise in medicine or court—the inspection of complicated cases such as unfortunate surgery or prejudiced sentence consists of the same surgeons and judges who can find themselves in a similar situation.[11]

The pattern of krugovaia poruka is well portrayed in a cartoon by Vladimir Romanov.[12] His caricature (figure 4.1) depicts people standing one behind the other in a circle, each pointing a gun or knife at the person in front of him, while being threatened from the back at the same time. A post-Soviet westernized Moscow looms in the background. Although these guns and knives should not always be taken literally, the element of fear and circular control should be.

Although the Soviet system of power was radically reformed in the 1990s, its dependence on krugovaia poruka changed little. Many scholars explained the strength of the Soviet legacy by the continuity of elites in post-Soviet Russia, especially in contrast with the experiences of Central European countries such as Poland, Hungary, and the Czech Republic in the 1990s (Kryshtanovskaya and White 1996).[13] Yergin and Gustafson (1994, 50–51, 61, 204–5) argued that the former party nomenclature has successfully managed to establish itself in the new society. A typical example is the former party official who creates a company in which the shareholders are his former colleagues, still employed in the state apparatus. From them he obtains a license to export wood. This wood is then bought at low state prices by another former colleague and another shareholder who is the director of a local paper factory, and they become rich together. This is how the old krugovaia poruka is still in effect today.[14]

Whereas krugovaia poruka in post-Soviet Russia is a relatively unex-

Figure 4.1. Vladimir Romanov, "Krugovaia poruka." At http://www.caricatura.ru/parad/rom/460. By permission of editor in chief of Caricatura.ru.

plored subject in academic literature, its coverage in the post-Soviet press is extensive.[15] As a rule, press reports identify krugovaia poruka with corruption[16] and with practices of bending the law in the interests of bureaucracy and law enforcement officers, protecting the "honor" of their "uniform."[17] Cases of krugovaia poruka among "people in uniform" (*liudi v pogonakh*) in the regions are common and follow a similar pattern. A prosecutor shot dead a teenager who infringed on the common area in his apartment block. A judge beat up a boy who scratched his car. In a lawful society the parents of the boy would have paid for the repairs of the car and the judge would have been sentenced to a maximum of two years in prison (according to Russia's Criminal Code). Moreover, he would have lost his job for an offense like this. Under krugovaia poruka, however, the judge's colleagues protected the "honor" of the legal profession and covered the incident up as if nothing had happened. Similarly, militiamen routinely cover up for one another whenever a breach of legality takes place. In fact, breaking the rules in operative and investigative work is so common that people get suspicious when someone is punished for it. It might be the case that the exposed officer crossed the path of a powerful circle, as happened to the officer investigating corruption case in the aluminum industry.[18] As Latynina put it,

What's worse than bribery, corruption, the overall idleness of the Interior Ministry, and even the corporate interests of the generals is krugovaia poruka *silovikov* [coercive ministries]. That very krugovaia poruka that forces courts to acquit an investigator who killed a suspect during interrogation, to acquit a drunk traffic police officer [*gaishnik*] who killed somebody in an accident, or a special services officer [*omonovets*] who shot somebody by mistake. (1999, 231)

Krugovaia poruka is also found in relation to the Russian corporate sector and abuses in corporate governance.[19] Gazprom was involved in a series of scandals associated with insider dealing, asset stripping, transfer pricing, share dilution, and other practices that violated minority shareholder rights for the benefit of an inner circle of managers.[20] This started to change only when the key figures of the circle—ex-Chairman Rem Viakhirev and ex-Premier Victor Chernomyrdin—"retired." But there is no guarantee that new ties are not being formed at the same time.

A well-known case against the former Kremlin property chief Pavel Borodin, who was associated with the Mabetex scandal in which President Yeltsin's family became implicated, is often interpreted along the lines of krugovaia poruka.

When Geneva prosecutor, Bernard Bertossa, fined Borodin 300,000 Swiss francs ($177,000) for laundering $30 million in alleged kickbacks from Swiss firms,[21] Borodin's lawyer, Eleonora Sergeeva, told the Associated Press that Borodin wouldn't pay the fine, because he didn't think he had committed any crime either at home or abroad.[22] Meanwhile, the Russian Deputy General Prosecutor Vladimir Kolmogorov confirmed that there were Swiss bank accounts to which Borodin transferred millions of dollars, but indicated that a court case will not be filed as this money was transferred by mistake."[23]

Commentators claimed that Borodin was confident of being bailed out of Swiss prison and left in peace in Russia because of his potentially explosive knowledge of Kremlin affairs: Borodin was able to use the kompromat in his possession as a bargaining chip and to turn the ties of krugovaia poruka to his advantage. Yeltsin and his inner circle received similar treatment in escaping punishment for the charges against them.[24] Such patterns can be found in smaller and larger communities, during and after elections.

When asked about the role of elections in providing legal immunity for deputies and elected officials, my respondent instead emphasized the aspects of access, power, and mediation indicative of krugovaia poruka.

Political immunity might be in the interests of certain candidates but their percentage is not significant. Rather, people become candidates for elected positions in order to achieve a new level of power, not necessarily the key positions, but significant enough to have access to decision making about budget funds and to influence the development of their business or other interests. Of course, one does not have to take an elected position oneself. As elsewhere in the world, one can serve one's own interests through the trusted people in positions of power—a scheme of mediation in politics. [2.5]

But the ties between those elected and those financing elections are even more inevitable.

On the one hand, candidates receive political support from political parties and advertise their own trademark (consumer goods, services) actively during the election campaign. On the other hand, political parties, especially those with underfunded regional branches, make alliances with people able to support them financially. In accordance with the 2002 legislation, regional parties as well as federal will be able to trade their party list "places" in exchange for funding and other dividends. One does not have to be a member of the party to be put on a list but can also acquire a membership. The financial contribution from such a candidate is very difficult to trace; it can formally arrive at the electoral fund from a charity organization or be passed over to the leaders of the party on a handshake. In both cases, whether it is a fully accountable charitable transaction or an informal contribution, the fact of exchange cannot be legally proven. [2.5]

Some evidence on the continuing importance of informal leverage and the ways in which it is created or avoided in electoral campaigns comes from an expert in political technologies.

One of the rules in the elections one has to try to follow is to avoid difficult victories. When you do not win comfortably, you are too much indebted to those whom you had to come to help, financially and otherwise. This puts one in a weak position in relation to the elite. . . . Regional governors pride themselves on their victories when the votes approach 80 percent or so. Technically, the absolute percentage is not important, but for them it is the proof of their power and independence. [2.3]

This is indicative of their position within the pattern of krugovaia poruka. Kurtov and Kagan illustrate an interesting set of dynamics during the 2000 presidential elections.

It was the first and foremost task for Putin's ideologists to distance Putin from Yeltsin. The polls showed that as soon as Yeltsin became close to a candidate, the rating of that candidate plummeted. It was the most serious problem for Putin. Moreover, a careful observer must have noticed: Yeltsin did appear in the presidential campaign a number of times. . . . Despite his retirement, Yeltsin was a real politician with an adequate understanding of his own anti-rating. Yeltsin was interested in the victory of Putin and understood how difficult it was for a candidate to start from the position of Yeltsin's successor. But suddenly, during that election campaign, Yeltsin held a press conference (press conferences are an extremely rare occurrence for Yeltsin) and made a radical statement about the inevitable presidency for Putin as *his* successor. "He will follow my steps," Yeltsin said. This was hardly a help. Quite the opposite, commentators agreed that it was an attempt to show Putin that his ratings could go down further if Yeltsin kept "helping" with the campaign. This forced Putin to negotiate with the "family." Why was it necessary? So that the victory would not be easy for Putin and so that he would ask for help and would be indebted to people who would stop Yeltsin from further statements. This is despite the fact that Yeltsin was interested in Putin's victory. (2002, 122–23)

After the elections, some observers suggested, "Putin does everything in his power to remove members of the political and economic elite recruited by Yeltsin and to break up the ties of Yeltsin's family krugovaia poruka."[25] Skeptics said that the maximum Putin could do was to replace Yeltsin's clientele with his own while the pattern of krugovaia poruka persisted. Reflecting upon this effort, *Vedomosti* awarded the "Politician of the Year 2001" title to "Collective Putin":

Putin appointed his St. Petersburg contacts to key posts: Minister of Defense—Sergei Ivanov; Interior Minister—Boris Gryslov; he "helped" Sergei Mironov be elected to the post of Speaker of the Federation Council; he "made" Aleksei Miller become the head of Gazprom, Russia's largest company. And this is just the tip of the iceberg. St. Petersburg appointees are now in charge of Sheremet'evo airport, the nuclear complex Tvel and a number of nonpolitical but strategically important structures. All these northwest migrants represent a political unit known as "President Putin." People with neutral appearances, sad eyes, quiet voices, and cautious judgments work in a coordinated way and without much publicity. Maybe this is the secret of success, and we will witness some positive changes analogous to those taking place at Gazprom.[26]

No legislation is sensitive enough to prevent such a personnel policy or forms of behavior prescribed by a certain legal and political culture. But even if it were the case that legal aspects of krugovaia poruka were defined as "mutual assistance and concealment in some organized group" and were addressed in the anti-anticorruption legislation, this legislation has been discussed in the State Duma since 1994 (Lopatin and Lopatina 1998, 486), and after each discussion the law tends to become more and more toothless. According to Pavel Burdukov, vice chairman of the State Duma Anticorruption Commission, "the present version of this law does not pose a threat to those who practice corruption."[27] Even if the anticorruption legislation were adopted, the issues of law enforcement and people's respect for laws are not likely to be solved without a radical change in the existing legal and political culture. The pattern of krugovaia poruka and its impact on legal institutions are central to understanding Russia's legal and political culture and thus requires a historical overview.

Change of the Pattern or the Pattern of Change

In contexts in which administrative and judicial institutions are insufficiently developed to oversee the enforcement of legal rights and responsibilities, the system of collective responsibility holds a certain logic. In the case of imperial Russia, krugovaia poruka was a clear reflection of the weakness of the state in the countryside and the imperative the state felt to guarantee the regular receipt of taxes. Krugovaia poruka was not advantageous for the Russian state alone, however. The institution of krugovaia poruka also shielded peasant communities from arbitrary interventions by outside authorities by placing the whole collective, rather than individuals, before creditors. Over time, however, the conditions that enabled krugovaia poruka to function began to change. The economic differentiation within peasant communes made the practice problematic and heightened internal tensions and friction within villages. Krugovaia poruka was no longer a neutral leveling mechanism but an increasingly powerful tool that the wealthy could use against the weak. Rather than leading to a convergence of interests, it appeared to fuel the growing divergence of peasant interests. Because krugovaia poruka was failing to fulfill its fiscal objectives, the state moved toward direct engagement with individual taxpayers—in both levying tax assessments and collecting tax payments. Thus the role of krugovaia poruka in Russia has been double-edged. Although intended by the state as a type of coercive measure in the battle over taxes, it was simultaneously used by peasants as a type of buffer that allowed them to soften budget constraints and reproduce traditional customs, practices, and hierarchies in local areas. After the formal institution of krugovaia poruka had been abolished, it reestablished itself in various informal practices in the Soviet state, spread particularly widely in the period of "the ruralization of the cities" in the 1920s–30s (Lewin 1985), when an intense peasant migration into the cities took place. As shown above, familiar practices of vigilance and control were omnipresent in Soviet bureaucracy (Easter 2000), communal apartments (Gerasimova 1998), and work collectives (Hosking 2004). Contemporary informal practices of krugovaia poruka, just like their legalized counterparts in the past, operate in both a protective and a disciplinary way for insiders and are conducive to informal orders that could be used for the purposes of informal politics by the state.

What sustains these practices is the continuity of legal culture grounded in fear and disrespect. Specific to krugovaia poruka, Yaney suggests that fear played a key role.

> The basic attitude that collective responsibility inculcated in each "peasant" was a constant fear that one or more of his fellows might leave, or fall sick, or for some other reason fail to render their share of the tribute obligation, thus increasing the burden he himself would have to bear. Unless common desperation drove all members of a village or tribe to depart (or revolt) together, they were anxious to prevent any action of any of their number that might bring punishment down on them all. Each villager, therefore, was likely to feel the need for an authority that could keep his fellows in line. When he felt this need, he found himself deeply dependent on the authority of the collector, and his sense of dependence was likely to make him generally anxious that his fellow villagers regard the collector with awe. Under a stable tribute-collecting hierarchy the villagers needed or wanted not kindness and "justice" for their community but an authority strong enough to keep their neighbors from defaulting or departing. (Yaney 1973, 138–39)

The liberal Russian thinker Aleksandr Herzen, whose statement from the mid-1800s sounds just as familiar today, summed up the features of the Russian legal culture:

> The legal insecurity that has hung over our people from time imme-morial has been a kind of school for them. The scandalous injustice of one half of the law has taught them to hate the other half; they submit only to force. Complete inequality before the law has killed any re-spect they may have had for legality. Whatever his station, the Russian evades or violates the law wherever he can do so with impunity; the government does exactly the same thing.[28]

The centrality of the legal and political culture to institution building in post-Soviet Russia has facilitated debates on continuity and change in atti-tudes and behavior of Russians in the post-Soviet period (Mel'vil 1998; Hahn 1991; Maher 1997). Some researchers suggest that Soviet citizens are inclined to accept the authority of a "strong" leader (Vainshtein 1998) who will protect and suppress them at the same time. They assume that con-formism and continuity will reside in the political culture of "antimodern" institutions (Rose 1999) in the years to come. Others have demonstrated the possibilities of change within Russian political culture (Miller, Hesli, and Reisinger 1997; Hughes 1999; Hahn 1991). The available empirical data confirms both hypotheses, which has led to the emergence of the view that Russian political culture is, to quote Ekshtein, "formless" (Alexander 1997, 110), meaning that "in people's mentality and behavior . . . both old and new cultural patterns, perhaps conflicting with each other, coexist" (Batalov 1997, 704). For instance, the "new" value of private property is combined with the "old" ties of krugovaia poruka.

In a way, the new and the old do not have to come into conflict. It has been suggested that a rapid change in the institutional framework has also caused a return to the most rudimentary forms that support continuity (Afanas'ev 2000; Zudin 1999, 60). In rural settings, "the typical adaptive re-action of local communities . . . to post-Soviet modernization was the re-birth of the most archaic social relations" (Markhinin, Nysanbaev, and Shmakov 2001, 54). This view is supported by the findings of Il'ia Shtein-berg (2002) and other authors researching the role of rural communities and informal networks in the post-Soviet transformation (Shteinberg 2002; Shanin and Kovalev 1996; Shanin, Nikulin, and Danilov 2002).

Those subscribing to the neoinstitutionalist approach (see Iasin 2002) rationalize such a rebirth by arguing that the institutional vacuum created by the breakdown of Soviet institutions was to be filled in by alternative strategies aimed at coping with the deficiencies of an institutional framework. These alternative strategies rely on both existing (such as krugovaia poruka) and emergent informal institutions (such as alternative contract enforcement) that compensate for the defects of formal institutions of the newly established market democracy. "The institutional weakness of the Russian state structures . . . is actively compensated for, complemented, or substituted by various informal models, which are representative of shadow forms of power and of administrative and political connections" (Solov'ev 1998, 155–56). Rosalina Ryvkina (1999, 38) observes that an "institutional vacuum" in the economy is coupled with a "moral vacuum" in society, produced by the impoverishment of the population and the marginalization of many social groups, that reveals the basic patterns of Russian mentality and political culture even more. The revival of krugovaia poruka in the post-Soviet context can thus be read as an indicator of both the powerful grip of Russian traditional political culture and the adaptation of forms and contexts of krugovaia poruka to post-Soviet change. The focus on krugovaia poruka highlights the following continuity in Russian political culture:

- The individual is viewed as a part of a bigger system (such as a circle of *svoi liudi* [one's own people] or a network of interests) rather than isolated and working for oneself.

- Individuals are encouraged to seek protection and to repay favors.

- Long-term relationships are kept and nurtured, thus creating mutual dependency rather than operating on the basis of short-term individual gain.

- Governance is by flexible ethical standards rather than by the strict rule of law.

The existence of practices of krugovaia poruka in the post-Soviet period testifies to the continuity of these features, but at the same time there is significant change in the institutions that these informal practices sense and shape. The constituency has changed as well: if it was people at the bottom who were tied by chains of krugovaia poruka in the past, it is now the people at the top who are most subject to it. In other words, krugovaia poruka has morphed into a mode of informal politics accessible for the few.

In contemporary contexts, krugovaia poruka could be thought of as neotraditional collaborative politics at a regional or local level (*v regionakh vse poviazano*) or at a corporate level (*krugovaia poruka silovikov*) aimed at undermining control from the center or at self-protection.[29] Both are exercised through a recruitment strategy by which every boss supports his own people not only because they are his and it is best to work with them, but also because by providing protection to them he creates an indebtedness and a guarantee that they will protect him in return.[30] Alternatively, as a rudimentary form of "mutual surveillance" krugovaia poruka can also operate in the criminal underworld, for a collective responsibility for a murder or to enhance order. As Foucault observes, techniques of surveillance were used in seventeenth-century Europe to control the spread of diseases and prison inmates [by inducing in people a state of conscious and permanent visibility that assures the automatic functioning of power] (Foucault 1977). Like inmates, people facing a system of suspended punishment also have a sense of vulnerability. This would be one way to interpret Oleinik's findings that practices developed in a "small society" in prison mirror and influence the developments of "large society" in Russia (Oleinik 2003).

The most important implications of the present-day forms of krugovaia poruka are for the workings of legal institutions. With krugovaia poruka in practice, no equality in the face of the law can be observed, laws are not enforced universally, and little respect is paid to the law. Krugovaia poruka practices help reproduce obstacles to the establishment of the rule of law and reinforce traditional features of political culture that in turn impede the possibility for a radical change. Awareness of the features of legal and political culture and its anti-individualistic nature could lead to a change in the pattern of krugovaia poruka. However, the individual will not be seen as a sustainable economic and political unit until people start trusting formal institutions and until impersonal systems of trust replace the existing practices based predominantly on interpersonal trust, thus enhancing ties of dependence. This can be achieved only with the elimination of the fundamental divide between us—insiders (*svoi*)—and them—outsiders (*chuzhie*)—and closing the gap in respective ethical standards.[31] But ultimately, the change in legal and political culture can occur only in the context of a change in the nature of political power in Russia—that is, change in its dependence on a system of suspended punishment and the use of informal leverage, which comes into direct contradiction with individualism and liberal values.

Chapter Five

Tenevoi Barter: Shadow Barter, Barter Chains, and Nonmonetary Markets

I am not in the least afraid of foreign capital, since I consider it is in the interests of our country. No country has been developed without foreign capital. What I am afraid of is just the opposite, that our way of doing things has such specific characteristics, so different from the way things are done in civilized countries, that not many foreigners will want to do business with us.

SERGEI WITTE, RUSSIAN PRIME MINISTER AT THE END OF THE NINETEENTH CENTURY

While the previous chapters have explored why the Russian political order might be not as much of a democracy as its leaders have declared, this chapter presents the case of the market along similar lines. As one of the players in the economy in the 1990s put it, "A few people know how the system operates. Those who are successful know but do not tell . . ." [3.16]. In what follows I explore the informal workings of the post-Soviet economy with help from my respondents, all experienced and successful players. I identify the informal practices that compensate for defects in market institutions and enable the functioning of the Russian economy, often contrary to its laws. As Boris Berezovskii put it after his resignation from the Duma in 2000, "Everybody in Russia who did not spend the last decade staying in bed has willingly or unwillingly violated the law."[1] Characteristically, Vladimir Makarov, the deputy head of the Interior Ministry's economic crime department, told Interfax that up to 45 percent of the country's goods and services fall within the shadow economy, and that over forty Moscow banks are currently involved in what he called "serious" shady deals. Duma committee chairman Aleksandr Kulikov told RIA-Novosti that the shadow economy accounts for the fact that the treasury receives only 5 percent of taxes due.[2]

When asked to assess the extent of the informal economy, one of the key players in Russian industry observed that it all depended on how you count:

> In a sense, the shadow economy in Russia is everywhere. In practice, at least some activities of any firm are run through semilegal or extralegal schemes. I am not saying that such and such a company uses such and such schemes; I am saying that activities of such and such a company are impossible unless somebody in it is continuously or at least periodically using such shadow schemes (*tenevye skhemy*). In this sense, 99.9 percent of the Russian economy is of a shadowy nature. [3.20]

Other respondents suggested various axioms of post-Soviet business life along the same lines.

- All firms work without profit (*vse rabotaiut po nuliam*).
- All firms keep double books (*u vsekh dvoinaia bukhgalteriia*).
- One has to share profits through payouts (*nado delit'sia*).
- One has to respect the informal order (*nado uvazhat' poniatiia*).
- One has to make and keep friends (*nado imet' druzei*).
- One should avoid dealing with formal institutions by reaching informal agreements with their representatives.

In tune with the insights of the most successful players, all pointing to the weakness of the institutional and legal framework emerging in the 1990s, the general advice to foreign investors even before the August 1998 crisis went as follows:

> Only invest in Russia, say old hands, if you can afford to—and can't afford not to. Companies building factories and brands in Russia face formidable difficulties. . . . Investment deals negotiated with the federal government are often not recognized by local authorities. . . . Taxes, operating licenses and regulations are all subject to change at a moment's notice.[3]

Needless to say, such difficulties were faced not only by outsider investors but by everybody, and this made resorting to shadow schemes almost a forced practice.

I offer one view here of the workings of the Russian economy through the lens of informal practices that have become predominant in the 1990s. It would be wrong to assume that these shadow schemes disregard the law. On the contrary, the law is a constituent element of the schemes but is used manipulatively. Often schemes are designed to formally comply with the law, but at the same time they violate its spirit. They enable one to conceal one's true identity in a formal contract or to escape formal responsibility in other ways. Avoiding responsibility can be achieved through untraceable spin-off firms: shell firms, scam firms (*pustyshki*), monkey firms (*martyshki*), and firms on the side (*levye firmy*) that are built into barter and capital-flight schemes. Such firms are often registered under the names of "dead souls" (when documents of the deceased or missing people are used) or under the names of people who would not be sentenced harshly (pregnant women or single mothers) if found guilty of financial abuses. Shadow schemes involve a lot of ingenuity based on the ability to manipulate formal constraints by falsifying documents in order to "construct reality," thus documenting "properly" something that never happened. The practices of backdating (*zadnim chislom*), issuing false invoices or empty receipts (*vydat' pustuiu kvitantsiiu*), over- and underreporting amounts received, preparing a backup pack of false documents (*paket podlozhnykh dokumentov*), and creating an indebtedness to oneself that does not really exist (*sozdat' zadolzhennost'*) are so common that the corresponding terms constitute the everyday idioms of post-Soviet business. Some of these practices are similar to those employed in the Soviet planned economy, but in place of overreporting to satisfy plan targets one now finds underreporting of profits for tax purposes.

Informal practices in the corporate sector are common but secretive, pervasive but difficult to pin down. The ethnographic material presented in the following chapters suggests that those involved in informal practices view them as an economic necessity. It is often the case that discourses on economic necessity, referring to everything from ineffective legislation to the pressures of the production cycle, lead to acceptance of these practices. At the same time most of the activities of shadow economy indicate how blurred the ideas of necessity and personal interest have become and how much both of them are tied to, merged with, and mediated by personal contacts. The informal practices combine formal rules with informal codes, thus creating the know-how that enables one to manipulate the system to one's own advantage.

Barter as an Indicator of the Russian Economy

One of the paradoxes of the Russian economy in the 1990s is that with the development of the market, a growing proportion of market transactions are being conducted using various nonmonetary forms of exchange and different substitutes for money.[4] Barter has been referred to as a "survival kit" for Russian industry in the context of omnipresent arrears and a high-risk environment. It is commonly agreed that the reason behind this situation is the liquidity crisis of companies, helped by the fact that arbitrary pricing in barter transactions allows for tax evasion and creates possibilities for the private use of the income of companies not controlled by regulators, owners, or other stakeholders in companies. If the former reason is likely to explain the emergence of barter and an overall consensus that everybody would prefer to work without it, the latter explains why barter scheming might continue to operate despite such a consensus. One respondent whom I interviewed a number of times is the director of one such enterprise. He argued:

> I have to emphasize again that barter chains are not done on the initiative of enterprises. Of course, barter schemes are used for covering up some underhand operations such as manipulation of prices and discounts, hiding profits and so forth. But this is a direct consequence of the overkill of governmental policies, supported by the IMF, in order to stop inflation. [5.41]

Most respondents emphasized the forced nature of practices associated with barter, practices rationalized as survival strategies and cooperation in the face of high risk associated with distrust of state and banking institutions. Just as unofficial networks were used in the Soviet economy to protect enterprises from the exigencies of the *plan,* now one can say that the reliance on schemes in some way protects companies from the exigencies of the *market.* Moreover, in both cases economic agents behave as if they need protection against the state.

In this chapter I consider informal practices associated with barter as indicators of 1990s developments in industry and in medium and small businesses, relying on a combination of publications, press reports, survey data, and fieldwork interviews. I sum up trends in the evolution of barter schemes and discuss the variety of these schemes and their functions on the basis of ethnographic material collected in the peak period of barter in 1997–98.

Tough economic reforms have had a particular impact on enterprises of the military complex because, in its efforts to meet strict budget deficit targets agreed on with the International Monetary Fund (IMF), the government has simply failed to pay hundreds of defense contractors. Those firms in turn have defaulted on their taxes, dues to monopolies in natural resources, and other payments, which has resulted in even lower revenues and nonpayment of wages in the state sector, thus creating a vicious circle known as an "economy of arrears" (*ekonomika neplatezhei*). The economy of arrears consists of (1) budgetary arrears—debts incurred by federal and regional authorities to fund organizations and enterprises; (2) tax arrears—debts incurred by state-owned and private companies to budgetary and nonbudgetary funds; (3) inter-firm arrears—debts incurred by state-owned and private companies to corporate suppliers and banks; and (4) wage arrears—debts incurred by state-owned and private companies, and budget-funded organizations, to employees.[5] These components are interlinked, forming complex chains of indebtedness that are exceptionally difficult to break. For example, tax arrears cause the federal and regional authorities to cut, or withhold, expenditures and incur debts to budget-funded sectors. Enterprises in these branches of the economy then pass the arrears along to their suppliers. These companies in turn fall into debt with their suppliers and pile up tax arrears to the federal and regional budgets, which cause the authorities to cut public spending further, thus producing another cycle of arrears to the budget-funded sectors. It was these conditions to a large extent that caused nonmonetary payments to become so prominent in the 1990s.

According to Russian experts, the first barter boom took place in the first quarter of 1992, when the share of barter in economic transactions within Russia rose from 8 to 58 percent in coke supplies, from 3 to 25 percent in coal, from 8 to 34 percent in metal supplies, and from 12 to 35 percent in supplies of machines and equipment.[6] Woodruff (1998) reports that at the beginning of 1994 around half of all payments to electric power companies were made in kind, and barter seems to have continued to rise from that point; in some regions barter accounted for over 75 percent of payments by the summer of 1994. In 1995, in a few Russian regions the volume of barter transactions accounted for 40 percent of regional budgets.[7] In their study of seventeen big firms in the machine-construction, chemical, electronic, light, and food industries of Moscow, Ekaterinburg, and Ivanovo in 1995–96, Makarov and Kleiner (1996, 5) found that almost 70 to 80 percent of inputs were acquired through barter transactions.[8] Other estimates of the scale of barter in 1995–6 range from 34 to 50 percent of gross industrial output.[9] According to Grigorii Iavlinskii, then a leading

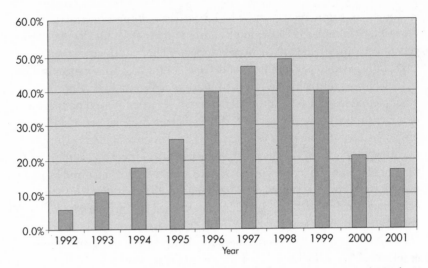

Figure 5.1. Barter shares in industrial sales, 1992–2001 (fourth quarter, in percentages). Numbers from 1992–99: S. Aukutsionek et al., *Survey Statistics/Russian Economic Barometer,* 1999, no. 4; from 2000: *RIA Novosti,* Russia, December 5, 13:02; from 2001: *Segodnia,* January 31, 2001.

pro-Western advocate of the market system, 75 percent of the country's domestically produced goods in 1997 were traded in barter.[10] For 1998, he quoted 85 percent. A study of small and medium-sized firms producing nonconsumables has shown that 75 percent of the sample firms had resorted to barter.[11] My own fieldwork in the Urals area in 1998 indicated a range between 60 and 90 percent use of barter in industry depending on the type of product and the firm's well-being [5.42]. I also discovered a great deal of "shadow" (officially undeclared) barter transactions taking place in the small and medium production sectors, none of which were being reported in the firms' books or accounts. Official figures (see figure 5.1) drawn from the Russian Economic Barometer, the 1998 EBRD Transition Report, and other sources show a steadily increasing incidence of barter across the 1990s and its sharp decrease after the 1998 financial crisis, a period that has been referred to often as a "healthening" of the economy (Aslund 2002; Hanson 2003; Ahrend 2004; EIU 2001).[12]

Is Barter in Russia Different?

Barter is a payment in kind (Dan and Valeksa 1998). In an ideal case, it serves matching demands. The commodities traded are those directly required by both parties—for instance, payment of wages can occur in the form of the enterprise's own output. This kind of transaction requires what has been known as "a double coincidence of wants": each party to the transaction must not only demand what the other supplies but supply what the other demands. In practice, such an occurrence is rare.

Three aspects of barter should be made clear before I turn to the details of barter schemes in the 1990s. First, the time frame for the evolution of barter has to be widened—barter schemes had been used in international trade long before the barter boom of the 1990s, and their impact on the development of barter schemes and intermediary firms in Russia may have been underestimated. Second, what is referred to as "barter" in the post-Soviet context in effect covers a variety of practices associated with complex barter transactions, also including mutual offsets (*zachety*), shift-a-debt deals, the use of promissory notes, and surrogate money. Third, the barter economy cannot exist without institutionalized intermediation. Let us consider these points in turn.

Pre-1990s Origins of Barter Schemes

Given the nature of central planning, there is some reason to expect barter to have played a significant role in the early phase of reform. Under central planning a distinction between barter and monetary transactions did not really exist, since apparently monetary transactions were no more than the accounting counterparts of the flow of goods and services determined by planners. Consequently, once price liberalization and other features of the market economy were introduced, unless they could be expected to work effectively, it would not be surprising to find enterprise managers continuing to work in habitual fashion. Under this view it would not be barter that was a novelty but ordinary market transactions. This argument finds support in the fact that barter schemes worked successfully in international trade before the early 1990s Russian reforms.[13] The share of barter in Russia's export-import transactions in 1992 reached as much as 40 percent (Makarov and Kleiner 1996, 14). Exported Russian goods were deliberately priced lower, while imported goods were priced deliberately higher—the exporter usually "received an additional payment from his foreign partner through a money transfer to his private account in a foreign bank or through an unregistered (cash) payment in Russia" (Tikhomirov 1997, 593). One respondent with firsthand experience of export-import operations from the late 1980s onward explains the advantages of schemes based on the mispricing of goods:

First, there was no need for capital to fund the transaction—no need to borrow from banks. Second, the guarantee was provided by a letter of credit from the end-buyer and was used as collateral to fund the entire transaction. Third, profits could also be made on the contra-goods (consumer goods and foodstuffs) because of the price differential between the world and Russian markets. Finally, under the loose customs control and legal regulation at a time, barter contracts served the purposes of the capital flight. [5.30]

Thus, the following steps had to be undertaken in order to complete a barter transaction (the documents indicated below are prepared as a package, all of them at once) [5.30].

Step 1. A supplier-intermediary contract has to be signed according to which a supplier-seller will provide product P to the intermediary as a buyer.

Step 2. A license for the transaction has to be received by an intermediary. Organizing a license for export requires a signature from the ministry of a given industrial branch and an approval by the Ministry of Foreign Trade.

Step 3. An intermediary—end-buyer contract has to be signed. An intermediary acts as a seller in this transaction and one of the major trading companies in the West as an end-buyer.

Step 4. The end-buyer provides a letter of credit from its bank to the bank associated with the intermediary. This letter is an irrevocable guarantee to pay an agreed sum within thirty days of the end-buyer's taking ownership of the goods in satisfactory condition and upon receipt of adequate documentation (customs papers, quality certificates). No mutual risk is involved.

Step 5. The bank associated with the intermediary issues a letter of credit to the supplier guaranteeing payment for product P in case the intermediary-buyer for some reason does not pay. The bank is happy to guarantee this because it is already a holder of the letter from the end-buyer secured at step 4. The bank would be released from this guarantee upon the closing of the contract, whereas the intermediary does not have to invest its own means in the transaction.

Step 6. A "countergoods" contract between supplier and intermediary should be signed under which the intermediary provides the supplier (now in the role of buyer) with counterdeliveries to balance off the supplies of product P. The supplier-seller would normally send people to select countergoods to import (equipment or consumer goods and foodstuffs in short supply at a time). This is a "payment in kind" contract with no sums of money figuring in. The intermediary bank controls the intermediary's spending of the funds arriving from the end-buyer of product P used either to pay the supplier directly or through the use of countergoods (barter transactions allow flexibility in pricing the exchanged goods and create loopholes for leaving capital outside Russia).[14]

It was these kinds of schemes that were responsible for early millions and further fortunes being made. Needless to say, the use of barter schemes in international trade was restricted to a few "authorized" agents. In support of an opinion that such barter operations took place in the context of the legal vacuum of the late 1980s, one can see in appendix 4 that the first piece of legislation on barter, found in a legal electronic database in Russia, was indeed adopted in 1990 and is concerned with the export-import operations. The consequent decrees applicable to domestic barter schemes are dated from 1992 onward.

Changes in conditions and new legislation presented in appendix 4 are the most important factors in the development of barter schemes over time. Domestically, the proportion of offsets has increased over time relative to voluntary barter, as could be expected from the growth in indebtedness of firms. As I will show later, barter schemes have grown in length and complexity, especially with the use of surrogate financial instruments.

The Inclusive Concept of Barter

What is referred to as barter in the post-Soviet context covers a variety of practices associated with the give-and-take of barter transactions, mutual offsets (*zachety*), shift-a-debt deals, and the use of surrogate money [3.23].[15] Barter transactions have normally been documented by an "additional agreement"—*dopsoglashenie*—allowing payment in goods to substitute for payments in money outlined in the main contract. Quite often, though, a barter transaction is used to clear a prior debt—a financial obligation incurred on a previous supply of goods or services that is later settled in material goods. In these circumstances the transactions are called offsets (*vzaimozachety*) (Bryzgalin et al. 1998). They are clearly a distinct phenomenon since they may imply a degree of coercion, or at least an acceptance by the debt holder that the debt value is less than it was once hoped to be. Therefore, many transactions between firms in post-Soviet Russia are highly complex deals that involve both matching demands and the use of commodity currencies, as well as combinations of offsets and intentional barter, as part of a scheme with many different links. Apart from debts, they also involve a number of other surrogate financial instruments such as promissory notes (*prostoi veksel'*), bills of exchange (*perevodnoi veksel'*), and interest-bearing notes.[16] These differ from the complex financial instruments in market economies not so much in their intrinsic character as in the fact that there are no organized markets for them; instead, they are typically exchanged in a bilateral, ad hoc, and often fraudulent fashion (Gudkov 1998, 5). The standard use of bills of exchange is illustrated in the following examples.

> Lukoil pays me for oil and gas equipment with a two-year *veksel'*. They know I won't be able to keep it for two years. The devaluation (discount) would be enormous, 80 percent or so. So they give me an informal promise that if I take it to their oil-processing firm in Perm', I will receive oil products at today's market price for the nominal sum of the *veksel'*. So I choose barter, take oil products, and trade them further. Still better than cashing that bill of exchange at a bank. [5.42]

On other occasions, barter might not be an option if you have to make some urgent cash payments because of the time factor. Intermediary firms, which have cash, benefit from this.

> Now that gas offsets have been made illegal, we use promissory notes. But the logic is the same. Every promissory note brings profit to those with cash and power. For example, we receive an oil *veksel'* in payment for our supplies but have to pay wages urgently, so we are forced to sell it at a 20 percent discount to an intermediary. They trade this promissory note for oil and sell it at current prices—it takes just a couple of weeks with oil—easy profit on our troubles! Intermediaries benefit from the situation and a lot of people have vested interests in sustaining this. [5.43]

The status of intermediaries is often backed up by other parties. Although it would not perhaps be any firm's choice to include intermediary structures in a transaction, the request to do so, the pressure to trade with a certain intermediary, and the guarantee of trustworthiness of this intermediary may occur on an informal basis (say, a word from the director of a large enterprise).

> Sometimes the bills of exchange they pay with are issued not by Lukoil but by some association or organization. If the latter goes

bankrupt, Lukoil won't have any responsibility for their promissory notes. These promissory notes are coupled with personal agreement that Lukoil will buy them back in a year, or that in a Perm' Lukoil oil-processing firm the note will be accepted as a Lukoil one. Smaller and dependent firms are forced to agree to these conditions in the face of such monopolistic pressure, whereas certain intermediary firms benefit from it. [5.41]

The intermediary functions are not always fulfilled by firms specializing in intermediation. Any firm will engage in this practice when it can in order to get access to cash. The prevalence of institutionalized mediation, however, adds an interesting and essential dimension to the analysis of barter.

Institutionalized Mediation

According to some assessments, only 5–10 percent of all barter transactions take place between industrial companies directly. All the remaining barter deals involve barter specialist firms that (1) facilitate transactions by matching the needs of various industrial companies; (2) supply industrial companies with some cash to cover their cash needs, however small; and (3) use the difference in products' exchange ratios and relative values in cash equivalents to their own benefit.[17] Energy distribution, one of the most lucrative sectors since the collapse of the Soviet Union, was done almost entirely by barter transactions. Russia's electricity monopoly (RAO UES) collected only 6 percent of its Russian revenue in cash, according to UES chairman Boris Brevnov. He said about three hundred intermediaries went between the company and its biggest customers.[18] On the receiving end, the respondents reported high risk when dealing with intermediaries:

> We try to work without intermediary firms. Once we've established our own connections, we use intermediary firms less. I work as a go-between myself—it's much better because dealing with intermediary firms is high risk. Once, we needed an offset for 300,000 rubles for electricity. We had already signed the papers and everything, had already shipped one-third of the oil (for 100,000) to the intermediary, but the offset didn't go through. . . . We received a letter from the electricity people that we still owed them; meanwhile the intermediary firm sold our oil and still didn't pay us back. . . . Typical fraud. They play tricks with false promissory notes. Or worse, they wait until we've shipped the product over to them and then "disappear."

> You know, they open a firm, sign a contract, make a quick profit and
> close. Half of the firms in Moscow are like that. They close in order to
> avoid taxes and reopen again under a new name. [5.43]

According to the *Moscow Times,* 4,658 companies were registered at a
single Moscow address in May 1997, making it practically impossible to
find tax offenders.[19] Finance Minister Aleksei Kudrin estimated in August
2000 that two-thirds of Moscow's enterprises do not report to the tax office
at all (Iakovlev 2000b, 140). Under these circumstances it is not easy for
local inspectorates to oversee all corporate actors. The possibilities for intermediary and shell firms increase (Humphrey 2000a). The scale of financial fraud and economic crime with promissory notes is so overwhelming
that the semilegal barter schemes serving the needs of production and intermediary firms exploiting the situation become less of a concern for authorities.[20] Financial fraud seems to be a feature that is, from top to bottom, characteristic of a high-risk environment. Consider the following
mutual dissatisfaction between firms on the ground and at the center.
Those on the ground say that they are forced to work with intermediaries
because of the extreme centralization of companies, which makes direct
links with actual partners impossible.

> We have a complex situation with Gazprom gas fields. They—the
> producers of gas on the ground—do not have a say over which equip-
> ment they buy. Everything is decided in Moscow and often in the in-
> terests of Moscow officials rather than actual production. The offi-
> cials in Moscow chose to import equipment, which is 70 percent
> more expensive, but they get to go abroad and receive their broker
> fees. So we cannot go directly to the producers as they don't decide
> anything themselves. [5.43]

On the other hand, as another respondent has pointed out, the Moscow
headquarters had to centralize and to block the direct contracts with suppliers because there was too much fraud on the ground [5.41].

At every level, these schemes seem to be uniformly tied up with intermediary firms that are either direct spin-offs or associated with the interests of
certain circles. Moreover, not only are they beneficial for a certain group,
but they cater to the needs of the economy and are implicitly endorsed by
state. Some argue that intermediation could assume such an institutionalized role only as a result of the tax relief policies (*nalogovoe osvobozhdenie*)
introduced by the government. Most "authorized" intermediaries have ini-

tially dealt with "tax relief" surrogates, according to which the government offsets taxes to be paid by the firms to the federal budget against the budgetary payments owed to the firms. This kind of currency emerged out of necessity to make up for the defects of the institutional framework and resulted in complicated schemes invented by those who tried to make things work.[21] Later on, the government clamped down on intermediary firms and banned nonmonetary offsets between firms and the federal budget. However, other schemes have come into being. As one industrialist explained:

> Despite the fact that officially the government has made the offsets with the federal budget illegal from 1997, Livshits initiated a scheme of monetary offsets in order to work with particular sections of the budget.[22] For example, according to the budget, the Ministry of Finance owes the Ministry of Defense, and the Ministry of Defense owes us for the supplies. The idea was that the Ministry of Finance allocates funds (in rubles) on paper. The Ministry of Finance pays us the same way, whereas we pay exactly the same sum as tax to the budget. In reality, money does not change hands. After Livshits, the same scheme was used by Chubais, only he also included a bank in the scheme (there were ten authorized banks that could conduct such operations), so that it is not an offset but a set of monetary transactions via a bank [laughs]. So the banks benefit too as they charge enterprises for the conduct of such an operation, sometimes even some extra for a speedy transfer. [5.42][23]

The deal for the government was to go through the market reforms at any expense, even if it meant turning a blind eye to the awards that schemes might provide for their practitioners. Here I consider the multiple functions that barter had in the 1990s.

Barter Schemes and Their Functions

First and foremost, barter became notorious for its association with the nonpayment of wages and salaries. Although many employees agreed to accept payment in kind in lieu of wages, their "choice" was determined by the fact that monetary payment was not an option. Indeed, employees often found themselves having to act as an unpaid sales force for their employers since their own ability to consume the firm's output directly was limited. To make payment in kind more desirable for their employees, a firm often engaged in barter transactions with other producers or demanded payment for its products in the form of food or consumer goods that could be used directly to pay its workforce. In this case, payment in kind was accepted as a medium of exchange. The use of barter for payment of wages in industry was widely reported. Makarov and Kleiner (1997, 26) compiled a list of items used as payment to workers of big industrial firms in 1996 from the press: foodstuffs (sausages, cucumbers, sugar, flour, meal tokens); *dacha* equipment (shovels, buckets, spades, chainsaws); household items (refrigerators, TV sets, bicycles, gas-guns); items of personal consumption (underwear); and so on.

> Our people are so inventive, they immediately start finding ways around everything [*krutit'sia*]. They go to trade their goods at the local markets on weekends. On weekdays, they make deals with intermediaries who walk around organizations offering goods. We work at a "closed-regime" enterprise, so we only see the traders at the lobby. But they are everywhere you go, at the tax inspection offices and commercial structures, everywhere one can enter even if you have to sign in and leave your passport at the entrance and where people have cash. These intermediaries trade what they've got, ask what people need, and take orders. They have their own routes and customers. When I worked in a bank, we had everything you can imagine delivered to the workplace, from socks to videos. [5.46]

Apart from payment for labor, industrial barter served all the needs of production: inputs and other supplies; energy; federal, regional, and local taxes; and social payments. Barter was instrumental, whether intentional or forced, as an alternative currency where money was in short supply. When asked about the liquidity of barter currencies, respondents tended to agree on the following hierarchy.

> In the order of liquidity, it's money, promissory notes, oil, and gas. Oil gives us profits because prices are high. Barter is unprofitable if the sale of the product takes more than a month. Oil and gas take about a week. The foodstuffs consumed by both the enterprises [to pay wages] and the population are also liquid. Because the population mostly now only spends on food, foodstuffs can be sold relatively quickly at a regular price, both in urban and rural areas. What is not profitable in terms of barter are goods that we cannot sell for three to four months, everything from furniture to clothes. [5.42]

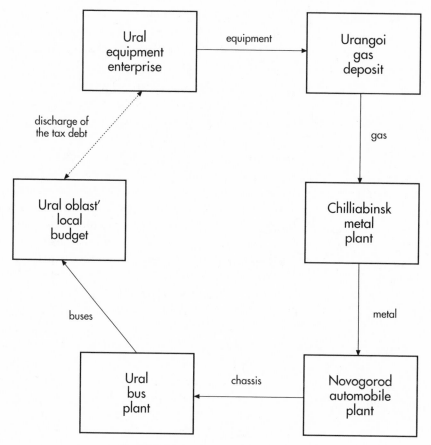

Figure 5.2. Scheme for payment of local taxes.

Another powerful association with barter is taxes. Taxes paid or avoided by means of barter schemes were at the center of debates in the 1990s about the policies of tax collection. The complexity of barter schemes does indeed allow for flexible accounting.

As barter schemes involve interrelated (though nonsimultaneous) transactions between multiple trading partners, any given transaction could not be understood without knowing the scheme of which it forms a part. Let us start with one example of how barter schemes help to pay taxes, illustrated in figure 5.2.

The deputy director of a Ural enterprise producing industrial equipment reports that his firm owes taxes to the local budget. Oil and gas equipment is supplied to Urangoi, one of the Gazprom deposits, which pays gas to the Chilliabinsk metal plant. The Chilliabinsk metal plant supplies metal to the Novogorod automobile plant, which supplies chassis for buses to the Ural bus plant. The latter now has a debt to the former, but instead they agree that the output of the Ural bus plant—buses—is accepted by the city budget in payment of local tax from Ural oil and gas equipment enterprise. [5.42]

As for tax evasion, there are two reasons why barter schemes were assumed to make tax evasion easier. First, it used to be possible to cite lower prices than the cash price for both sides of the transaction in order to reduce liability to value-added tax (VAT) and profits tax. Before 1997, the use of lower prices in barter transactions inside Russia was an underregulated area (see appendix 4). Although transaction prices were meant to be calculated according to "market prices" published in *Ekonomicheskaia Gazeta*, in practice not all commodities could be included in the list, and there was flexibility in pricing commodities with somewhat different characteristics in contracts between parties. Second, a barter transaction itself may be easier to hide because it does not pass through an account (if not hidden, every link in a barter scheme is taxable separately, which increases the tax). This has become particularly important in Russia since a decree of August 1996 that imposed draconian restrictions on legal persons in arrears to the budget or nonbudgetary funds. When it appeared, *Kommersant Daily* commented that it would treat any tax debtor as virtually bankrupt and would deprive managers of control over or interest in the profitability of their enterprises.[24] The decree also contradicted several articles of the civil code. Under the decree, any enterprise or organization that falls behind in its payment either to the budget or to nonbudgetary funds is required to open a special "tax debtor's account" (*schet nedoimshchika*) or designate an existing current account for this purpose. All funds from the organization's other accounts must be channeled to the *schet nedoimshchika* (and this is what every organization would try to avoid!), as must all income (no cash may be withheld even for minor expenses), with the exception of funds for wages, payment to the budget and nonbudgetary funds, and the financing of budgetary programs. This includes all funds from accounts opened by all representative offices and other branches of the company that are not "independent subjects" of tax legislation.[25] *Schet nedoimshchika* was intended to make it more difficult to evade taxes and to facilitate enforcement of regulations that would allow the tax authorities considerable scope for dictating the order of payments made by a tax debtor; in reality, however, every enterprise engages in practices that circumvent such accounts—organizing financial flows so that no money is ever deposited in the main company's account:

> We work with *veksel'* very actively, because it provides a legal way of acquiring cash. Because if any money comes to my account while I am an enterprise in arrears, it's all automatically taken to the budget. Whereas if I am paid by a *veksel'*, I can use it as collateral and get a loan from the bank, which I can spend for paying wages, for inputs, etc. I could redeem the loan with this *veksel'*. Today we ask all our partners to pay us by *veksel'*. So *veksel'* is really liquid. A Sberbank *veksel'* is 98 to 100 percent liquid. We also ask them to pay us by a *veksel'* of the bank where we receive loans. So instead of paying us directly they go to our bank and buy a *veksel'*. [5.42]

Given that in 1998 the State Tax Service estimated that 80 percent of Russian firms had tax arrears, nearly all enterprises regularly confront the problem of frozen accounts, whether their own or those of their key trading partners (Hendley, Ickes, and Ryterman 1998, 104). But instead of folding, tax debtors remain in business. The availability of *schet nedoimshchika* also implies that no loan can be given to this firm by a bank, even if a loan is meant to discharge the inherited stock of debt. As reported by another respondent:

> As far as the *schet nedoimshchika* is concerned, these accounts do not increase the collection of tax revenue, so the government keeps pressuring Viakhirev at Gazprom and the like. We feel that pressure indirectly.[26] Whenever money appears on any of our accounts it automatically goes to the *schet nedoimshchika*. We cannot take a loan to pay off our taxes because of this. Meanwhile we have to live somehow. So we find another mechanism. Legal or semilegal, but at least the tax authorities can't charge us with anything. So we distribute our income ourselves: something for taxes to be paid directly (not to lose days by transacting this through *schet nedoimshchika*), something for the pension fund, something for wages to be paid. [5.41]

Another respondent summed up such a self-regulating system in the following manner:

> In these conditions, it's pointless to pay too much attention to which rate of tax should be paid on profits because the whole country lives

by different laws. The country does not pay taxes on profit. Rather, the country distributes the profit. People decide themselves how much they will pay and on which grounds. Lots of opportunities are provided by "imaginative" accounting. So we first decide how much we want to pay and then adjust the books accordingly. One can argue for ages about tax rates on profit—24, 23, or 22 percent—but this does not really determine our life. [6.28]

These respondents refer to the possibility of circumventing the *schet nedoimshchika* procedures by registering a spin-off firm whose account would be used instead of the tax debtor's. This firm would normally be established by senior managers of the enterprise (supplementary employment is not against the law, so managers as individual persons can establish an independent firm for this purpose). The spin-off firm seeks to sell the product of the enterprise, at the same prices and to the same partners, and charges commission for services accordingly. To the partners the firm tries to prove that it is not separate from the main enterprise; to the tax authorities the firm presents legal documents indicating it has independent status from the main enterprise. All costs are thus carried out by the enterprise, whereas the spin-off firm signs contracts and conducts payments (monetary ones, of course) through its own account. Although such spin-offs may be technically legal, as everything is done in accordance with existing laws, it contradicts the spirit of the law and presents an obstacle to creating an environment based on the rule of law.

Where payments could be made through the use of barter schemes, thus avoiding the tax debtor's account, the use of spin-off firms is unnecessary. Figure 5.3 provides an example of this situation.

A Ural equipment enterprise supplies its product to a Chernigorneft' oil reservoir. Instead of paying for it directly, the latter makes a shift-a-debt deal, by which another oil company, say, Sidenko, becomes a payee. Sidenko does not pay the Ural enterprise either; it supplies oil products to a refinery company, which, following the chain, supplies diesel fuel to an automobile plant in Novogorod. The Novogorod plant pays with cars, which are accepted by Uralenergo and the local telephone station as payment for the Ural enterprise's debt. [5.46]

The barter schemes often require trust and "personalization" (*doveritel'nost'*) of their links, normally in response to the operational risks of such complex transactions [3.23]. For example, when offsets of federal taxes were still al-

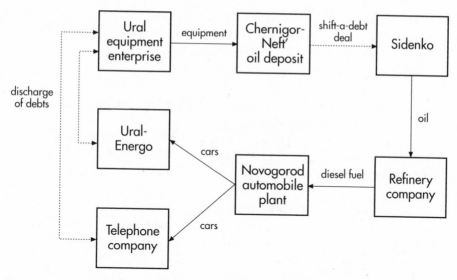

Figure 5.3. Scheme for payment of telephone and electricity arrears.

lowed (until 1997), very often they would not be agreed upon unless the dependent enterprise used a specific intermediary firm. The monopolistic position of enterprises with more liquid products gave them an advantage in pressuring the rest of the firms. To make them agree to offset or buy its product for money rather than by barter, the company had to have good contacts in high places. The unwillingness to offset is reflected in the following statement by a director of an enterprise:

> The Ministry of Finance has to pay for the military orders fulfilled by a metallurgical plant but doesn't pay. As a result, this metallurgical plant can't pay its debt to Gazprom. We owe that metallurgical plant for our inputs and would be happy to conduct a mutual offset for them, as Urangoi Gazprom, one of the Gazprom branches, owes us 2 million. It's been more than a year already, but Gazprom just won't accept the metallurgical debt through us as a mutual offset. Iamburg Gazprom owes us more than 3 million, also for more than a year. ZapSib Gazprom owes us 1 million. This would make 6 million. But being monopolists as they are, they simply don't take their indebtedness to us into account and instead try to squeeze cash out of producers like that metallurgical plant under threat of its closure. [5.41]

Whereas the lack of contacts means that the most obvious offsets would not be conducted, the presence of contacts means that even the monetary funds could be made available. When asked about the sources of monetary funds at the enterprise, the same respondent admits:

> There are very few sources. A number of oil and gas enterprises regularly pay us with money. They not only pay: one company even used to finance our innovation program, helped to reorient our products, and gave us an experimental field. We have certain ties there; they know us well and we have made an arrangement that is working well. [5.41]

Firms normally rely on personal contacts in schemes where access to cash is targeted. On a local level, small businesses may get involved as intermediaries. Let me illustrate the way in which municipal services payments can be used as a source of cash for small businesses (see figure 5.4).

This barter chain includes Techcom, its shell firm, water and heat companies, local housing departments, and households. The local housing departments, in charge of housing, owe the water and heat companies for their services. Techcom finds fifteen, twenty, or thirty households in arrears on their housing charges. Both the water and heat companies require Techcom's product. The contract includes the delivery of Techcom's product in exchange for discharge of the indebtedness for certain apartments (people engaged in the scheme list with their address, the housing department, and sum of indebtedness). The total sum of this contract can reach the significant sum of 30,000–40,000 rubles.

Through this scheme Techcom pays the housing dues for all its employees and their acquaintances and thus gets hold of some cash. There is also a young employee in Techcom who is in charge of finding people in arrears for housing payments. People are interested in this because Techcom offsets the indebtedness for three months, while in cash it charges only for two. According to the barter contract with the water company, Techcom's product barter price is 348 rubles, while its cash price is 250 rubles. The difference means that people get one month free. This is one of the high-trust patterns that help schemes to work—the point emphasized by the businessman himself.

> We trust these people because we have known them for a long time. Almost all of them are our acquaintances, so they trust us. We can even wait on providing a three-month credit, as it were. As we work permanently on this, some cash always comes back. Some people pay

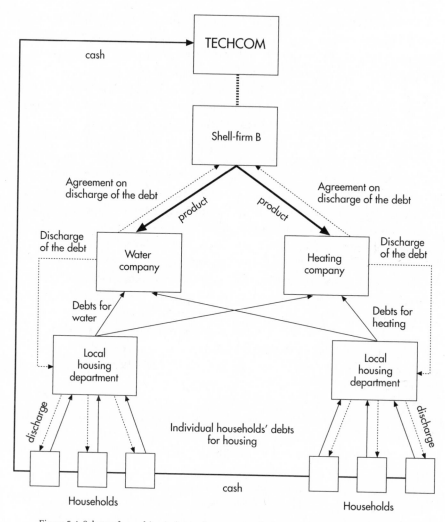

Figure 5.4. Scheme for cashing in barter by payments for housing services. For more details, see Ledeneva 2000d.

straightaway, some people ask to wait. As we give a whole month's equivalent as discount, people appreciate it and pay. We give each person a copy of the mutual offset contract, in which their debt is paid by our shell firm. For tax inspection these deals are of no interest; they won't even check on less than 100,000 rubles. In principle, such mutual offsets are allowed. It's useful for people, especially in cases of long-term indebtedness. As we offer conditions of one-third off, people can pay for nine months, rather than for the whole year. [5.47]

In certain circumstances big firms are also forced to become intermediaries. In ordinary bilateral transactions it can usually be presumed that the terms of the transaction depend only on the preferences of the two parties involved. In a complex transaction a particular exchange in the scheme may be undertaken because of the requirements of some third party. This fact may be important for understanding both why transactions are structured in this way and who benefits from them.[27] Consider the following account of the head of a firm on how barter schemes come into being.

> For producing oil and gas equipment I need metal forms from KMZ, which has a monopoly. The director of that plant can dictate his terms. He gives me a list of their priorities: say, payments for energy, for timber, for metal, or supplies of aluminum—perhaps twenty of his problems. I decide which ones I can solve, choose three or four areas, and start building schemes around them. It is understood between us, permanent partners, that we cannot change direction every time. They know the problems I solve: I can pay their electric energy expenses, I can pay for their gas or supply gas for their heating and technological needs, I can arrange aluminum supplies—these are my four areas. On top of this I pay their transport expenses, since it so happens that the railway owes me as a result of another barter chain. [5.41]

Thus, it is the director who is engaged in initial negotiations about the basic links, and it is an agreement between directors that guarantees the stability and enforcement of transactions. On the one hand, such personalization of barter schemes implies strong reliance on trust between partners, as most agreements are done on a handshake. On the other hand, all directors feel the pressures of the system, and they bear joint responsibility for regional development and the social sphere that could be conducive to the ties of krugovaia poruka. These aspects should be viewed as important implications of barter schemes for the economy.

Implications of Barter Schemes: What Do They Tell Us about the Economy?

There are a number of distinct, though not necessarily mutually exclusive, hypotheses about the causes of barter (see Ledeneva and Seabright 2000). In the 1990s, barter was associated with a flight from money due to hyperinflation; a response to the high cost of working capital; a lack of trust in the banking system; a response to interenterprise debt arrears; a means of evading taxes; a means for firms to collude in overvaluing their output to soften budget constraints (the virtual economy hypothesis); a means of increasing the enforceability of private contracts in the absence of a credible system of civil law; and a more general symptom of a breakdown of trust in those economic institutions that depend on collective confidence about the functioning of the market economy. The implications of these various hypotheses for the effects of barter on the economy are discussed in the economics literature (Seabright 2000).

What do we learn about the economy if we consider barter schemes from the perspective of informal practices? Two sentiments emerged most strongly in my interviews across the spectrum of respondents: blaming the state for its conniving role in the rise of scheming in the 1990s, and emphasizing the self-defense aspects of this scheming. Following up on the arguments found in ethnographic data, I suggest that the use of nonmonetary schemes both helped the post-Soviet economy and recompensed those economic agents who chose to bear its crises on their shoulders, provided that they did not further their interests too far (as in the cases of financial fraud with promissory notes or setting up nonexisting firms, as discussed earlier). I also suggest that "barter schemes were not pure exchanges in kind" and that "they did not operate purely according to economic logic—they hid financial flows sometimes diverted to serve private interests" [3.16], but they constituted a phenomenon different from cases of financial fraud. Barter compensated for defects in the formal economy, and was regulated by the state. In a certain sense barter schemes implied some connivance by the state, which made the state to a large extent responsible for the excessive scale of the shadow economy in the 1990s.

In earlier work, I analyzed the shadow aspects of barter practices in small businesses (Ledeneva 2000d). A microperspective into the informal workings of a small provincial firm, trading almost entirely in barter, included a graphic description of barter networks, discussed possibilities of shadow production and all the multiple functions that barter schemes can play from paying of the telephone bills to the tax evasion. Most important, the analysis illustrated the range of shadow practices deployed in barter operations, such as the use of double books and fake documents for defrauding tax authorities, "laundering" cash in barter transactions, dealing with criminalized businesses, and giving and receiving bribes, gifts, and favors. These practices were presented as logical by the participants and were justified along the lines of "Look what the government does!" By contrast, they looked absurd in purely economic terms and criminal in purely legal terms. Such microanalysis adds a further dimension to the results of large-scale surveys of tax-paying firms, as it addresses deals and activities off the record—those routine practices that define the background of the Russian economy and block organized attempts to transform it.

I do not repeat that analysis here but would like to emphasize again how those exercising shadow practices often view them as a compulsory activity to which the term "economic necessity" applies. At the same time, most of the shadow economy's activities qualify as economic fraud. The discourse on economic necessity, referring to everything from ineffective legislation to the inevitable pressures of the production cycle, leads to an overall acceptance of shadow practices, while the self-interested nature of such economic necessity—an important factor supporting the existence of barter—remains unnoticed. I illustrate in detail how blurred the discourse on necessity and the logic of personal interest have become and how much barter schemes rely on personal contacts.

The personalization of transactions can be seen as a substantial, although indirect, transaction cost that has important implications for the economy in general. It goes without saying that where parallel currencies are involved, substantial investment resources may be diverted into stocking, protecting, transporting, and using products that are bartered. But there may also be a large diversion of management time, effort, and ingenuity into solving situations in which there is no double coincidence of wants. Barter is a terrible headache for directors.

> If every partner paid us in rubles, it would take me half an hour a week to discuss incoming payments. As it stands, I have one hour meeting everyday, have to go on business trips all the time, to negotiate, and to put some pressure where necessary. Barter is an endless process of problems that I have to be personally involved in. [5.41]

There are also costs of sustaining personal contacts in an increasingly "divide and rule" kind of environment. The so-called red directors used to be a powerful lobby group. But as the leader of one regional union of entrepreneurs acknowledged in 1998, this is no longer the case: "All we care about is to keep our own businesses afloat." Nevertheless, good personal contacts are vital for making the offsets agreed upon between the parties, for designing schemes, and for making these schemes work. Negotiation skills may help to acquire weak links for the schemes—partners engaged on a rather short-term basis—but it is personal contacts that provide strong links in these schemes, those characterized by absolute trust or long-term technological partnership.

> Long-term partnership is not about help or solidarity. These have long gone. We have a tough relationship with our suppliers but if we satisfy their conditions, they won't let us down. My deputies and staff solve a lot of problems but there are situations where they would not "pass," where everything has to be agreed on the top level. So then I will have to go and act as an icebreaker or a tank in order to solve problems which seem dead-end. That's why they value me. [5.41]

Anyone who doubts whether Russian entrepreneurs have adequate talent to make the transition to capitalism cannot but marvel at the ingenuity and re-sourcefulness deployed in putting together barter deals. Inevitably, operating in a high-risk environment also means that such entrepreneurship is used up in circumventing difficulties and scheming to go around formal rules and procedures rather than focusing on improvement and innovation.

Thus, practices associated with barter schemes are supportive of the market and advance business but are also subversive as they rely on the anti-market-type alliances. It is another important consequence of person-alization that there is the possibility of a lock-in effect, in the sense that partners for such schemes are chosen on the basis of reliability and preex-isting relationships with managers, rather than according to any financial logic.[28] Barter schemes can thus be divisive in their implications—they help the insiders and exclude the outsiders; they protect the firm against the ex-ternal pressures but impose their own internal ones. In a way, there are similarities between the barter schemes locked into certain personal or technological alliances and the practices of krugovaia poruka described in chapter 4. Just as the collective tax responsibility of the peasant commune attached to their land brought into being the practices of krugovaia poruka, the external tax pressures on the industrial community brought into being a complex web of mutual debt obligations, with richer partners establishing their "monopolistic" dues. However distant a modern industrial firm may seem from a peasant family, the pressure of taxes, dependence on neigh-bors in their technological network for obligatory payments and inputs, and an inability to "disappear" as many small or shadow businesses do make krugovaia poruka a poignant metaphor for the predicament of many enterprises in the 1990s.

The so-called lock-in effect, where one is limited by the interests of one's network, means that the decisions of individual firms will influence not only their own financial performance and survival prospects but also those of other firms in the scheme. This insures individual firms to some extent against the economic storms in their environment but also stifles their incentive to innovate and improve. As the then prime minister, Sergei Kirienko, put it in an interview on the TV program *Itogi* on March 29, 1998, "A mechanism of krugovaia poruka has been formed, aimed exclusively at avoiding responsibility." He implied that bankruptcies were not taking place where they should and vice versa. But in view of my respondents, krugovaia poruka does not always help. One of the managers explained:

> If there are no officially processed bankruptcies, it does not mean that we do not have bankrupt enterprises. There are thousands of them. They are the ones that nobody works with or works with on very unfavorable terms. There is a certain degree of trust involved in a chain, as every party comes in with a known interest and a known product. If they say that they will pay with oil products, I trust they have them. But parties do not provide guarantees for one another. Rather, everybody pushes everybody else to a collective bankruptcy by increasing direct transaction costs and indirect, hidden ones (the longer the chain, the more costs it involves and the more harmful it is). [5.41]

Despite the overall inconvenience and inefficiency of barter, these schemes have continued to be used even after the dramatic change brought about by the financial crisis of August 1998. The fact that there are substantial transaction costs attached to barter schemes does not in any sense imply that firms are foolish to undertake them. In fact, all the explanations I have heard from my respondents imply that barter is a privately rational response to a distorted economic environment. The problem is the absence of attractive alternatives such as a well-functioning macroeconomy or banking system. If one believes that informal practices are the best indicators of defects in formal rules and procedures, one should conclude that the intricate schemes on the ground simply counteract the pressure from the state, often representative of and coupled with high-powered private interests (the theme discussed by Wedel 1998; Freeland 2000; Klebnikov 2000). The inconsistency between the state's interests and those of its economic agents, along with the state's inability to create conditions in which small and medium-sized businesses can exercise initiative and creativity to benefit the economy, points to the engagement of the state with big business. In other words, the state cannot be expected to act as a guarantor of declared rules and procedures. State institutions are used selectively and manipulatively to keep businesses off balance, whereas businessmen protect themselves from the exploitative system by layers and layers of clever scheming. Although this statement might be universally applied, it is essential to distinguish among small, medium-sized, and big businesses in our analysis. So far I have been addressing schemes undertaken by small and medium-sized businesses. In the next chapter I touch upon big business and focus on the generically double-edged nature of financial scheming, outlining both its supportive and subversive aspects.

Chapter Six

Dvoinaia Bukhgalteriia: Double Accountancy and Financial Scheming

To paraphrase an old saying, "excessive taxation in Russia is compensated by its partial payment."
KAKHA BENDUKIDZE, *KOMMERSANT*, DECEMBER 16, 1998

If a company has a profit, it has a bad accountant.
POST-SOVIET SAYING

Few claim to understand fully either the origins of the August 1998 financial crisis in Russia or the postcrisis recovery. Post-1998 analyses suggest that reforms did not work as expected because the institutional environment required of a market democracy was not in place. This in turn was explained by sociohistorical and cultural factors responsible for the lack of civil society, civic responsibility, and business ethics. As the *Economist* put it in 1999, a healthy banking system requires

> honest administrators backed by determined politicians, a legal system in which loans make sense and a financial climate in which people want to lend. All the above are missing in Russia. This is why a whole year since August 1998, not a single significant bank pushed into insolvency has been properly wound up. The World Bank estimated that at the top 18 banks alone, liabilities exceed assets by $9.8 billion. Of the few banks that have lost their licenses in 1999, most were those trying to deal honestly with their creditors. . . . Strangest of all, there has been no official censure of the widespread asset stripping and book-fiddling which followed the August crisis.

According to a leaked report from the World Bank, the bad habits in Russian banking are deep-rooted. Apparently, most of the losses incurred by the banks were not on short-term government debt, on which Russia has defaulted to the tune of $40 billion, but on wild loans (presumably to cronies) which were never repaid. The report notes that "the largest banks actually seem to have led the way in developing techniques for concealing basic imprudent conduct."[1]

The lack of transparency, insufficient accountability, and consequent spread of corruption have often been identified as important self-reinforcing sources of Russia's woes. As a result, the economy continues to be looked upon as governed by nontransparent rules and unattractive to foreign investment.

Although one has to agree that fraudulent and largely corrupt practices are the main obstacles to economic development, it would be wrong to blame the practitioners or to create anticorruption policies without an in-depth understanding of the genesis of these practices, their functions in the economy, and the best ways of addressing them. Many reforms to date were designed to remedy capital flight, tax evasion, and abuses of corporate governance, but they failed at the stage of implementation. Why? Rather than looking only at what does not work and why, we should concentrate on what firms actually do to run their businesses. I argue that there is a set of extralegal—or "practical," as anthropologists call them (Blundo and Sardan 2001; Bourdieu 1990)—norms and practices in Russia that serve to compensate for the shortcomings of state and market institutions, thus undermining the course of their intended development. Instead of simply stigmatizing these grassroots practices as corrupt, I concentrate on understanding them from the participant's perspective and provide an ethnographic description of what firms do under specific circumstances based on their own "common sense." Respondents to a survey regularly referred to such practices as matters of necessity, so I start with a note about the nature of this blanket self-justification and offer some historical background on such patterns. I then illustrate how these patterns reproduce themselves in the post-Soviet context with emphasis on the ambiguity of roles that informal practices play in the functioning of the most widespread financial schemes. I rely on the opinions of my respondents in offering some conclusions on whether these substitutive financial schemes have present and future costs for the economy or whether they represent a uniform substitute for the workings of market institutions.

Practices "Out of Necessity"

Given the nature and scale of the informal economy in Russia, there is no shortage of examples to illustrate how the weaknesses in the banking system are compensated for and/or manipulated at the grassroots level. While these everyday practices (such as the use of "black cash" and various forms of financial fraud) can be perceived as corrupt by outsiders, they are regarded as a matter of necessity by insiders. The explanation, "I had to do it in order to survive/to stay in business/to be successful" was most frequently cited by survey respondents.

Rather than rigid inevitability, however, the notion of necessity in this context implies various strategies of coping with situations involving risk. Historically, practices considered necessary are associated with the need to protect resources from robbery or from excessive levels of taxation.[2] It is both intriguing and reassuring that the basic patterns of self-protection repeat themselves across time and space while taking different names. They are shaped by similar risks and comparable economic and legal situations, even if in different historical circumstances. For example, during the T'ang dynasty in China, the growing tea trade between regions and the imperial capital underscored the necessity for a safe money transfer. In response to the need, a medium of transfer poetically named "flying money," or *fei-ch'ien,* evolved. According to Larry Lampert, provincial governors maintained "memorial-offering courts" at the capital. Provincial merchants paid the money they made from the sale of goods at the capital to these courts, which then used it to pay tax quotas due from the Southern Provinces to the central government. In return, the courts issued a certificate to the merchants, which they presented to the provincial government and were paid an equivalent sum of money. In this way, both the merchant and the government avoided the risk and inconvenience of carrying quantities of copper and silk.[3]

Another product of necessity is a *chit* system, considered a British colonial invention. The word "chit" itself is the derivative of "chitty," a word of Anglo-Indian origin borrowed from the Hindi *chitthi,* meaning a mark. From the late seventeenth century, the word came into English usage as meaning a note, pass, or certificate given to a servant. The chitty went to China in the nineteenth century by way of British custom. Foreign residents in the treaty ports found handling strings of Chinese cash or silver ingots a major inconvenience. A system was devised to eliminate this inconvenience: "The salary of foreign employees was paid by check drawn on the Chinese compradore, who then held the funds against which the employee wrote chits . . . memoranda acknowledging debts for retail transactions. These were accepted by the shopkeeper and passed for collection to the firm's compradore."[4]

This scheme also makes use of the offset mechanism and implies trust in the accounting system and/or certificate paper, chits. Both the flying money and chits systems are somewhat similar to the tax and arrears offsets practiced in Russia in the 1990s. Offsets have commonly been used to clear obligations among groups of firms, between firms and tax authorities, and between firms and utilities or government. Multilateral offsets were originally introduced in 1994, primarily in the form of treasury obligations and tax offsets, and were used to clear enterprise tax arrears and budget payment arrears through chains of mutually indebted enterprises (Commander and Mummsen 2000, 115–16).

Despite the linguistic diversity of terms, these schemes are in no way unique. They are based on a triangular model involving a principal, a client, and a third party (an agent) and based on a relationship of trust among them. If the principal and its agents (such as provincial governments, their memorial-offering courts, or the Chinese compradore) are trusted by clients, the schemes work as designed.

A different outcome occurs if the relationship between principal and agent is far from transparent, particularly if this relationship is outweighed by trust or personal interest shared by agent and client, as in the classic model of corruption.

Finally, if the principal (state) and/or its agents (bureaucracy) are not trusted, horizontal relationships of trust and alliance among clients arise in order to avoid dealing with the principal or to "beat the system." Such models make use of kinship and personal networks and constitute forms of informal exchange like blat (Ledeneva 1998); forms of petty corruption (Ledeneva 2000b; Varese 2000); and illegitimate activities (illicit transactions in black cash, money laundering or underground banking). A historical example of a scheme of underground banking is replicated in present-day drug dealing.

Historically, in China, if you had a quantity of raw opium and I wished to purchase the opium, I would give you a quantity of silver. The silver would become a medium of exchange with which I obtained a commodity. If there was an unsatisfied debt and I had the ability to pay in raw opium, that opium would be a means of payment and a form of money. I accepted the opium from you at the rate of one kilo for each one hundred taels of silver you owed me. I stockpiled silver in anticipation of future purchases, and you did the same with your opium. Suppose I wish to purchase 500 kilos of opium from you. You live in Burma, I live in China. I do not want to transport 50,000 taels of silver, so I tell my cousin in Burma to pay you and I promise to settle with him later. You deliver 250 kilos, but you receive 50,000 taels of silver. I now have a 50,000 tael liability on my cousin's books, a 25,000 tael asset on your books and a commodity worth 25,000 taels on my books. I sell my opium for double its unit cost and have 50,000 taels of silver in my possession. My cousin tells me to pay a 50,000 tael debt he owes in China and thus settle my debt with him in Burma. I have caused the transportation of 250 kilos of opium from Burma to China without moving my silver and have 25,000 taels in Burma which the Chinese authorities will never see. During the course of this transaction my "money" has taken the form of raw opium; silver taels; notes between my cousin, myself and a third party; and has been alternately (various) mediums of exchange, including a means of payment, a standard of value and a store of value.[5]

Perhaps the best-known underground banking system is *hawala*, which is an Arabic word used in non-Arabic Muslim countries with the spelling *hawallah*, the transfer of money or information between two persons using a third party, a practice that predates Western banking by several centuries. This system also originated as a means of avoiding robbery and repressive tax measures but continues to be used in India by those involved in illicit activities such as tax evasion, drug trafficking, money laundering, political corruption, and arms smuggling.

According to Lampert, the fundamental scheme in Chinese and Indian underground banking illustrated above is still at work today.[6] Agencies that specialize in gold and precious stones, currency exchanges, and import/export businesses form a network that facilitates the swift and efficient movement of cash and commodities with little or no documentation. Guarantees of payment are assured by relationships between the "bankers" and their clients. Failure to meet obligations has reportedly led to reprisals carried out on the families of bankers. As a result, payments are generally handled with care and dispatch.[7]

Hawala is grounded in personal or criminal networks and is associated with local culture. In India, *hawala* routes are used to bribe politicians. At the same time, this system can operate globally, making it difficult for governments to track illicit funds, halt money laundering and capital flight, or control financial support provided to subversive organizations. Underground banking has historically proven itself one of the safest methods for transferring large sums of money without a trace. Less is known in law enforcement circles about underground banking systems than about any other form of money laundering or cash movement both because of a lack of understanding of the cultures in which they operate and because of the elusive nature of participation in these systems.[8]

Similar principles of operation can be traced in present-day Russia. Some of them become legalized schemes, such as barter and mutual offsets (*vzaimozachety*), and have been used at every level of the national economy in the 1990s. Some of them, such as black cash serving the needs of small and medium-sized businesses, have remained underground, while others, such as money-laundering schemes serving large networks, have come to the public's attention.[9] The use of the term "underground" is slightly misleading here because the constituent practices of financial scheming make use of the existing legal framework, have a seemingly legal appearance, and are characterized by a high degree of law observance. The next section explains the origins of such underground financing in Russia, gives basic examples of financial schemes, and offers a participant's view on the commonsense responses relied upon to survive (or thrive) and remain competitive amidst pervasive uncertainty and high levels of risk.

The Genesis of Financial Scheming

In Russia, the informal practices of *pripiski* (false reporting) that were omnipresent in the planned Soviet economy have a certain continuity with present-day practices and endure despite various legislative attempts at reform. While fairly universal, these practices also bear the distinct imprint of the Soviet planned economic system, where false reporting was employed to keep production targets manageable and to secure bonuses for plan overfulfillment (Shenfield 1983). The types of Soviet *pripiski* are summarized below.

Types of Soviet-Era *Pripiski*

Underreporting. To safeguard against a potentially unsuccessful future production period, accountants understated production output figures. The managerial team also had to be wary of reporting an overly successful production period which might have resulted in unrealistically high production targets in the future period (Shenfield 1983, 245).

Overreporting. To avoid punishment or to win bonuses, promotions, or simply the approval of the ministries and the party committees, plan fulfillment was overstated. Referring to his experience in the labor camps of the 1940s, Alexander Solzhenitsyn writes of *tukhta* (prison slang for *pripiski*), which flourished because work standards were onerous to achieve. When the targets for woodcutting were unrealistically high, the reports would simply read that the unfulfilled portion was rotten and not fit for delivery. Each member of the chain of command, realizing that this was the only way out of an impossible formula, would falsify his reports. The minister of the timber industry himself reported to his superiors that the rotten portion had been allowed to float downstream to the sea.[10]

Wage falsification. To compensate for a lack of skilled labor and unrestricted labor mobility in the postwar period, enterprises were forced to use extralegal payments (*namazki*) based on falsification of work orders (Berliner 1957, 171–73).

Shuffling of accounts. If one planned item was overconsumed, it could be stated that the money had been used for the purchase of another material or service. The most common example was the shifting of funds from production accounts to the account for entertainment and cultural events (Ibid., 169).

Borrowing of output. Instead of pulling numbers out of the air, the factory valued output that had not yet been completed at the end of the planning period at a considerably higher percentage of completion (Ibid.,161).

Today, the comparable practice of underreporting profits is used to reduce tax liability and other obligations to outsiders, while the use of multiple bookkeeping (at a minimum, one set of books for corporate insiders and one for tax services) and false documentation (counterfeit contracts, fake invoicing, false offsets) ensures compliance with the law or its creative use. To cite two examples, a business transaction can be invalidated through the use of a backdated dismissal order, falsely reflecting a signatory's dismissal prior to concluding the deal, or alternately, a contract may be voided by deliberately replacing the stamp of the firm and then claiming that the stamp on the contract is wrong.[11]

The more recent types of financial schemes have flourished in legal loopholes left by market reforms. Those that most damage the transparency of Russian business involve so-called corporate identity split, by which firms abuse corporate registration procedures to insulate themselves within a sophisticated financial network made up of at least two *front companies,* also known as spin-off firms, shell firms (*levye firmy*), scam firms (*pustyshki*), or monkey firms (*martyshki*). Offshore companies are created with the specific intention of channeling assets to an insiders' club of shareholders or managers while obscuring the benefits of ownership. Such schemes are organized according to another "splitting" principle (*matrioshka*) in which a bigger *matrioshka* is owned by the smaller one inside it, which is in turn owned by a smaller one inside it, and so on. In *The Godfather of the Kremlin,* Paul Klebnikov (2000) claims that this was the organizing principle of Berezovskii's empire. According to Klebnikov's sources, the ownership ties of AvtoVAZ, the giant auto manufacturer that accounted for half the Russian market for passenger cars, were linked to the company Forus Services S.A. in the town of Lausanne, Switzerland, which was owned by Forus Holding (Luxembourg), which in turn was owned at least partly by a Lausanne shell company named Anros S.A., with Berezovskii behind it.

Financial schemes, the hybrid produced by Soviet legacies and post-Soviet opportunities, represent mechanisms deployed by businesses to intentionally mislead outsiders by misrepresenting the true nature of their affairs. From the insiders' perspective, they may be divided into two broad classes. Some are designed to organize a company's *internal* finances, that is, to minimize taxes, divert profits, and confuse outsiders. Normally, these involve satellite firms that belong to an enterprise head either directly or through the people he or she trusts or controls, as in the examples above. Others are designed to organize *external* deals: outgoing capital flows and payments for the services of important external institutions such as the customs services, railway authorities, regional administration, or private protection companies. These schemes make use of intermediary firms in order to pay for services and protection, to offset taxes, or to transfer bribes and political payments.[12] The most elaborate schemes involve multiple stages of transactions between upwards of a dozen ostensibly independent economic agents. Yet despite their complexity, financial schemes are used almost universally and are guided by a simple principle—the diversion of payment to a front company, also used in the basic mechanism of transfer pricing (see Adachi 2005).

The diversion of payment implies that somebody whom you trust will pay for your purchase in exchange for a similar favor in the future. The central principle of financial scheming, to misrepresent the state of affairs, is founded on a basic imperative—"If you have money you should pretend that it does not really belong to you or that you owe it to somebody"— which turns every transaction into a circular chain. The banking sector demonstrated this phenomenon in the use of so-called show capital. A bank would give a loan to one client, who would then forward it to another client, who in turn would transfer it back to the bank's capital base (see a similar case in Tatiana's story in chapter 7). Repeating this operation could enlarge the capital base as much as desired.

Originally, circular schemes in the 1990s were associated with barter and mutual offsets, which were used to operate in the economy of arrears internally and to export capital. As shown in chapter 5, the evolution of these schemes for exporting capital through foreign trade began with barter schemes in the late 1980s to early 1990s. With the further development of the financial sector around 1993, sham credit schemes emerged. Tikhomirov describes sham credit as a "semi-legal scheme . . . [in which] a Russian-based company failed either to receive payment for the commodities supplied to a foreign partner or to receive goods from abroad after making all necessary payments. In both cases the foreign partner (usually a small company established by Russian emigrants or by locals with the help of Russian-connected capital) disappeared leaving the Russian company with 'losses'" (1997, 593).

As the government later took steps to regulate abusive barter transactions, financial schemes, and trade deals, double invoicing became the preferred means of facilitating capital flight. According to Tikhomirov, double invoicing requires a close business partnership between Russian and foreign companies and is based on a high level of trust. It essentially involves signing two contracts for the same deal: the "official" contract used for reporting and taxation and the "unofficial" contract that spells out the division of profits between the two colluding parties. The foreign partners accept a small proportion of the earnings as payment for their services, while the remainder is transferred to accounts held by Russians in foreign banks.

More recently, sophisticated schemes for exporting capital without foreign trade were developed to overcome complicated export procedures (transportation, customs, licenses, and so on) and difficulties associated with excessive reliance on foreign partners. These do not involve any export procedures and permit conversion of rubles to dollars without the need for cumbersome intermediary transactions in products or material resources.[13]

Capital Flight Scheme (Adapted from Aleksashenko 2000)

Enterprise A wants to transfer some funds to a foreign account. Legally such a transaction is restricted by regulations on currency conversion and bank transfers (see figure 6.1).

Step 1. Creating a regional monkey firm. Enterprise A registers a firm,

M1, usually in the corrupt area K. According to the contract signed between A and M1, A pays M1 $1 million for fuel oil supplies.

Step 2. Linking the monkey supplier with a real supplier. The firm M1 is actually an intermediary and does not produce anything. M1 subcontracts with Enterprise B, which is controlled by A, to supply the fuel oil to A. M1 pays B in promissory notes (*vekselia*).

Step 3. Creating a central monkey firm and setting up the real supplier. Enterprise B sells the promissory notes at a generous discount to M2, a firm created to have access to an account with a large commercial bank and to disappear when necessary. M2 will never use those promissory notes, so they are removed from circulation and can be written off as a "little debt" when M2 is liquidated a couple of years later. As a result, enterprise B either has to supply its product for free or must become indebted to A (which can serve as a basis for launching an insolvency procedure).

Step 4. Creating an offshore monkey firm. An offshore firm, M3, is registered in Cyprus. With a minimal sum, M3 opens a special "I-type" investment account at a large Moscow bank. There are no limits on the repatriation of capital back to Cyprus with I-type accounts. Money from this account is supposed to be spent on portfolio investment, which in this case enables the purchase of junk shares in Russian enterprises.

Step 5. Linking the offshore monkey firm with the regional monkey firm. Some of the junk shares purchased by M3 are sold to M1. The latter pays with its $1 million, which is then transferred from the regional bank account to account I at the large Moscow bank. In effect, the Cyprus firm makes an investment and repatriates the capital gain (capital gains were not adequately taxed until 2000).

Since 1992, the Russian government has made attempts to halt capital flight, first by modifying the financial and currency regimes and second by enacting controls over foreign trade. These measures have been ineffective, in large part because they falsely supposed that a system of bureaucratic controls was in place. But instead of curtailing capital flight, they have caused bureaucratic corruption to proliferate from foreign trade to other areas of the state apparatus and into banking. Simultaneously, these reforms have caused financial schemes to grow even more intricate while only marginally diminishing capital flight. No efforts have addressed a major contributing factor behind capital flight—the high degree of public distrust of Russia's government and its financial institutions. The government is partly responsible for the lack of trust. Some respondents reported on financial schemes that wouldn't have been operational without the endorsement of or at least connivance by the state. These schemes involved

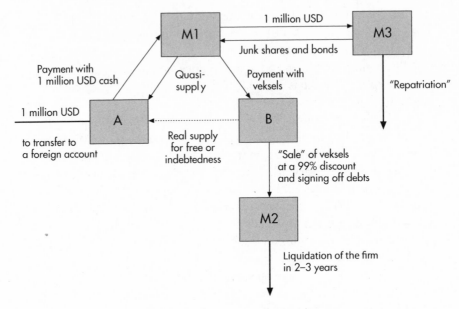

Figure 6.1. Scheme for capital flight in the late 1990s.

budget funding that was released or intermediated by the banks associated with the gatekeepers of budget allocations. For example,

> When somebody is entitled to some budget funding but the funding is not coming through, there comes a benefactor, say, from Menatep or some commercial bank, who will "help" to deliver the funding and will also take the lion's share as a "commission." This commission will subsequently be shared with the budget gatekeepers as well. In other words, the budget allocation would not materialize without these so-called enforcement costs paid by the recipient of budget funds. [5.42]

> In Soviet times, access to budget funds, allocations, special quotas, priority funding, etc. used to work through the party programs, central planning mechanism, and lobbying for the "interests of the Soviet people"; now they operate through privatized financial institutions at the expense of those people who are dependent on the budget funding that gets siphoned off on the way. [6.32]

Because some of these activities in the banking sector resemble authorized robbery, it is not surprising that many Russian owners believe that maintaining foreign accounts is more secure than investing at home, while managers have their own commonsense reasons to deprive shareholders of their dues.

Restrictions on asset sales imposed by the director of a company can also be circumvented with the aid of financial schemes and a cooperative board of directors. Such was the case in October 2000, when representatives of the government occupying five of the eleven seats on Gazprom's board raised objections to the fact that large quantities of assets were being transferred to companies related to the senior management. A contract had been signed with Stroitransgaz, 50 percent of which was owned by those at the upper echelons of Gazprom's management, according to 1999 financial records: 6 percent by Vitalii and Andrei Chernomyrdin, the sons of Viktor Chernomyrdin; 6.4 percent by Tatiana Dedikova, the daughter of Rem Viakhirev; 20 percent by Arnold Becker, the general director of Stroitransgaz and one of Gazprom's corporate directors; and another 12.3 percent by three of Becker's relatives.[14]

It is important to note that asset stripping can be instrumental in defending a company's assets from a takeover. When somebody tries to gain control over a company through bankruptcy procedures (which will be described later), and it is known that the court's decisions would certainly be prejudiced against the company, the company may opt to strip its assets. The ownership structure (controlling blocks of shares of this company and its subsidiaries) can be manipulated. Company buildings and residences will change hands (diversion of ownership). All contracts under which the company should receive payments will be consolidated in a "shift-a-debt" contract (*pereustupka prav trebovaniia*), so that any incoming funds will be transferred to some other firm belonging to the management indirectly (diversion of payment). If the company holds more than a 51 percent share in any of its subsidiaries, this must be reduced to 25 percent minus one share, and so on. In rare cases, the deliberate bankruptcy of company subsidiaries can be undertaken with the subsequent exchange of their devalued shares for shares of holdings belonging to management and its inner circle.

When asked about the current state of affairs with respect to financial scheming and the prospects for change, one banker from a medium-sized bank gave an extended answer that could be summed up as the following.

First of all, it is crucial to distinguish between financial schemes in big business, operating mainly with transfer price mechanisms,[15] and the rest of them. A particularly widespread practice today involving intermediary firms is the illegal conversion of rubles into hard currency. In this area, progress can be seen in the fact that these intermediary firms are not "black" or "monkey" as before. They are registered firms and they pay taxes, though not all of them. They might function for two years or so, whereas it used to be three months. The only feature that does persist is that these firms only have "dead souls" as directors or chief accountants.[16] Because the regulation of conversion is ineffective (for example, the ban on Latvian banks has brought an extra link into the chain and Belarus's banks into operation), illegal currency conversion does take place. However, one should understand that the currency does not stay in the West. It comes back into Russian businesses, serves their needs, and contributes to the economy even if it still goes through gray channels.

Trust in business partners is extremely high. These days, for example, one gets insurance payments for fire damage even though supplies have been delivered without documents or contracts. One cannot secure white (legal) guarantees when business operates in the gray domain (extralegal). Offshore business is where this degree of trust is the highest.

An important indicator of progress is the share of offshore companies in business. It is going down, but slowly. Most payments for services, supplies, shipment, and storage space are still made through intermediaries. Even the largest suppliers ask to be paid through their offshore companies, and the financial schemes are organized in such a way as to make everything appear lawful, whereas intermediaries are created specifically to break the rules [6.28].

A general idea behind these financial schemes is to obscure any direct connection between a company and its operations. Asset ownership is hidden by channeling funds through intermediaries, while companies that bear liability are stripped of assets and have nothing to lose. The level of financial schemes is therefore much more central to understanding how business is done than the level of institutional fictions that are created, used, and eliminated for the sake of the schemes.

Decoding Financial Schemes

To decode a scheme, one has to establish its functions, the true identities of all agents involved, and the connection or relationship of control between them. According to Yulia Latynina's account, published in the *Moscow Times*, all of Aeroflot's hard-currency turnover passed through two Swiss companies, Andava and Forus, and probably remained abroad. Nikolai Volkov, the former lead investigator on this case, reported that "Aeroflot engaged a Russian company called FOK to collect its foreign debts. FOK, in turn, hired an Irish offshore company and that company then collected the money from Andava."[17] FOK, the Irish company, and Andava are controlled by the same people (78 percent of shares belonged to Glushkov, one of the heads of Aeroflot, and Berezovskii). In this particular case, FOK and the Irish company collected the spectacular fee of $38 million. Basically it was a scheme by which Aeroflot borrowed its own money and paid a percentage for the privilege.

Did Berezovskii's people do anything illegal? No. There is no law against paying a middleman to perform a service, no matter how ridiculous the service or how high the fee is. Latynina, a journalist and the author of a series of fascinating "economic thrillers," argues that this scheme is routinely used. The same pattern applies to Sibneft', Tiumen' Oil, and Noril'sk Nickel, where Andava is replaced by such companies as Runicom, Crown Trading and Finance, and Norimet.[18]

To establish the identity of offshore companies and other links in a chain is a daunting task. It is normally true that the more successful the enterprise, the more complex its identity split. In the most elaborate cases, financial flows link the main enterprise with its "pocket bank," its *veksel'* (promissory note) center, and more than a dozen firms whose functions are known only to the top management. To reveal the functions of financial schemes is even more daunting.

Although the activities described above are directly related to tax evasion and capital flight, Latynina's commentary strongly suggests that this is what good companies do. First, in order to earn big money, a company needs a skilled and qualified management. Second, the revenues generated must be concentrated in foreign companies, or else the efforts of the managers will come to nothing and any revenues will be consumed by Russian taxes.[19] To evade or, rather, avoid taxes, a company has to simulate arrears. Latynina (1999) describes a variety of financial schemes that serve that purpose. For example, firm X sells its product to a Cyprus firm Y at a low price (to avoid making any profit), and firm Y pays for the goods in 180 days. Meanwhile, firm X takes a loan from its own pocket bank Z, in dollars at an inflated rate of 60 percent per annum. When the money comes from firm Y, it is shifted immediately to repay the loan to bank Z. If the money is kept in the firm's account, it will be levied as tax. But, Latynina argues, taxes will be siphoned by corrupt bureaucrats, as happens with all government funds. However, if the money goes offshore, it will not be stolen but will find its way back to the enterprise.

The use by enterprises of financial scheming as a protective strategy has also been prominent in the context of hostile takeovers since the 1998 Law on Insolvency, which made bankruptcy procedures relatively easy. Many enterprises suffered from having their debts bought by third parties, accumulated, and used to initiate takeover.

The most widespread are the schemes aimed at tax evasion. They serve fairly routine functions such as paying salaries to employees or renting office space. The most primitive of them are associated with the use of black cash (*chernyi nal*). Apart from the widely available anecdotal evidence that the salary of employees is regularly underreported, there are estimates that 50 to 95 percent of employees' salaries, and an even higher percentage of managers' salaries, are paid in black cash (Iakovlev 2000b, 138). By declaring only a fraction of their employees' salaries, enterprises evade social taxes that until January 2001 were payable to the pension fund (28 percent), the social security fund (5.4 percent), the medical insurance fund (3.6 percent), and the state employment fund (1.5 percent).[20] In January 2001 payments due to the pension, social, and medical funds were consolidated into one social tax (36.6 percent for most incomes).

> In other words, in order to pay a ruble of salary, you have to pay 37 kopeks to the state, after which employees are going to be taxed for the income they receive. A variety of schemes were invented to avoid payment of the social tax. There were schemes based on "loans-deposits" (*kredit-depozit*) with the use of insurance companies, which was blocked by the tax restrictions later on. [6.33]

Evading taxes through insurance schemes is based on an imperfection of the law: payments for life insurance aren't taxable if they do not exceed the amount of the premium (*strakhovoi vznos*). One scheme was described like this. The employees of a firm receive a loan from a bank. This money is deposited into an insurance company in the form of an insurance premium. The loan is paid off on the same day at the expense of a loan from the insurance company (this is important, so that there is no material gain). Next, according to the insurance policy, the employees receive income each month at a high rate. So as not to operate at a loss, the insurance company gets resources for such payments from the management of the firm in the form of a premium for an insurance policy with extremely low risk (for example, the firm insures itself against fire).[21] An accountant of one multinational company explains,

> We would sign a contract with some sort of insurance company, and we would send along a certain sum of money to this insurance

agency. At the same time we would sign a contract about termination of the previous contract, a contract that the insurance would be paid directly to employees and a contract about the return of the money. The insurance company would kindly suggest that we open an account (they are generally related to one bank or another) for individuals (*fizicheskie litsa*)—the employees of the enterprise. So these sums would appear on the accounts of the employees, which signified the end of the contract for insurance. As a rule, however, terminating the contract with the insurance company is not evidenced. So it would appear that the money would be returned to individuals who were insured. And these incomes were not liable to income tax, to the social tax, and in fact just appeared in the bank accounts of these individuals, with a bit of a commission having been withheld by the insurance company. [6.34]

Boris Fedorov began the battle with insurance schemes in his role as tax minister. In 1998, the Ministry of Taxes and Collections (*Ministerstvo nalogov i sborov*) published a letter calling upon inspectors to publish schemes they came across in the course of inspections, because without the help of universal public condemnation it would be impossible to fight them. The subsequently adopted sections of the Tax Code on income tax strip these schemes of their former attractiveness.

The basic option of the insurance scheme has been blocked by the regulation that insurance expenses are taxed at 13 percent from January 1, 2003, but everybody is working on it at the moment—organizing brainstorming sessions with the leading experts on taxation in order to figure out if there is still a loophole there or not. I think there must be; it can't be that there isn't. [6.29]

Unlike the use of black cash, such schemes are grounded in legal loopholes and can be qualified as tax avoidance rather than tax evasion. They exploit defects in the tax legislation, which, according to some respondents, may themselves have been left there on purpose as an outcome of state capture or lobbying by the powerful insurance business. One respondent described an amazing loophole that is used by banks as a service to big clients for paying salaries.

Imagine that on the one hand, you do not want to pay 37 percent social tax and then another 13 percent as an income tax, and on the other hand, you do not want to operate in the shadow (*v teni*) and want to legalize some money. So, the fantastic loophole is the 6 percent tax on dividends received from foreign companies (juridical entities). That is, if an individual (*fizicheskoe litso*) received dividends, they are taxed at 6 percent. Nothing stops us from buying shares of western companies, which is perfectly legal; you can spend up to $75,000 for the purchase of shares of a foreign (or any) company (this sum is rather strange, as it is too small for people who are engaged in this sort of activity). But the main trick is: you buy $2,000 worth of shares of an offshore company that performs so well that it can afford to pay you dividends at $10,000 monthly. As it is an offshore company, you have limitless possibilities; you can pay yourself as much as you want (it's your decision). The question is how to transfer money offshore in the first place, but this is not a problem—the market infrastructures are developed to such an extent that the differential between the costs of money here and there is fixed and there are tariffs for cash and noncash (*beznal*). Despite the awful competition in the offshore sector, the degree of trust is the greatest as everything in this business works on a handshake; there is no documentation of the transfer to the offshore whatsoever.

These days the offshore activities are organized so that they meet audit standards: the incoming funds, say, consulting activities resulting in absurd profits, which enable the offshore company to pay absurd dividends that are taxable only at 6 percent. [6.28]

Another basic scheme applied fairly widely involves renting office space through an insurance company.

According to the last Tax Code there are no limitations on insurance payments. Technically, 100 percent of your expenses can go for insurance. It is as if the state decided "OK, use the insurance scheme but we'll charge VAT on your insurance payments" (firms will lose the VAT). The profitability of rental business is substantial: the cost is $60–$70, the rental pay is $300–$400. To minimize profits, the difference is taken out of balance sheets through insurance companies. How? There are two contracts signed: one for rental (at a modest rate), one for insurance (for a huge sum). The insurance company returns everything minus 5 percent for services. This is the simplest scheme and it is not even illegal. Every type of activity involves some kind of scheming. [6.28]

Similar schemes serve the purchase of housing in Moscow. Any estate agent offers two contracts: one with a property developer, one with an insurance company (to insure the risk of the transaction). The property developer receives his money from the insurance company (the difference between what's written in the first contract and the actual price for the square meter) and thus avoids taxation (the housing estate business is very profitable and it would be necessary to have it on the balance if it were not for the insurance company, serving to take the profit out of the books).

> For example, if a square meter costs $800, the first contract will quote a price of $500, whereas $300 will go through the insurance company. Clients are also interested in this scheme because they show that they pay $500 per meter, and if the tax inspection requests, as they do, documents confirming the source of this money, it is easier to account for. So the scheme as such is legal. The problem starts when the insurance company has to pay back to the property developer, because they also have to show it on a balance somehow. . . . but it's not too bad. [6.28]

Overall, these schemes are aimed at minimizing profits for the purposes of tax evasion by taking the profits out of the books through the use of shell companies, offshore companies, insurance companies, and fake contracts. Given the skills and the determination to invent such schemes, it is unlikely that the reduction of the profit tax will be a sufficient stimulus for companies to give up these practices.[22]

Implications of Financial Scheming for the Post-Soviet Economy

What are the implications of these practices for the Russian economy and for the fate of reforms that do not take informal practices into account? From the participants' point of view, financial scheming is not only a substantial component of the post-Soviet economy in Russia, but it is also perceived to be indispensable to the functioning of that economy and historically rooted. Financial schemes enable economic agents to protect their property and business operations from the exigencies of market reforms, from the arbitrary judgments of tax inspectors, corrupt authorities, and the deformed institutional framework in general. At the firm level, financial scheming is represented as a survival strategy. Whether the need-based argument is a genuine one, whether the boundaries between such necessity and manipulation can be defined, and whether the long-term effects of these necessary practices are not more harmful than helpful for the institutions exploiting them are issues that remain to be explored. It is likely that the answers will be sector-, size-, and manager-sensitive.

At the same time, the universal principles of false reporting, corporate identity split, and diversion of payment that underpin financial scheming in the new Russian economy have contributed to the economy's inadequate responses to reforms and the poor investment climate in the following ways.

- The official documentation that backs up financial scheming does not reflect the real flow of resources; it undermines the basic economic distinction between sellers and buyers (particularly in multi-link chain schemes) and creates statistical problems.

- As a result, changes in economic legislation have little direct influence on real economic processes in the shadow economy. Being protected by nonexistent economic agents (shell firms), real economic agents either avoid appearing on paper altogether or refrain from showing real transactions or their volumes. Thus, changes may considerably influence the "paper" level of transactions, but they may not necessarily reach the level of the real economic agents.

- The use of shell companies is not confined to profitable firms. It is also a vital tool of survival for inefficient and loss-making companies. The wide use of shell firms helps explain the puzzle of Russia's "virtual economy," depicted by Gaddy and Ickes (1998): that it is replete with loss-making and tax-owing, but nonetheless persevering, enterprises. At the end of 1999 more than six hundred thousand enterprises had tax arrears (Aleksashenko et al. 2000, 261), and in early 2000 total tax debt amounted to more than 440 billion rubles (more than $16 billion).[23]

- Apart from the direct detrimental impact on the economy, financial scheming is even more damaging in the long term in that every legal firm or structure is forced (in order to preserve itself) to engage in underground financial scheming, usually having to do with its ownership structure, concealed profits, and multiple accounting systems.[24]

- Financial schemes present numerous opportunities for a firm's owners and managers to gain by transferring costs to clients and customers (in particular, through tax evasion, asset stripping, and mismanagement).

- Moreover, financial scheming on the current scale is indicative of a strong network of vested interests committed to its continued existence, which in turn replicates obscure ownership patterns and insufficiently defined property rights.

The existence of financial schemes thus creates a vicious circle: they compensate for the deficiencies in formal institutions and enable business activities, but, by the same token, they undermine formal institutions and retard their effectiveness. I have come across a very common sentiment among accountants and their ways of "legalizing" the plans made by directors of companies, which is indeed identical to the mode of interaction between PR specialists and their lawyers (see the discussion of lawyers in chapter 2). As one accountant of a multinational firm acknowledged,

> If a director comes up to the accountant and says, "I want the numbers to look this way," the accountant has to have a high level of qualification to get it all carried out legally. . . . to look at what angle it is read from, and to review all the documents that need to be attached. So maybe it is possible to do this, but you need the right documentation. . . . only then is it legal. [6.34]

Such close surveillance of legislation is symptomatic of the specificity of the regulations themselves, leaving ample room for market agents to navigate them. The continuous changes in legislation make the life of an accountant a misery but also create new opportunities. Between 1992 and 1997, no fewer than fourteen major changes were enacted by the Ministry of Finance to the profits tax section of the Tax Code. In the year and a half that passed after January 2002, twenty-one federal laws, five federal resolutions, nine orders of the Tax Inspectorate, five orders of the Ministry of Finance, and literally dozens of other laws, regulations, letters, and edicts were issued by the regulatory organs on accountancy.[25] Summing up the trend, one successful banker was both optimistic, outlining important positive trends after 2000, and cautious, pointing to the persistent features of the political system inconsistent with the development of small business and civil society. On a positive side, he noted positive general tendencies; a greater role for legal principles; takeover of private protection services and criminal "roofs" by state security agencies; disappearance of barter and the more efficient workings of monetary schemes. At the same time he emphasized reliance on informal connections at every level of business.

> The problem lies deep in the mentality of people—especially in a distrust of the state and state institutions. Exploitative attitudes toward the state are likely to change maybe only in three hundred years or so (an optimistic estimate). And it is not only the mentality as such; the problem is also the ways it is dealt with. The tax reform is but one example of the inadequate, or rather, incomplete, dealing with the problem. Take the situation with the tax on profit, in itself an intelligent and useful piece of legislation.[26] Regrettably, the best way to describe the context is as follows. There is a long fence and a gate in it. The gate is first fitted with an automatic lock, then a censor lock, finally equipped with video security—really good work is done on it! But right next to the gate is a huge hole though which anybody can go. While the government is busy improving the locks, people go through the hole. What the government should also be doing is thinking how to motivate people to use the gate, how to change people's mentality, their attitudes to the state, by creating new traditions. What is worrying is the political resistance to seeing the "hole." [6.28]

Despite the advances that have been made in these areas since the 1990s, it is clear that the spirit of accountability and disclosure in Russia is far from sufficient. Organizations continue to rely on clandestine means of accounting in which information diverges substantially from that required for external use. The continued use of these informal practices hampers the development of the Russian financial sector. A new timeline adopted by the Ministry of Trade and Economic Development in March 2003 for the transition to International Accountancy Standards promises to bring enhanced investment and credit opportunities to the Russian financial sector. However, this is not the first time the deadline has been postponed. Focused political opposition and widespread public incredulity have delayed this process numerous times. The July 2003 transformation of the Russian Ministry of Taxation and Collections (formerly subordinate to the Ministry of Finance) into the Federal Economic and Tax Crime Service (a division of the Ministry of Internal Affairs) aims to consolidate the law-enforcement function of tax collections. Practices of tax minimization have become widely disseminated through glossy magazines and Internet publications enabling accountants in remote districts to legally avoid the snares of tax liability. Assuming that informal practices compensate or substitute for the defects in formal rules and procedures, it is easy to miss other significant factors associated with the manipulative use of law from above (such as lack of political will, state capture, creating and sustaining loopholes) and from below (lack of respect for the law and aggressive exploitation of the loopholes by firms).[27] Despite the generally positive tendencies, the manipulative use of the law and law enforcement poses a serious obstacle to the efficient working of the market.

Chapter Seven

Post-Soviet *Tolkachi:* Alternative Enforcement and the Use of Law

Before analyzing informal practices in the domain of enforcement, I would like to offer insight into the environment of the mid-1990s—the early days of democracy and the market—in which criminal groups played a significant role, alongside emerging private security services and reformed law enforcement institutions. It is difficult to explain the complexity of this emerging system in the span of a chapter, but it is possible to convey the atmosphere with the help of an eyewitness who has been on "the barricades" of the market and who is frank about what it meant at the time.

Tatiana's Story

Tatiana is the chief accountant in a spin-off firm of a medium-sized industrial enterprise in my home city of Novosibirsk. Initially she agreed to do an interview about an entirely different subject in 1998, but our conversation seemed to go in all directions, and we chatted for hours. Her story captures the spirit of the 1990s, wild and difficult enough to drive many people off the rails and make the survivors tougher than tough.

    T: I used to work as an accountant at the same enterprise I work in now but left three or four years ago to take up the post of director of a regional branch of a bigger bank. The unemployment was awful, especially among women. When I came back after all my troubles, my director here said, "Well, you wanted to achieve something for yourself, now look what hap-

ГОРОДСКИЕ БАЙКИ

ЗАЯЦ И ЛИСА

СОВРЕМЕННАЯ СКАЗКА

К-а-ароче, жил один раз такой пацан, типа - Заяц. Держал недвижимость -правильную реальную хату, чекак, ну, блин, - бунгало ваще. А рядом, два лаптя по карте, одна Лиса-кидала крутилась - ну, типа, деловая, блин, в натуре. А тут по весняку контору Лисы - бац! - спалила налоговая, и осталась Лиса не при делах.

Она, такая, имидж на морду прицепила - и до Зайца. Сдай, типа, Заинька, халабуду свою в аренду, че, я потом тебе баксов отстегну немеряно.

Заяц, в натуре, клюв разинул и лоханулся конкретно. Сдал свой квадрат, покатил на Канары оттянуться. Взад подгребает, а Лиса хату уже втихаря на себя зарисовала и сидит, такая, типа, все пучком и с понтом, здесь выросла. Заяц, такой, в обиду и баклант: "Домой пусти, что ли, коза, блин! " А Лиса лыбу отшарила до макушки и тянет:

- Ты че, лох ушастый, гонишь, ваще нюх оторвало? Давай вали отседова на фиг и не возникай, пока в череп не схавал. Моя собственность.

Заяц, лошара, по горю двинулся и пошел в мусорник слезу давить.

- Ой, кинули меня, ментики-братики, продинамили по полной программе! Выручайте-спасайте, закона вчинь.

Подорвался такой весь из себя опер Волк, пошел закон исполнять. Тычет свою ксиву в окно, маузером машет, хвост напружинил:

- А ну, Лиса, освобождай помещение!

А Лиса высунулась, пальцы веером, и гонит:

- Слышь, мент, не доводи до разборок - башка, блин, у тебя что ли бронированная? Я не фраер позорный - ксиву мне в нос пихать! Иди комаров пинай.

Волк хвост к носу, прикинул: на фиг надо за такую зарплату беду себе цеплять? Отвял. А Зайцу откорячку слепил: тут, мол, чисто не наше ментовское дело - по закону все строго. Тебя ж не бьют? Не нравится что-то - в суд подавай.

Побежал Заяц к судье Медведю.

- Какой-такой, - кричит, - закон есть, чтоб с хатой кидать?! Хочу иск вчинить. Нате вам пять штук баксов для подмазки и давайте халупу мою взад по суду.

Взял Медведь бабки, пошел на Лису наезжать согласно закону.

- Нате вам, Лиса, серьезную бумагу с реально набитой картиной. Суд решил вас выселить.

А Лиса, типа, зевает:

- Слышь, ваше благородие, не волоси. Тебе чего дали за это решение? Пять? На еще десять, чтобы его не исполнять. И не размножай мне мозги всякой чепухой. Вот тебе еще две штуки за то, чтоб я тебя тут в жизни не видела.

Медведь баксы по портфелю распихал и Зайцу-терпиле докладывает:

- Все, мол, ништяк, дело свое вы выиграли, поздравляю. А остальное, в смысле, - не наша забота.

Пошел Заяц стрелку вешаться. Хаты нет, бабки ушли, куда ни кинь - везде облом. Расклад - только лапы надуть. Но тут катит мимо такой правильный пацан Петушок-стриженый гребешок в спортивном прикиде. Даванул косяка, как Заяц петельку мастырит, и спрашивает:

- А ты че тут ваще?

- Да вот. . . - говорит Заяц.

Кароче, доложил обстановку. А Петя ему бодряка:

- Да не хнычь, братан! Я за тебя впрягусь. Перетрем щас тему с ней конкретно, а не врубается, так замочим эту отмороженную - и без базару!

Забил Лисе стрелку на разборки. Лиса является в малиновом смокинге, при "мерсе" и всех делах.

- Ну че, - говорит, - надо? Горя хочешь?

- Слышь, сестрила, в два горла жрешь, - говорит Петушок. - Пацаны обижаются. Верни братку хату.

- Да ты ваще под кем ходишь, козел? - удивляется Лиса. - Да я чисто братве своей свистну... Да за меня сам Лев подпишется! Да я... Да мы!..

- Крутая, блин, аж башню сносит! - ухмыляется Петушок. - А вот подписку от всего Московского зоопарка видела? А с братанами с Северного Ледовитого хошь побазарить?

Как услышала Лиса про северных отморозков, тут ее на измену и пробило. Утухла конкретно, свернулась в тряпочку и без вопросов из хаты слиняла.

- Живи, братила! - говорит Зайцу классный пацан Петушок. - Весь чулан твой будет! Суетись, бабки делай, меня корми. А я буду твоя крыша.

И зажили они, кароче, с тех пор, как белые люди.

Figure 7.1. Post-Soviet folklore on alternative enforcement. "Zaiats i lisa: sovremennaia skazka" ("Hare and Fox: Modern Tale"). A modern improvisation on folklore themes combined plots of traditional fairy tales ("Hare and Fox" and "Cockerel and Fox"), placed in the context of early market developments of the 1990s, and told in practically untranslatable contemporary slang that was often imported from criminal jargon. All the cliché references to tax inspection, police, courts, and alternative agencies engaged in market scenes, Canary island holidays, dress codes, traps and let-downs for amateurs in property deals, mechanisms of debt recovery, and the rationale for protection, or the "roof," are grasped with formidable precision. By permission of the Editorial Board, Telemir.

pened. It's hard to get anywhere, especially for a woman. One has to have *svoi* contacts everywhere, in militia, in the regional and local administration, even in criminal structures. Our times are very difficult." Our bank provided services to the corporate sector and individual clients: currency exchange, bank transfers, and other banking services. It was a small branch, twenty-five people.

AL: Did you give loans? Nonreturned loans?

T: Yes, we had a lot of nonreturned loans. The loans were substantial, and the turnover was large. In those years (now it has all changed, of course) everything came down to legal defects. For example, we would accept someone's apartment as collateral for a loan, but this perfectly legal contract was not enforceable, even if court executives had a right to dispose of this property. This was because according to the Civil Code, one could not evict a child registered as residing at that address. The two laws contradict each other, so nothing could be done about it. Another example: an arbitration court might make a decision to discharge a debtor's assets, but these were hard to dispose of. Barter could not be used, so in order to sell anything they announced an auction. The minimum price at the auction was the sum of the debt, but in practice the price went down in the auction, not up.

AL: What else could you use as collateral?

T: Cars, guarantee letters of other people and organizations, guarantees of other banks and assets in storage. We came across so many fake documents—it's extraordinary how inventive our people are. The government comes up with one plot, the people come up with another.

AL: You must have seen a lot of the dark side of human nature in your job. Do you trust people at all?

T: Well, I can tell my story and the price I paid for my job in the bank. Taking into account that I tried to do everything by law, and not only by law, but also by conscience, I made a lot of mistakes. First of all, I took over a bank that had arrears, all the nonreturned loans, etc. I should have done it differently, but it's too late to talk about that. It had been a couple of months since I started, and we'd been doing well, but there were a lot of problems too. What I discovered was that the previous director had planned his own independent bank and had used this branch for it. In preparation for his departure he had given loans to a number of firms, which then invested these funds as contributions [*uchreditel'nyi vznos*] toward the start-up capital [*ustavnoi capital*] of his new bank. It goes without saying that these loans were meant to be nonreturned. Everybody just shrugged their shoulders. As the new bank was not registered yet, all the money was put in a savings account in the government-run Central Bank, but according to law, it was impossible to withdraw. Naturally I went to the arbitration court right away. But to start the procedures costs 10 percent of the sum in the appeal—it's a state fee that is paid in advance by those who appeal. The nonreturned loans amounted to 100–200 million rubles, so I had to pay 10 percent of that sum![1] People in headquarters withdrew from the situation and were just watching from a distance to see whether I could manage or not. They knew our branch would be closing, so they helped neither by loans nor by moral support. They even criticized me for going through arbitration, claiming that we wouldn't be able to retrieve enough money even to cover the state fee because even if the defendant actually had that money, it would be all in black accounts [*chernaia kassa*]. What does one do under these circumstances?

AL: Alternative enforcement?

T: Yes, access to black accounts could only be gained through alternative means: either through a criminal group or through FSB, whose methods are practically identical. Both charge a lot. Naturally everything was done with the consent (even the prompting) of the chairman of the bank. But in the end I had to resign. I just couldn't take the pressure. I resigned with difficulty—only the third letter of resignation was accepted. Directors would come from all branches, they begged me to stay, and offered rewards. Now I understand they simply wanted to finish off certain deals, to cover up for it while I was still there. Not surprisingly, the director of the branch after me came into conflict with the top management right away.

. . . We did work with criminal organizations on the recovery of those loans, which I was forced to do both by circumstances and by my top managers, and I had to pay them. So we made the payment in the form of a loan, which we hoped to sign off as a nonreturned loan later on. I didn't plan my departure but rather left in haste, in panic, under pressure that I just couldn't take any more. As I was leaving, the top managers assured me that this loan wouldn't be a problem—everybody knew about this payment for the recovery of debts. But the new director questioned this loan though the court. So when they started to investigate, they easily found that all the details in the documents were made up. They opened a criminal case against me and arrested me, right in my new workplace (when I resigned from the bank I became the head of the Department of Checks and Controls—a structure analogous to tax inspection). Imagine, they took me straight from work and kept me under arrest for three months. When it was happening I just didn't believe it, I just couldn't take in that this was happening to me (my parents brought me up very gently). They pressured me at the interrogations and they planted people in my cell who tried to make me talk. I didn't say anything until the chairman of the bank came to see me.

AL: Do you think they wanted to get hold of the criminal group though you?

T: Of course not. Do you really think that FSB is interested in some bandits? They know them all by name. Moreover, the relatives of the regional leaders are engaged with them. What they were really after were the directors of other banks. They wanted kompromat on the leadership of the region and the city. They found a lot of interesting people in my address book. I knew the prosecutor of the region and the city prosecutor. There is no way the latter would have sanctioned my arrest.

... As for the criminal organization in the case, I was put though the court case together with it. Not the organization itself, of course, but some scapegoat from them, like me. All the rest was conveniently forgotten; we were not even categorized as a "donor" and a "recipient" of the loan. We were charged as allies, colluding to receive and split the loan [author's note: a common scheme at the time]. This was the formula for a sentence. My "ally" went to prison as this was his fifth criminal record. I was sentenced to two years of corrective labor with part of my salary being withheld to recompense the damage.

I am grateful to the director of the enterprise where I used to work and where I work again now. He wrote to the court, sent his deputy to make a speech at the proceeding about the support of colleagues, etc. They treated me really well but also reproached me with a kind of "What did you expect?"

... As I said, I didn't say anything until the chairman of the bank came to see me and refused to give evidence as to what really happened. So they just let me down, or rather set me up. When my investigator and my lawyer spoke to me in confidence after all those cross-examinations, the investigator asked me, "But why did the chairman do this to you, do you think?" I was so scared I didn't even understand at first what he was asking. But then it came to me, so I said, "Well, if it's not me, it's him!" Somebody had to take responsibility. The chairman of the bank told my lawyer informally that they would cooperate and help. When they let me out on bail for 4 million, I went to see him. I just wanted to look him in the eyes. He apologized, of course, and felt sorry, I think; he acknowledged that it was his fault and named the other guy who was involved, but he also said, "We are guilty, but I hope you are not going to waste your life on revenge. . . . Rather, go to church, light a candle, and live in health and prosperity." That is exactly what he said.

AL: I can't believe they didn't give you any money afterwards. . . .

T: My sentence included complete confiscation of property; everything was registered, every chair I had was taken. Also I had to pay the bank 24 million rubles, which I didn't pay in the end as they canceled the request. The chairman said he would help with money but not through the head bank (it would be clear then that he was paying me off). So I went to another regional branch up north. The director of that branch said, "Yes, he did ask me to give you a loan; of course I can't say no but how can I give it to you? What for? How do I show it in the paperwork? The chairman himself did not want to do it though a "material help," so instead he made another person do it. So that branch director just gave me his own money, which I returned with time. Without interest, of course.

AL: So the chairman did not give you anything in the end?

T: No, but the most awful thing is not that. It's my criminal record. It's there and it will always be there, the black mark on my biography. The court decided not to give me any restriction on employment [author's note: it seems as if some helping hand did indeed influence the decisions of the court], so I have come back to the post of the head of the Department of Checks and Controls. Twenty percent of my salary was withheld throughout my two-year corrective labor period. Then I had a baby and was released before time. It's revealing that when I came back to be the head of this department and continued the inspections of the regional tax inspection and other regional and city authorities, the FSB told all of them that they didn't know anybody more honest and decent than I was. This was after they told me time after time when I was under arrest, "The whole city knows you are corrupt." Total inconsistency, in laws, in life!

AL: Perhaps you shouldn't be so hard on yourself—you were used in that situation, but you didn't use other people. One's reputation does not necessarily correspond to the decisions of the courts, especially in that time. People know the courts themselves became instruments in the hands of those with power and money.

T: Oh, no . . . It all happened in 1993–94 but feels as if it were yesterday. I still react to every noise and telephone call. I just never understood the proverb "trust but check" [*doveriai, no proveriai*]. If you trust somebody, how do you also check on them?

AL: What is the atmosphere like around you now? Isn't that criminal group after you?

T: Well, nobody reminds me of it here at work. As for the others, the one who went to prison is not out yet. His friends could of course bug me even now, but they don't; they stay in touch with my friends. I have a number of friends and acquaintances from that path of life. Sometimes, it seems to me that those people are even more normal than those in our system; at least they follow their own laws, their mutual "understandings" [*poniatiia*].

What Tatiana was not able to conclude was that her story is in any way unique. It was often the case that framed victims in the court cases (often vulnerable single mothers, receiving small sentences, released into community care) enabled those behind them to end up with accumulated capital, nonreturned loans, and newly formed banks.[2] Despite the one-sided nature of the story, the dominant features of the 1990s were the inevitability of the use of alternative forms of enforcement on the one hand and the manipulative use of the legal system on the other.

It is clear from Tatiana's story that alternative enforcement is often the only option available in an environment where organizations engage in providing informal services and favors (see also figure 7.1). Another bank director testified some years later:

> We provide a number of banking services discretely. They are typical services banks offer these days. For example, somebody comes and asks me to keep some money at the bank, so that it wouldn't be kept at home. Not on deposit under his name (so that the client has to declare it) but just to keep it in the bank, say, $1 million or so. Only I and one of my aides (just in case something happens to me) are going to know about this. This money is deposited in some company account, hundreds of millions, simply on a handshake. There can't be any paperwork here, just trust. I pay them interest on this money. It's good for the bank and good for the client. Or, say, another typical service—to give a loan to a client with his own money. Someone comes to the bank and says: I'll put money in the bank and you give me a loan. A lot of businesses in Russia involve offshore companies and banks for storing money and for conducting financial operations, all of which imply an enormous measure of trust in people you deal with. [6.28]

When such trust is broken, as in Tatiana's story, the only way to retrieve the money is through the use of extralegal enforcement—one always keeps in mind, "Who do I call in case there is a problem with this client?" [6.28]. The role of informal contacts and networks of control in this respect should not be underestimated. The same respondent explains in more detail:

> While my trust in the state and in the business community overall is extremely low, trust in those with whom I do business is extremely

high, because many deals go through without any documentation whatsoever. I am a banker and my bank gives loans. Of course, I build my relationships with clients on a formal basis as much as I can, but there are no ideal defenses and it's impossible to put every nuance in the contract. You have to trust your clients. The informality comes in when I have to think about the informal leverage I could apply to a client who might choose to ignore my demands. The court system is still useless in many ways, but there are many situations where it takes just one call to the right person who would then get in touch with the client advising him to pay. [6.28]

In a high-risk environment with underdeveloped legal institutions, which do not ensure contract enforcement and property rights, alternative forms of enforcement may become an integral part of the implementation of financial schemes, thus creating a niche for "progress pushers"—the enforcers of contracts, financial schemes, takeovers—to complement or substitute for the workings of the legal system by the use of informal practices. Even more detriment is incurred when the law and legal institutions become instruments in the hands of these progress pushers—either the existing laws are manipulated or new laws are pushed through to serve certain interests. To illustrate the logic of the deliberate manipulation of the law and the use of alternative forms of enforcement, let us consider a basic scenario involving an insolvency case.

Firm C is owed a substantial sum of money by firm X, which cannot or will not pay its debts. Firm C initiates insolvency proceedings against firm X in an arbitration court and has the largest claim among all of firm X's creditors. According to the January 8, 1998, law on insolvency, the arbitration court must appoint an interim manager (*vremennyi upravliaiushchii*) to oversee firm X's affairs while the case is under review. The interim manager—who watches over the firm X's assets, monitors the actions of its management, and oversees major transactions—is chosen from among qualified (licensed) managers nominated by firm X's creditors. The appointment of an interim manager is a pivotal decision yet one that is not transparent: the arbitration court is not obliged to accept the nomination of the main creditor (firm C) and instead appoints an interim manager nominated by a creditor (firm P) with a much smaller claim than firm C.

The management of firm C suspects that the provisions of the insolvency law are being deliberately manipulated—that the appointed interim manager and firm P are controlled by a competing enterprise with links to criminal organizations. If the interim manager were to allow firm X's assets to be stripped, for example, and firm C were not to recover its claim because of its already precarious financial standing, it could be ruined. What options does firm C have at its disposal to prevent this from happening?

There are only a few legal defenses open to firm C to prevent the predatory acquisition of firm X and the loss of its claim. Once interim managers are appointed by the arbitration court, they are very difficult to change because the law does not contain any provisions for appeal. Thus, the stage is set for an informal intervention. Firm P has made the first move by exploiting the loopholes within the insolvency law in order to file a claim against firm X and to arrange for one of its own people to be appointed as interim manager—a move that it knows is difficult by law to contest. Because firm C has no available legal options, it resorts to extralegal sanctions to remove the initiator of the problem. Among its extralegal options, representatives of firm C might arrange to have the license of the interim manager revoked, thereby disqualifying him legally from serving as interim manager. Alternatively, they could threaten to release compromising information (kompromat) about him, or about the relationship between firm P and criminal groups, in an attempt to pressure him to step down. In particularly high-stakes cases, threats of physical violence may be employed. This case illustrates a range of ways in which the public methods of enforcement are infringed upon by private interests: from the manipulation of what otherwise look like perfectly legal procedures to the informal pressure and violence exercised by formal law enforcement organizations. Let us consider these informal practices in more detail.

Sanctions as Part of Informal Practices

The informal practices that are used to assist with cases such as the one above come in diverse guises, but together they comprise a toolbox of techniques for enacting what their protagonists perceive as "informal justice" through the manipulation of the formal rules. The main types of sanctions initiated at informal requests are summarized in table 7.1.

Let us briefly consider each of these areas in more detail.

The first area encompasses a set of administrative sanctions that can be organized through well-placed links to official structures such as regional administrations, the tax inspectorate, tax police, the fire department, and the departments of sanitation and public health. It is possible to arrange for a firm's access to water, gas, electricity, and sewers to be cut off by the re-

TABLE 7.1
Types of sanctions

Type	Action	Institution manipulated
1. Provoking administrative actions	Arranging for raids, inspections, and citations for administrative violations; arranging clashes between local/regional/federal levels of administrative control	Administrative institutions
2. Interfering with legal procedures	Opening, suspending, and closing cases and official investigations and sanctions	Legal institutions, tax police, state security organs
3. Interfering in personnel issues	Forced resignations and fixed appointments; staff reorganization	Employer institutions Use of blackmail files (kompromat) collected by private security firms
4. Applying financial pressure	Freezing assets, demanding repayment of debts, raising the level of kickbacks, and purchasing debts	Financial institutions
5. Organizing informational pressure	Using kompromat	Media institutions, PR agencies, private security firms
6. Using violence/threat of violence	Informal negotiations (*razborki*) and physical attacks	State and private security services and agencies

gional authorities on the pretext of arrears. These techniques have been practiced widely and remain one of the most common ways of neutralizing opponents.[3] The formal system exploits the informal, while the informal ones exploit the formal:

> [P]repaid business attacks [*naezdy*] can assume legal form and make a use of a fire inspection, tax police, sanitary-epidemic station (the most frightful beast in the region) ... And vice versa, these inspections can be just a way of extorting bribes. [7.39]

In other words, inspections conducted by formal organizations are used manipulatively for purposes different from the claimed purposes of the inspections—to impede and intimidate (*meshat' rabotat'*).

A second area in which informal practices are employed is in influencing the status of official investigations and judicial proceedings.[4] By using connections in various federal and regional authorities, it is possible to arrange for a criminal case to be opened or closed (*zakon zakrytykh del*), for tax evasion charges to be pursued (or conveniently forgotten), and for law enforcement officials to continue an investigation (or abandon it).[5] Local police and militia can be persuaded to initiate cases against purported suspects by setting them up or by planting falsified evidence. At a higher level, influence with judges and prosecutors can yield desired results in criminal and civil trials, and if unfavorable judgments are handed down, there are ways to ensure they are not enforced. One former judge, Sergei Pashin, gave the following testimony:

> Q: We hear a lot about political pressure put on judges. How does this work?
> A: The mechanism is traditional—distributing favors and privileges. Let's say you are the chairman of a court, and you want to become a member of the Supreme Court. Are you going to refuse to take the advice of the chairman of the Supreme Court? No, you're not. Or for example, the mayor calls you up and says you're really in debt. But I'll pretend not to see it, he says, and, by the way, I have a libel case in your court tomorrow. For some reason, the mayor always wins.[6]

A popular area of orchestrated interventions has to do with banning shareholders meetings in order to win time. According to the Moscow arbitration court, this trick is used in one out of every five cases. This is done very easily. A court officer comes to the location of the meeting for a certain reward or compensation. The trick is that after the announcement of the ban some important shareholders leave the place while the meeting resumes its work and makes certain decisions without them (Golikova 2001, 40–41).[7]

A third target for promoting desired outcomes is to orchestrate changes in key personnel. This can mean forcing someone to resign through public or private channels, or arranging for staff reorganization in order to ensure that loyal individuals occupy strategic positions. Interfering with the formal appointment procedures and personnel policy is yet another way of infringing on formal procedures through informal means.

These first three types of practices are similar in the sense that they are all informal; that is, they involve the manipulation of formal laws, measures, and procedures by individuals with personal links to those who wish to have the sanctions enacted. As a result of a bribe, a long-standing personal relationship, or an exchange of favors, a public official or bureaucrat agrees to use the authority of his or her position in a way not intended by the written rules. In today's Russia, as in Soviet times, the ability to solve a problem is dependent not so much upon one's own capacity as upon the power of the network that one can mobilize. Thus, formal procedures and formal justice are often replaced by personalized versions that maintain the trappings of legality while the logic of law is subverted.

Financial pressures comprise a fourth area of sanctions that can be levied through the use of informal practices. Here the permutations are extensive. Examples include arranging for an opponent's shares or assets to be frozen, refusing to renew the terms of a loan and demanding immediate repayment, threatening a firm with insolvency proceedings, and increasing the level of bribes and kickbacks demanded as part of a quasi-legal business deal. Sometimes a firm can achieve the seizure of a competitor's property through the court in order to prevent that competitor from making a certain deal. One lawyer specializing in property conflicts, Spartak Markin, provides the example of a company that was brought to court by a plaintiff demanding the seizure of property as a guarantee for the suit. It quickly became necessary to bring the defendant company's balance to zero (*obnulit'*). The company transferred all the property to a third person, and when the necessary court decisions were taken, there was no property left to seize (Golikova 2001, 40). To prevent such incidents from occurring, a ban on property management must take place in the beginning of the trial when a case is brought to court. This provision is abused by those who want to stop the transactions of their competitors.

If the previous four types of practices rely heavily upon manipulation of administrative sanctions in order to make them part of a certain business strategy, a fifth type is based on the manipulative use of information, channeled through legal, criminal, or media institutions for the purposes of personal blackmail or legal prosecution. According to the respondent involved in law enforcement, such compromising information—*kompromat*—can be legal, investigative, and journalistic in nature [3.13]. The best kompromat includes already existing legal documents: sentences for criminal offenses served in the past (especially those different from the more ideological offenses such as "anti-Soviet behavior" and "speculation" prohibited under Soviet statutes); information about opened and closed cases (*vozbuzhdennye i prekrashchennye dela*); information about community service (*peredacha na poruki*); time spent in Kresty (such as St. Petersburg's *sudebno-sledstvennyi izoliator* and prison); and records of administrative sanctions (violation of customs, traffic, tax, fire, health, and safety regulations). The distinctive feature of such information is its documented nature, in records, protocols, and acts of confiscation. These documents can be interpreted in various ways, viewed as insignificant at one time (serving the function of suspended punishment) or brought into action at another (serving the function of punishment if there is reason for it).

The difference between documented and nondocumented information, as suggested by one respondent, is similar to interrogation and questioning (*doprashivat'/oprashivat'*). Interrogation is a formal procedure of collecting testimony sealed by signature. Questioning, by contrast, is the collection of information and opinions with no precision or responsibility involved. Nondocumented information will not work in court, but its collection is an important part of the investigative process, and it is often referred to as investigative information (*operativnaia informatsiia*). A respondent with a background in law enforcement explained:

> We keep our own database [*kartoteka*], which supplies a variety of information: "connected with Tambovskie" or "was involved in dealing stolen cars in Kiev." I look at it and say "Oh, that's what kind of goose *you* are!" This might go against human rights, as it is about suspicion that cannot be put on paper, but it is useful in investigative work. To give you an example, in the press Mr. X is often called the leader of the Tambovsk group [*gruppirovka*]. But there is no documentary base on which this could be proved. Was convicted—yes, lived in Tambov— yes. But "a convict from Tambov" is not the same as the leader of Tambovskie! Therefore, Mr. X can sue everybody and will win! [3.13]

Outside the legal sphere, kompromat information does not have to be of a formal nature—in other words, usable as evidence in court or proven to be authentic. "For a criminal group, for example, the legal status of the documents is unimportant—if they have a printout of a problematic telephone conversation they will follow it up, regardless if it's real or not" [3.11]. In the media, the documentary status of information is often unclear. The above example of "a leader of Tambovsk group" is representative of journalistic discourse.

> In present-day Russia there are so many phobias, manias, alternative sects, and witchcraft rituals that it gives perfect grounds for kompro-

mat of all journalistic types, which is not in contradiction with the law but would make one unpopular. Homosexuality, for example, is not a crime, but it can serve as kompromat. If a political leader is gay, this is lawful, but the public reaction to this fact will bring his ratings down. [3.12]

Thus, kompromat can include documented evidence, useful information on lawful but socially uncomfortable behavior, and even entirely fabricated stories. The manipulative use of information for the purposes of legal investigation and prosecution or for protection against legal investigation and prosecution implies that "just as the law can work for you or against you depending on other factors, so *kompromat* can be allowed to rest in peace or put to use according to the circumstances" [3.13].

The sixth area covers a full spectrum of practices ranging from informal business negotiations conducted by security personnel on behalf of formal institutions (privatization deals, contract enforcement, conflict resolution) to the use of physical violence (threats, physical shakedowns, beatings, and the roughing up of potential witnesses or opponents, coordinating violent attacks and contract killings) in order to influence certain formal situations. One keen practitioner and the director of a private security business was convinced that "for the time being, one can't do without violence in Russia—people are to be taught the order of things [*uchit' umu razumu i kak nado*]"[8] [3.11]. In other words, the lack of efficiency in law enforcement institutions and the lack of people's respect for the law create conditions for the emergence of an alternative institution of *tolkachi*, which operates with more efficiency by manipulating sanctions available to formal institutions but also using only partially legitimate methods.

Post-Soviet *Tolkachi*

Under the Soviet system, *tolkachi* ("pushers") were employees of enterprises whose official task was to support the command economy and to make it function according to the plan (Berliner 1957; Nove 1993). Their responsibilities were essentially to close the gaps in the planned economy to make it possible for enterprises to meet production targets. In practice, this meant manipulating the centralized system of allocation to procure resources needed to fulfill monthly plans, or maneuvering within the bureaucracy to get targeted outputs reduced. The managers of factories depended upon tolkachi to push for the company's interests. Tolkachi did this through a whole range of informal methods: manipulating paperwork, cultivating good relations with bureaucrats and officials, and thinking outside the box in order to solve problems. The only way that *they* could perform these functions was by violating the very principles of planning, and by subverting the rigid system of bureaucratic allocation (Ledeneva 1998, 25–27).

Once the centrally planned economy was abandoned, Soviet-style tolkachi, with their expertise in procurement and plan reduction, became redundant. However, the concept of tolkachi remains useful as a generic term for designating those who bridged the gap between the formal rules and the informal workings of the system during the "wild accumulation of capital"[9] or those who made use of the six types of sanctions outlined above. Just as Soviet-era tolkachi enabled enterprises to operate within the planned economy, a new generation of Russian tolkachi allows private businesses to survive within chaotic market conditions. Modern-day tolkachi compensate for deficiencies in the legal framework by assuming functions that the state and market institutions, for a variety of reasons, do not perform. Like their predecessors, today's tolkachi are also forced to manipulate and violate the formal rules of the existing legal framework in order to get things done. Just as the existence of Soviet tolkachi was a signal that the planned economy did not work according to its own declared principles, so the existence of the post-Soviet tolkachi testifies against the market.

Who are the tolkachi of today's Russia? As the elements of the command economy have fragmented and diversified, there has been a proliferation of agents involved in pushing forward transactions, deals, and market activities of all kinds. The tolkach seems to be no longer embodied in a single individual; rather, its functions are carried out by whole departments within enterprises or independent agencies hired to perform similar functions.

In mid-1998, twenty-five hundred banks and seventy-two thousand commercial organizations in Russia had their own security services.[10] In size, some of the security services of large banks and financial-industrial groups rivaled those of a small country. They were often headed by high-ranking former officers of the KGB. For example, the head of security at Stolichnyi Bank was a former commander of the Alpha Unit, a special counterterrorism force, while the former deputy chief of the KGB, Philip Bobkov, was in charge of security at the Most Bank group. By the end of 1999, there were 4,612 security services of this type (Volkov 1999, 2002).

Private protection companies that were used by smaller banks and enterprises made up the second category (Volkov 1999, 2002). These firms, which numbered more than 6,700 in Russia by the end of 1999, were contracted to provide protection and enforcement services.[11] Like the company security services, private firms often were founded by high-ranking former officers, or groups of individuals from security backgrounds who believed they could market their expertise to clients. Other security firms developed into formalized businesses after beginning as informal security providers for specific commercial deals. Their services were rather expensive, estimated at 15 to 40 percent of the claim (Volkov 2000b, 57–58).

If taken at face value, it would appear that the private security industry in Russia operates as it does elsewhere in the world, performing a relatively standard set of tasks aimed at protecting the rights and interests of clients in market transactions and in their interactions with representatives of the state. However, security services in Russia are notoriously associated with the sanctions described above, with debt recovery and other "routine" business tasks, all of which need to be accomplished in an environment of pervasive corruption and high risks.

The dissonance between how a market economy is supposed to work and the actual environment reflects the necessity for Russia's private security and enforcement agencies to fulfill a much broader set of functions than those enshrined in law (see table 7.2).[12] At the same time, this necessity leaves a wide margin for manipulation. This particularly applies to the methods of gathering intelligence used by these security departments in order to compile kompromat on clients, current or potential competitors, civil servants, and elected officials. In June 1997 Iurii Shkuratov, then Russia's prosecutor general, quoted a list of state organizations permitted to conduct phone tapping according to the rules for operational investigative activities adopted in 1995. These were the MVD (Ministry of Interior), FSB (Federal Security Service), GUO (State Department of Guard of RF), SBP (Presidential Security Service [Sluzhba Bezopasnosti Presidenta]), FPS (Federal Border Control), SVR (Foreign Intelligence Service), Tax Police, and Customs Service.[13] Although private security services do not have the right to conduct eavesdropping as part of their investigative operations, phone tapping is common, as are other forms of surveillance such as stakeouts, shadowing, and videotaping.[14] Owning one's own cell-net company was the only protection from interception by the "privatized" FSB. Despite all the restrictions on government monitoring imposed by SORM (*Sistema operativno-rozysknykh meropriiatii*) promising that electronic surveillance would be undertaken solely as part of counterintelligence and crime-fighting activities, cyberintelligence is also conducted by private security departments.[15]

Most of these semilegal activities have been given attention in literature

TABLE 7.2
The roles of security services

Declared role of security services	Actual role of security services
Protection (physical) Bodyguards (physical protection of citizens) Security (physical protection of property) Ability to deal with threats from organized crime groups	Compensate for failure of state to protect physical safety of entrepreneurial class; general law enforcement in the country Contribute to image of firm Serve as deterrent to "aggression" by opponents Serve as interface with criminal element (criminal culture, criminal slang); make and read threats
Informational support (information gathering and analysis) Information on competitors (market research to assess reliability of partners) Awareness of potential threats—economic and otherwise Awareness of economic and legal changes that can affect the firm Collection of Awareness of potential opportunities for growth, expansion Collection of kompromat Collection of data on lawsuits Security consulting Protection of commercial secrets and trademarks Investigations into biographies of potential employees Searching for people claimed to have disappeared	Compensate for failures of state and market to regulate and oversee the business sector Compensate for absence of transparent information about business activities of other firms (comprehensive annual reports, shareholder info, earnings data); minimize business risk; industrial intelligence Databases and kompromat allow for "preventive neutralization of potential conflicts and threats" (Volkov 2002) Kompromat files supplement financial reserves as currency for use in business expansion, takeover bids, privatization tenders Find rent-seeking opportunities unknown to others
Dispute settlement "Solving questions" Negotiation between enforcement partners	The process of "solving questions" allows business to carry on functioning Compensates for inability of formal mechanisms to resolve conflicts of interest between economic agents
Contract enforcement Debt recovery Sanctions Agreements Recovering lost property	State is unable to enforce business contracts and legal decisions By providing this service security services allow firms to keep operating, but also perpetuate a culture of violent *razborki* as a business norm

TABLE 7.2—cont.

Declared role of security services	Actual role of security services
Negotiation with state authorities	
Interaction with bureaucrats and state agencies	Foresee and forestall bureaucratic obstacles; Navigate through those obstacles as needed
Expertise in legal codes, tax codes, accounting procedures, licenses, registration	Allow firms to conduct transactions more efficiently by manipulating the formal system
"Facilitators" who guide the firm through complicated regulations and laws	Enable financial schemes to function (knowledge of the law and its loopholes is essential)
Ensuring that firm is "well known" at high levels	Use and reproduce the culture of personalized relationships and favors
	Position the firm to be able to organize intervention from above, or to mobilize the authorities on the firm's behalf

on alternative contract enforcement, economic crime, or violent entrepreneurship (Ledeneva and Kurkchyan 2000; Varese 2001; Volkov 1999, 2002). The focus here is not on violence or the rule breaking but on the rule following in the activities of tolkachi during the 1990s. The attitude to the law in this context was somewhat paradoxical: on the one hand, the law was perceived as little more than red tape that had to be formally satisfied one way or another; on the other hand, the law was followed zealously, particularly where legal procedures constitute an integral part of a larger business maneuver. In both senses the law was used manipulatively for purposes unrelated to the actual legal dispute. In other words, the law was used selectively and opportunistically aimed at initiating sanctions against political or business opponents (Ledeneva 2001b, 12–15).

Positive and Negative Implications of Selective Rule Following

At Russia Forum 2000 in London, a Western lawyer working in Moscow summed up the myths spread among Western companies about the legal system in Russia in the 1990s. He lamented that most foreign investors act as if "Russia is another planet and no rules apply; there is no law in Russia; you can't enforce your property rights; you never win in Russian courts; you can't do business in Russia if you are not prepared to give bribes." He emphasized the extraordinary achievements of the Russian legal system in the 1990s and turned his critique against Western investors, who believed those myths and acted accordingly. Since then, Russia, alongside Latvia and Slovakia, has reformed its regulatory system even more actively, as was noted in the World Bank report released in October 2003. According to experts from the International Finance Corporation at the World Bank (IFC), the authors of the report, the Russian legal system is ranked sixtieth out of the 130 countries included in the survey and precedes Poland (sixty-second) and Slovenia (sixty-fifth).[16]

Where is the catch? Both Russian and Western experts note that the fact that a court makes a decision does not mean it is going to be enforced. It is implementation that normally presents a problem (Hendley, Murrell, and Ryterman 2000, 646). In 1997, according to official statistics, only 56.1 percent of all court decisions were implemented (Kononov and Kokarev 1999, 74). This figure has certainly risen since bailiff service was introduced in the same year (60 percent in 1999; see Mel'nikov 2000), but it also shows that anecdotal evidence about the nonenforcement of many arbitration court decisions is not unfounded. Furthermore, the surveys conducted by the European Bank of Reconstruction and Development show that the perceived level of enforcement in Russia is pretty low compared with that in other post-Communist countries (EBRD 2002, 16–17).

In a survey of company managers, Frye (2002b, 127) concludes that the arbitration courts in Russia are rated as the second-best-performing institution, while the bailiffs are regarded as one of the poorest-functioning institutions.[17] The weakness of the bailiff institution often results in the selective enforcement of court decisions, often with the use of alternative agencies of contract enforcement.

Available research and statistics on the overall use of the arbitration courts are informative but may also be misleading.[18] First of all, it obscures the fact that the use of courts is strongly correlated with the size of the firm. One of the main players in Russian banking emphasized the key but manipulative role of arbitration courts:

To bankrupt an enterprise is elementary, but these conflicts do not get settled in court. And not at the *strelka* [informal dispute settlement] either. Big things are under control of the *silovye* structures [coercive government ministries]. Also, much depends on the status of their counterparts. With a medium-sized bank, one can rely on fair hearing of the case and the comparability of the bribes. With a big bank, a call from a superior will induce the arbitration court to make a decision desired by the big bank. An enterprise can win regional arbitration if the governor supports it, but to win in the district [*okruzhnoi*] and the higher arbitration court is an entirely different story [in terms of the level of support, influence, or the size of the bribe].[19] [3.19]

Another respondent, the chairman of a Moscow bank in the 1990s, confirmed that there is a big difference between a large company and a small firm:

There are no universally recognized rules. Rules are inconsistent and unclear. The Constitution, the Civic Code, and corporate laws are not compatible. But even if these laws were better, there would be problems with both court procedures and enforcement. These circumstances have facilitated the emergence of extralegal (*nepravovye*) methods of solving problems. Large companies can go to court, but at a lower level this doesn't work. [3.16]

According to survey data (Radaev 1998, 159–60), arbitration courts are used primarily by large and medium-sized enterprises (71 percent), while small enterprises use them quite rarely, especially those in risky environments (3 percent). Furthermore, state-owned enterprises—large ones in particular—seem to use the courts most, while small enterprises in wholesale, retailing, and the service industry use them least (Radaev 2000, 72–75).

It should be noted in the context of these data, that what might look like a more or less well-functioning legal system in the field of business conceals the role of courts as helpful servants in the interests of dubious business actions. In a survey of privately employed managers (Johnson, McMillan, and Woodruff 2001, 50), 54.3 percent of Russian respondents answered that they had used the courts in the most recent dispute they had, with 55.8 percent believing that courts could do their jobs. In most other countries polled in the same survey, comparatively more respondents believed in the courts, but fewer actually used them. This result can be interpreted in support of the argument that the court system is used manipulatively.

Characteristically, by the end of the 1990s even criminal groups paid attention to the legal basis of things and preferred to act in a "bailiff capacity" [5.42]. Varese's research indicates that entrepreneurs might simply be abusing the arbitration courts as yet another weapon in the arsenals of contemporary Russian business (Varese 2001, 50–51). In other words, the court system may be in use, but this does not mean that the law works (54).

Volkov (2002, 46) reports that some companies obtain court decisions in their favor but then, knowing how uncertain the state bailiff service is, they turn to private security companies to get decisions implemented. With a legal court decision in hand, there is a better chance that alternative enforcement agencies will succeed.

Meanwhile, we know relatively little about the tolkachi's manipulative use of the court system and the widespread ways of diverting the course of justice while still following the rules. Although arbitration courts are used more and more, they are reported to be subject to interference by authorities and to manipulative use by influential clients. As one of Latynina's characters explains, "If one can't win in court, one can win time by placing a complaint in FKTsB [*Federal'naia Komissiia po Tsennym Bumagam*], which will take two months or three if you pay more (1999, 158).

Often the plaintiff is interested not in winning the case but in the judicial process itself, while that process is influenced by the use of judicial tricks. The following tricks are reported to be common. A petitioner to arbitration court has to notify the defendant that a case has been initiated (Oda 2002, 337). If the defendant does not react to the notification (*uvedomlenie*), the trial can proceed without the participation of the defendant. As a result, some petitioners send the letter to an address where they know the defendant will never get it. In Russia, the legal addresses of many companies do not correspond to their actual addresses, a practice often used to avoid paying taxes. Knowing this, the petitioner can choose to send the letter only to the company's legal address. Having seen that no one is there to receive the mail, the postman then returns the letter. Alternatively, there are reports of petitioners buying fictional receipts for the mailing of a letter at the local post office, or just sending envelopes containing nothing but old newspapers.[20] Empty sheets of paper can also be sent to a plaintiff instead of a copy of a defendant's reply to a lawsuit (*otzyv na isk*). If sent by registered mail, the receipt of even a false letter will be signed for by the secretary of the plaintiff. However banal, this trick enables the defendant to conceal the official position and the arguments from the plaintiff at a crucial time and can define the outcome of the case. Golikova (2001, 39) reports that such tricks are not necessarily applied only by private companies but by state organs as well.

Multiple tricks are employed to reschedule trial.[21] There are numerous ways for a defendant to delay the judicial process if necessary—from presenting a medical certificate for sick leave to introducing a representative, a third party, to the process. For example, a court investigation may be postponed (every time for six months) so that a third party can familiarize himself or herself with the court's summons on the judge's request [6.35]. Fiddling with addresses again can ensure that the summons will not reach the defendant, causing another delay with the paperwork. To convince the court that the company didn't receive certain documents, company's lawyers will sometimes force a secretary to copy a book that records incoming mail. On the contrary, when it's necessary to prove that a document was received at a certain time, a fax machine can be reprogrammed (*perebit' faks*). According to lawyers with experience in arbitration, the court is very formal in its actions, and reasons to delay administrative paperwork can always be found—irrespective of common sense or the relevance of the pretext (Golikova 2001, 41). Barristers can help delay the hearing as well. "'One day, I had to faint, since our side turned out to be unprepared for the sharp change in the process of the session'—says lawyer Spartak Markin. As a result, the court postponed examination of the matter" (Golikova 2001, 41). Often the outcome of a dispute depends on the existence of a single document. If it is lacking, or its meaning is not obvious, companies turn to notaries. Notaries prepare a necessary paper and backdate it (*zadnim chislom*). The trick here is that the majority of notaries use fountain pens. According to Georgii Nechaev, an expert of the independent appraisal bureau Alfa, records made by fountain pens are impossible to date precisely. If the authenticity of the document is suspect, the court can appoint an expert graphologist. The catch here is that such appraisals can be done by the defendants themselves before the court even starts, so that when the judge requests one, an already existing result of an appraisal is available. Usually, the opposing side will demand an additional appraisal, but this rarely helps. According to Evgenii Zaikov, it is not acceptable among experts to question the opinions of their colleagues. Every expert knows that sooner or later he or she can be placed in the same kind of situation. So even if experts carrying out the additional appraisal discover counterfeits, they do not refute them (Golikova 2001, 41). This is a classic example of the workings of krugovaia poruka in formal contexts. As one of my respondents, a former diplomat, who had lived abroad for years summed up:

Generally, foreigners do not understand our specifics. We have a rural kind of arrangement of krugovaia poruka. Networks of interests are organized in such a tight way that it is impossible to target anybody without wounding oneself. It would be great if a younger generation of businessmen operated according to universal business ethics and in a more market-oriented and transparent way. What we witness, however, is the reverse: the economic logic of Russian conditions forces the younger generation to deal in shadow sectors even more than the older one. They have to develop skills allowing them to evade taxes and customs duties, to master practices of "solving problems" by extralegal means and of turning the legal procedures to their advantage. [3.16]

Apart from the manipulative use of arbitration courts by companies since the 1990s, the interpretation of arbitration court statistics should also include a more recent tendency. If the arbitration courts' biggest caseload in the 1990s was contractual disputes, since the late 1990s, when the tax authorities and tax police began a vigorous pursuit of tax offenders, the load of tax cases initiated by the state has exploded. Tax cases (207,485 in 2002) constituted about 30 percent of all approved cases, whereas contract disputes constituted about 29 percent. Cases about the nonpayment of penalties, interestingly, constituted about 80 percent of all tax cases. This indicated that the tax authorities had pursued an aggressive strategy of punishing offenders rather than forcing present taxpayers to comply with the law (Hendley 2001, 131–36). Besides this, their main activity was in bankruptcy proceedings, which constituted around 16 percent of all cases ("Osnovnye pokazateli" 2003). As opposed to tendencies from the 1990s, arbitration courts have slowly deviated from their prime purpose of solving commercial disputes between private entities. The percentage of the cases involving tax and property rights initiated by state agencies had increased by 2005 and in some regions reached 70 percent [6.35]. The entanglement of the legal system with the state (known as *telefonnoe pravo* [telephone justice]), as well as evidence suggesting that state agencies engage in opportunistic and manipulative ways of using formal rules and procedures (Golikova 2001, 39; Basmannoe pravosudie 2003), creates an additional impetus for these patterns to be replicated by other agencies at all regional levels.

The manipulative logic extends not only to law enforcement but also to the legislative process itself. In other words, paraphrasing a Hungarian proverb about sausages, "Those who like laws do not want to see them made." As one of the respondents working in the legal field explained:

Take, for example, a PSA lobby. Naturally, those who pushed it through were interested in the existence of this piece of legislation, as they would then become consultants to large international clients. Why would they want this law to be simple and easy to follow, why?

Naturally they shape it in a way that will create various possibilities for themselves. In this sense, our specialists are extremely intelligent. [3.20]

Another lawyer claims that similar practices are omnipresent at a local level, where certain decrees are pushed through in the interests of a particular group of people. When asked to give a recent example of such a decree, she quoted a ruling by local authorities the previous week on the privatization of garages in the center of town:

The formula—"those who had paid their garage rent for ten years from the date of the adoption of the decree are entitled to privatize these garages"—presupposes that only those who knew about this decree and had enough resources to pay rent ten years ahead would be able to acquire property in the center of town. [6.33]

Such day-to-day practices of the state are paramount in shaping people's perception of the law and law enforcement. As it stands, despite the judicial reform initiated since the year 2000 and the "dictatorship of law" rhetoric, the All-Russia Center for Public Opinion (VTSIOM) data show low rates of trust in all basic institutions of society, including the courts. Ninety-two percent think that law enforcement is selective and eighty-eight percent say that officials taking bribes are not likely to be punished, according to a survey conducted by the Levada Centre (http://www.levada.ru).[22]

How does one address the issue of the rule of law in a situation where the state seems to be "yet another player" [3.22] in the field rather than a referee responsible for enforcing the universally applied rules and protecting everybody's rights and freedoms? Is there really a political will to make the rules of the game transparent? One revealing answer comes from the owner of a medium-sized business:

There is no equality between the players in Russia, no transparent rules, no open competition, as one can't really compete with oligarchs. There are perhaps a thousand of them now rather than seven but it's even worse. The state is engaged with big business and in many ways is paid for by them, while businesses benefit from the sanctioned process of monopolization as this also increases the "manageability" of the economy for the state. In theory, the state admits the need to help small and medium-sized business and declares the political will to protect them, but in practice state bureaucrats receive payments from big businesses and are often in their keep. The antimonopoly trust and the lobbying organizations for support of small and medium-sized businesses are not powerful enough. Tax measures do not work. And every other institution in Russia (regional governors, Duma, other businesses) prefers to deal with big businesses too—it seems reliable and prestigious, just as it used to be with the state orders [*gosudarstvennyi zakaz*]. [6.28]

Yet big businesses are far from being in a secure position themselves. The very act of an informal agreement between the state and the businesses, made at a meeting between Putin and the oligarchs in July 2001, was seen by many as a sign of the state's refusal to outline transparent policies toward big business that could involve specific taxes to regain the hidden profits made in the 1990s. Instead, the state reserved the possibility of an assault on the oligarchs, thus creating informal leverage against them. Such leverage is required to control them and negotiate with them on terms favorable for the government. The informal component is an integral part of political power in Russia, which makes it both efficient and dependent on the unwritten rules, their nontransparency, and the selectivity of law enforcement (as illustrated on pp. 12–13 in chapter 1).

To make the rules transparent means to lose manageability and centralization, the strategy chosen to run the country after the events of September 11, 2001, in the United States and reenhanced after the terrorist threats to Russia's national security in later years. Not to make them transparent means to reproduce conditions for corruption and the poor investment climate, as well as to undermine the protection of the freedom and initiative of small economic agents. Putin's second-term political reforms, allegedly in response to security issues, run against the logic of separation of the state from business and civil society, a separation that is essential for creating a market democracy.[23]

Conclusion

In this book, I offer an interdisciplinary alternative to the mainstream accounts of post-Soviet Russian politics and the economy, focusing specifically on the nature and implications of informal practices. The book builds upon my previous book, *Russia's Economy of Favours,* moving the discussion into the post-Soviet period and accounting for a wider set of economic and political practices. With *blat* having lost its central significance, other informal practices have gained prominence in the context of market and democratic reforms. The reforms of the Soviet system have resulted in the spread of black and gray PR and krugovaia poruka in elections, kompromat in the media, barter and financial scheming in industry and business, and alternative enforcement in legal and security spheres.

An ethnographic perspective on the informal practices allows us to grasp players' strategies and perceptions of constraints—the enabling aspects of both formal rules and less visible informal norms in Russia. Conceptually, the category of informal practices helps us understand the origins of practices and dispels a number of commonly held stereotypes about formal rules and informal norms. By contrast with "informal institutions" or "informal rules," informal practices are guided by the opportunistic logic: they navigate between different sets of rules and manipulate not only formal rules but also informal norms. Rather than following a coherent set of principles, informal practices are in line with some, but contrary to other, widely held norms and values and are thus regarded ambivalently. They are usually condoned by some and condemned by others, and just as often, condoned and condemned by the same people, a phenomenon sometimes referred to as semicorruption (Etzioni-Halevy 1990, 115). The contradictory (and elusive) nature of informal practices accounts for their paradoxical relationship with both formal and informal sets of norms, which informal practices help both to reproduce and to exploit.

Both formal and informal constraints play equal parts in the genesis of informal practices. For example, krugovaia poruka constituted an informal norm before it became a formal constraint but then again was made illegal and became associated with informal practices. Historically, I chart a genealogy of informal practices, tracing them back to their Soviet and pre-Soviet roots, and attempt to find patterns common for Russia at all times, patterns shared by both political and economic players, and patterns universal in human societies. I also make suggestions concerning possible political and economic measures that might improve the development of market and democratic institutions in Russia.

I argue that informal practices were an integral part of the postsocialist transformation. Informal practices adjusted to and were shaped by formal and informal constraints: they supported formal rules and informal norms but also subverted them; they rapidly accommodated legal changes but also created an obstacle to further change; they were beneficial for certain individuals but also made them hostages of the system. These practices were not simply illegal but integrated the law into political, media, and business technologies, often manipulatively. Similarly, they did not simply follow or contradict informal norms but relied on some of them and played one set of norms against the other.

If one has to single out the most important trend in the transformation of informal practices, it is the centrality of law and the increasing expertise of players in its manipulation. Known as "from tax evasion to tax avoidance" in more mature market democracies, this trend has been more pronounced in Russia. Under any regime, informal practices can be a response to a form of governance that is top-down, prohibitive, and centralist; to situations of overregulation, underregulation, or cross-regulation; and to situations of inconsistency between formal rules and informal norms. No regime can be completely free of restrictions and regulations; likewise, "market democracy" in Russia has not simply liberated people from Soviet oppression—it has liberated and restricted, empowered and impoverished at the same time, thus creating new freedoms and new constraints.

Under socialism, people tended to develop similar responses in order to survive in conditions of shortage, insufficiently defined property rights, overregulation, and ideological predicaments. Informal practices made use of social networks based on noncontractual but binding relationships, such as kinship, friendships, and other trust-centered relationships in order for people to get what they could out of the existing system and to avoid the rigidities of economic and political regimes. Informal practices constituted a response that can be viewed as uniform across societies with state-centralized regimes. For example, *guanxi* and *blat* practices in prereform China and Russia played a similarly paradoxical role in these economies: on the one hand, they compensated for the defects of the formal rules, thus enabling the declared principles of the economy to exist; on the other hand, they subverted them (Ledeneva 2003). At the same time, informal practices had a paradoxical impact on informal norms as well—people were compelled to use their personal networks pragmatically, as well as socially. On one hand, they created solidarity and reinforced the power of informal obligations and principles of reciprocity; on the other, such pragmatic use of personal relationships undermined their voluntary nature and produced the divide between us and them (*svoi*—*chuzhie*). These tendencies enhance patterns of personalized trust, thus weakening forms of generalized trust, and trust in impersonal institutions, necessary for effective workings of politics, business, and civil society.

Given that informal practices navigate between formal and informal sets of rules and norms, they change their patterns when those rules and norms change, especially when changes are as radical as they have been in Russia. The post-Soviet reforms have changed Soviet-type practices to such an extent that blat has lost its key function to support and to subvert the centralized distribution system. Because of monetization of informal exchanges, blat has almost ceased to be a relevant term for the use of personal networks both in the state and in the new sectors of the economy. In contemporary China, where reforms are much slower and the practices of *guanxi* have a longer history than those of blat, the term *guanxi* has not only sustained but also given a name to the Chinese system—*guanxi* capitalism. There has been much more debate about the role of guanxi in contemporary China than about blat in Russia. In the Russian context, people speak of kleptocratic, crony, or oligarchic capitalism, whereas "*blat* capitalism" sounds like an oxymoron.[1] Despite the differences, the logic of transformation of informal practices in post-reform China and Russia is similar. Before the reforms, both guanxi and blat were often beneficial to ordinary people in allowing them to satisfy their personal needs and to organize their own lives, whereas now their shift into corruption benefits the official-business classes and harms the majority of the population.[2] Trust and social networks are vital components of both economies and continue to exist, but because of the exclusive nature and the monetary targets of informal practices in market contexts the ethics and traditional values that had once been the foundations of guanxi and blat have changed accordingly.

Just as elsewhere, contacts in post-Soviet Russia play an important role in establishing personal relationships with patrons, partners, and clients. Practices of networking and the use of networks for getting things done can be found in any economy or society, but in full-fledged democracies, these practices are better hidden and are constantly tested by procedures of accountability and independent media. They are not the only available channels and are integrated into modern institutions more subtly. These practices are associated with filters and channels of vertical mobility: clubs, references, introductions, invitations, kin- and class-based old-boy networks. The consistency between informal norms and formal rules can also account for the difference in the use of networking—for example, between Russia and the United Kingdom—where players can engage in networking without feeling the strain of having to engage in informal practices or to accommodate conflicting sets of rules.

Although from a legal perspective any practice can be qualified as either licit or illicit, the legitimacy of informal practices often causes controversy. If informal practices are widespread and more or less accepted, it indicates that (1) the formal rules are lacking legitimacy or informal norms predominate in determining the ways of behavior; (2) there are legitimate formal rules but there are also legal loopholes that allow informal practices to flourish in a controlled way (by closing and opening loopholes); or (3) there is a balance between the defects of legislation and the informal practices (as Russians say, *nesovershenstvo nashikh zakonov kompernsiruetsya ikh nevypolneniem*—the rigidity of our laws is compensated for by their nonobservance). Following Ken Jowitt's argument, Sampson (1985–86) argues that the informal sector moves from the phase of "benign aid" to the system in which informal practices are accepted into the "corrupting" and potentially "system-threatening" phase. Yet it is not the subversive nature of informal practices that creates the unwillingness of the authorities with certain political and economic agendas to acknowledge their pervasiveness. The subversive aspects are often stigmatized and fought against in various, however ineffective, anticorruption campaigns. What is less often admitted about informal practices is that they are as much a solution to certain defects in the workings of institutions as they are a problem, and it is their supportive role that should perhaps be researched more thoroughly and addressed in policy making.

The logic of modernization assumes that the role of informal practices should decline. With domains of informal norms becoming increasingly regulated (domestic violence, punishment of children, domestic slavery, animal rights, etc.), formal rules can undermine the power of informal norms (for example, litigation becomes an instrument in family disputes). Ethnographic research into informal norms and practices of informal politics can contribute to a similar trend. Although it is my intention to shed light on the areas of Russia's "antimodern" patterns of informal politics that contradict liberal and democratic values and to emphasize that it is impossible to understand the workings of institutions in Russia without understanding their reliance on informal practices, I am also wary of the consequences of a Western-type modernization. Let me first summarize the impediments created by the informal practices.

Informal practices preserve the vulnerability of an individual vis-à-vis the system, whether it's a family, a network, or a state. Vulnerability to kompromat (*komprometiruemost'*) enables pre-electoral attacks on a candidate's image and sustains ties of mutual dependence in smaller and larger communities. It provides bargaining power and channels for informal pressure and internal conflict resolution. It protects one from the selective workings of legal investigation and prosecution, but it can also make one a victim of the selective use of law. It may seem that these patterns of informal politics preserve stability by maintaining an informal order of mutual control, or induce instability in order to keep powerful players off balance ("divide and rule"), but they also create a substantial gap between the formal order and the informal order of things by their reliance on selective use of formal procedures and informal leverage.

By serving the needs of insiders (suppliers, intermediaries, and customers of the black PR and kompromat market or members of krugovaia poruka), informal practices also serve the needs of the political regime by undermining the principles of free and fair elections, independent media, and the rule of law and by exerting symbolic violence or manipulation of public opinion. By serving the regime, however, informal practices also entrap it by creating its dependence on them (addictive medication can make a good metaphor).

For an optimist, an obvious question to ask is whether the post-Soviet era of domination of informal practices is over. For a pessimist, the question is whether it is possible to solve the governance puzzle and break up Russia's dependence on unwritten rules in principle. It is hard to answer these questions without in-depth research into Putin's Russia and related data, which are a challenge to obtain. But if one is forced to make a judgement, Putin's second term does not look too promising. Take Khodorkovskii's case, re-

solved in nine years in prison for one of the most successful oligarchs leading the campaign for transparent corporate governance. A variety of interpretations exist, including those blaming the authorities for the selective use
of law and those blaming Khodorkovskii for his arrogance, notoriety, and
political ambitions. What most of these interpretations have in common,
however, is that Khodorkovskii violated the unwritten rules announced in
June 2000 at the meeting between Putin and the oligarchs, who were told to
stay out of politics.[3] Instead, Khodorkovskii was financing oppositional parties (including both liberal and Communist parties) and civil society, buying too much influence in the State Duma, and declaring his participation in
the 2008 presidential elections. He also launched a clean-up campaign in
Yukos, claimed business interests outside Russia, and planned sales to foreign investors without consulting the Kremlin where expected—initiatives
that have been now curtailed. Importantly, Khodorkovskii's case points to
the gap between formally claimed principles and informal agreements yet
again, and gives ground to Western lawyers familiar with Soviet courts to
suggest that nothing much has changed in Russia after all.[4]

The very fact of informal agreement between the state and big business
created a lack of transparency and the refusal by the state to outline clear
policy toward privatization. The government could set up selectively targeted but accountable tax policies to regain the profits that were made by
the oligarchs in the 1990s. But this would "liberate" the oligarchs, enable
them to play further with such clearly set formal constraints, and deprive
the state of informal means of control. Reserving informal leverage against
oligarchs in order to make them stay in line is an effective tool and an essential feature of political power in Russia. This form of governance makes
the ruler powerful vis-à-vis other influential individuals but powerless vis-
à-vis the system, which is trapped in its own dependence on unwritten
rules, the nontransparency of the rules of the game, and the selectivity of
law enforcement.

Some analysts argue that selective enforcement is better than none and
in many ways it is the only possible way forward (one has to start some-
where in order to, in Putin's words, "teach people to live by law"), but the
problem is that there is no good solution for the authority that "sits" on the
branch of informal leverage. In the short term, to make the rules transparent means to lose the manageability needed to run a country of such scale
and complexity. Not to make them transparent means to reproduce obstacles to the workings of the rule of law, the improvement of the investment
climate, and the freedom and initiative of political and economic agents in
the long term.

Given the context, it would be wrong to consider informal practices exclusively as an impediment to modernization and a legacy of the past. The role of informal practices is fundamentally paradoxical: they support reforms as much as they produce an impediment to their implementation. They are a channel for innovation at both the individual and societal level. In other words, informal practices are conducive to change but also resistant to it. They may have helped to bring about the collapse of the Soviet Union, but they also ensure that there will be no return to a Soviet-type rule. The changes that informal practices have introduced into the post-Soviet system are associated with economic rationality, political competition, and the centrality of the law. It is crucial to see these practices not only as an impediment but also as a resource for Russia's modernization.

Appendix 1. *Pravda* versus *Istina*

PRAVDA

Etymology

Pravyi is an Old Slavonic word derived from the Common Slavonic short form *prav':prav'. Some believe that the Common Slavonic *prav' may have resulted from the intersection (contamination) of *pret' (*priamoi*, or "direct") and *orv-p (*rovnyi*, or "even"). Others think that the Common Slavonic *prav' developed from the Indo-European *prouos ("pointed/directed ahead, located ahead"). The adjective *prav'* initially meant "directed ahead," from which the following meanings derived: (1) *priamoi, rovnyi* and (2) *istinnyi, takoi, kak nado*.

The root is *prav'*. Main meaning: as it should be (*kakoi dolzhen' byt'*). Compare with Latin *probus* (kind, honest, good)—*takoi, kakim dolzhen byt'* (Preobrazhenskii 1959: *Pravda*).

Usage

Pravda denotes a conformity with known facts or events.

Pravoe delo: the right cause; *pravil'nyi otvet:* the correct answer; *pravdivyi rasskaz, istoriia:* true story; *pravdivyi chelovek:* truthful person; *dobit'sia pravdy:* strive for truth; *pravdivost':* conformity with the facts.

Worldly notion

Relates to a state of worldly affairs knowable on the basis of human observation or intellect

May refer to a state of affairs that humans believe to be desirable and attainable

ISTINA

Etymology

Borrowed from Old Slavonic. Old Slavonic *istina*, meaning *deistvitel'nost', zakonnost', pravda, spravedlivost', vernost'*, was formed from *ist'*, meaning *nastoiashchii (podlinnyi)* (Shanskii 1980).

The root is *istyi*, meaning *nastoiashchii, sushchii, istinnyi*. Etymologically, relates to the word *iskat'*—that is, a person who searches for, exacts/recovers, or brings a suit (against someone). Long explanation of possible derivations (Preobrazhenskii 1959: *Istina*).

Usage

Istina denotes a truth beyond the known facts of the world.

Istinnaia nauka, znanie: true science, knowledge; *istinnaia religia, Bog, vera:* true religion, God, faith; *istinnyi drug, liubov:* true friend, love (reveals the essential nature of an entity); *otkryvat' istinu/istina otkrylas':* open up, reveal the truth; *istinnost':* the property of truth of a higher order.

Otherworldly notion

May be unknowable to the human mind, or a distant, elusive goal attainable only by a privileged few, a meaning conveyed in journey metaphors, e.g., "the path toward truth" (*put' k istine*)

May accord with ethical, moral, or legal standards of correctness

Attainable, e.g. "the revealed truth" (*pravda obnaruzhena*)

Refers to metaphysical, unchanging truths about life, existence, and the universe

Exists independently and may be considered superior to mundane notions such as justice, ethics, and morality

Relativistic

There can be degrees of *pravda,* such as *polupravda* (half truth) or *nepravda* (untruth).

What constitutes *pravda* may be subject to debate.

Nonrelativistic

There can be no quantification of degrees of *istina.*

Istina can be relative or contingent upon prevailing beliefs and knowledge.

Applications

Journalism, politics, social reform, history, storytelling

Applications

Mysticism, religion or theology, philosophy, poetry and literature

Appendix 2. Profile of the Leading National Media Outlets in the 1990s

These data are published by the Freelance Bureau at http://www.flb.ru. For more details about Freelance Bureau (FLB), which is responsible for the publication of compromising materials on 150 Russian politicians, businessmen, and journalists, see Anna Ostapchuk and Evgenii Krasnikov, "'Kontora' pishet: na rynke kompromata predlozhenie, pokhozhe, uzhe prevyshaet spros," *Moskovskie Novosti*, July 11–17, 2000, 3. For ownership structure of the Russian media, see "Komu prinadlezhit Rossiia: Sredstva massovoi informatsii. Rasstanovka sil v sredstvakh massovoi informatsii," *Kommersant" Vlast'*, December 18, 2001, 68. The scheme of ownership does not contradict the affiliation listed in the classification below and suggests further links.

Argumenty i Fakty: the most popular weekly with a multi-million circulation. The most expensive for publication of kompromat, $18,000 per page. Regardless of the fee, the final decision to publish is taken by the editor in chief, who is financially independent and keeps no political alliances, which means that any material can be published.

Komsomol'skaia Pravda: second place in terms of popularity and cost. During the November–December 1999 preparliamentary election period, the newspaper earned $850,000 in pure profit from political commentaries alone. "Special order" pieces appear under the following rubrics: negative ones in "Open Tribune," "Point of View," "Informational Wars," and "Disputes" (*Razborki*); positive in "Open Tribune," "Press-Release," and "Business People" (*Liudi Dela*). The kompromat markup may reach 200 percent. *Komsomol'skaia Pravda* is owned by Vladimir Potanin (Interros); therefore, it does not publish anything against the various favorites of the proprietor (Chubais and Nemtsov) or long-term advertising clients. But any regional governor can be criticized.

Izvestiia: maintains the status of a serious and conservative newspaper. It belongs to Potanin's media holding, with a growing proportion of ownership held by Lukoil. All "sponsored" articles are framed with a discreet border.

Moskovskii Komsomolets: has a "yellow press" reputation; it is loyal to Luzhkov and discredits Berezovskii free of charge.

Moskovskie Novosti: tends to remain aloof from PR battles; it attempts to be neutral while staying loyal to Luzhkov and Smolenskii.

Vedomosti: has declared itself to be incorruptible, but financial independence is hard to sustain.

Nezavisimaia Gazeta: is in demand for the publication of minor PR materials; for some time it has been known for its loyalty to Berezovskii.

Pravda: an old familiar title, is actively used during elections campaigns, but never against Communists.

Rossiiskaia Gazeta: is supported by the state and therefore is not dependent on retail sales; the editor in chief is extremely careful not to lose his position. This paper tends to take money ($5,000 for a quarter page) from regional "mini-tsars" seeking positive interviews highlighting their local success.

Profil': the journal of the banking sector. It is cheap to hire and unselective in what it publishes, although it avoids insults or sharp language. It is used in massive PR campaigns.

Segodnia: former competitor of the *Nezavisimaia Gazeta,* belonging to Gusinskii (it was closed in 2001).

Kommersant and its satellites *Vlast'* and *Den'gi:* has very high fees. The main client for kompromat materials is Berezovskii, who has overwhelming influence over this newspaper.

Novye Izvestiia: used to be absolutely loyal to the Kremlin and Berezovskii, as illustrated by the 1999 parliamentary elections; recently the paper has been called anti-Kremlin on the grounds of its coverage of Chechnia. PR questions are dealt with efficiently and at a reasonable price.

Trud and *Tribuna:* friendly to Gazprom and Rem Viakhirev personally. Gas sponsorship began in 1995, when these outlets were called to support Chernomyrdin's political movement, "Our Home is Russia," and this has continued. Within the media market, *Trud* is still considered a competitor of *Komsomol'skaia Pravda,* but is considerably more reasonable—$8,500 per page. Tribuna charges $5,000. Kompromat markup is from 20 to 100 percent of the standard advertising fee.

Sovershenno Sekretno and *Versiia:* belong to the same holding company and are both pro-Luzhkov. They attack adversaries of the Moscow government. *Sovershenno Sekretno* charges $14,000 per page, but the price goes down for particularly interesting kompromat. *Versiia* charges $4,500, with 100 percent markup for "controversial material" (kompromat).

Novaia Gazeta: from the mid-1990s supported and was supported by the National Reserve Bank, Iabloko, and more recently, by Sibirskii Aliuminii. Editor in chief is considered principled. Officially, *Novaia* charges $3,800 per page, and kompromat costs $5,000, while urgent orders and guarantees of future editorial policy on the same matter amount to $8,000–$10,000.

Ekspert: not a very popular business magazine. It is used for "white" PR, or for ratings and graphs that feature a firm favorably. It was initially financed by Oneximbank and has sustained friendly relations with Potanin.

Kompaniia: a very interesting journal, initially financed by the National Reserve Bank but after 1998 has been left to its own devices. Fees are relatively low: $3,500 per page.

Ogonek: since 1995 financed (rather badly) by Berezovskii and Smolenskii. Issues during the 1999 parliamentary elections period reflect the orientation of Berezovskii and Pavlovskii. A page in color costs $4,000, black and white $2,500.

Megapolis, SPID-info, Ekspress-gazeta: all yellow press outlets. The first two are extremely successful and prefer to avoid political involvement, whereas *Express-gazeta* is both active and not particularly selective on the kompromat front. It belongs to Interros holding company and charges $2,500 per page, plus an additional 40 percent for kompromat.

Sovetskaia Rossiia: used in emergencies, for material that no other outlet is willing to publish. It charges 1,900 rubles for a manuscript page plus an additional charge of 20–100 percent for anything of a "controversial nature."

Zavtra: has an original approach—it charges $1,000 for kompromat material that is in accordance with the views of the paper. Otherwise the cost is $4,000.

Appendix 3. "Bound by One Chain"

СКОВАННЫЕ ОДНОЙ ЦЕПЬЮ
(В. Бутусов—И. Кормильцев)

Bound by One Chain
(Viacheslav Butusov—Il'ia Kormiltsev)

1

Круговая порука мажет, как копоть.
Я беру чью-то руку, а чувствую
  локоть,
Я ищу глаза, а чувствую взгляд
Там, где выше голов находится зад,
За красным восходом—розовый
  закат,
Скованные одной цепью,
Связанные одной целью,
Скованные одной цепью,
Связанные одной . . .

1

Krugovaia poruka sticks like glue.
I want friendship but feel pressure,
I look for eye contact but feel watched,
Where the position is more important
  than what we think,
Following the red sunrise is a pink sun-
  set,
Bound by one chain,
Tied by one aim . . .

2

здесь составы вялы
а пространства огромны
здесь суставы смяли
чтобы сделать колонны
одни слова для кухонь
другие для улиц
здесь брошены орлы
ради бройлерных куриц
и я держу равнение даже целуясь
на скованных одной цепью
связанных одной целью
скованных одной цепью
связанных одной целью . . .

2

Here trains are slow and spaces are vast
Here joints are compressed to make lines
Some words are for kitchens and others
  for the streets,
Here the strongest are extinct for the
  sake of the weak,
And even while kissing I keep up with
  those
Bound by one chain
Tied by one aim . . .

3

можно верить и в отсутствие веры
можно делать и отсутствие дела
нищие молятся молятся на
то что их нищета гарантирована
здесь можно играть про себя на
  трубе
но как не играй все играешь отбой
и если есть те кто приходит к тебе
найдутся и те кто придет за тобой

3

It's possible to believe in the absence of
  faith
It's possible to be occupied doing nothing
The poor pray for their poverty to be
  guaranteed
You can think of change but only in
  your head
But whatever you think it will come to
  nothing

также скованные одной цепью
связанные одной целью
скованные одной цепью
связанные одной . . .

4
здесь женщины ищут
но находят лишь старость
здесь мерилом работы
считают усталость
здесь нет негодяев
в кабинетах из кожи
здесь первые на последних похожи
и не меньше последних
устали быть может
быть скованными одной цепью
связанными одной целью
скованными одной цепью
связанными одной целью . . .
скованные одной цепью
скованные . . .

And if there are those who come to talk
    to you
There will also be those who will come
    for you.
Also bound by one chain
Tied by one aim . . .

4
Here women are searching
    but find only old age
Here the measure of work is tiredness
Here there are no bad guys in offices
    made of leather
Here the highest in rank look like the
    lowest
And the former might be as tired as the
    latter
To be bound by one chain
Tied by one aim . . .

Appendix 4. List of Legal Documents Related to Barter Transactions in the Russian Federation, 1990–1997

Date	Reference	Issuing institution	Name of document
16 April 1990	24B	Ministry of Finance of the USSR	Letter "On accounting for barter-based export-import operations"
30 October 1992	16-05/4	Ministry of Finance of the RF	Letter "On rules for reflecting in accounting the exchange of goods or barter-based dealings"
12 February 1993	ЮУ	State Taxation Service of the RF	Letter "On rules of confirmation of barter-based dealings"
23 May 1994	4-06/17н 1006	President of the RF	Decree "On implementation of complex measures on timely and complete payment of taxes and other mandatory payments"
		Civil Code of the RF	Agreement about *Ustupka trebovaniia*, chapter 24, articles 382, 383, 990, 993, 168 (from 'Advice of the lawyer," October 1997; also includes cases from the arbitration court)
18 August 1996	1209	President of the RF	Decree "On state regulation of the export trade barter operations"
20 September 1996	C1-7/03-572	High Arbitration Court of the RF	Letter "About the presidential decree 'On state regulation of export trade barter operations'"
31 October 1996	1300	Government of the RF	Decision "On measures of state regulation of the external trade barter dealings"
31 October 1996	T-22488	State Customs Committee of the RF	Telegram regarding implementation of the presidential decree of 18 August 1996, No. 1209, "On state regulation of export trade barter operations"
24 December 1996	ВК-6-16/883	State Custom Service of the RF	Letter "On tightening control over the taxation of products sold on cash and barter basis"
13 March 1997	Ministry of Justice number 1296, from 24 April 1997	Ministry of External Economic Relations	Order for issuing licenses for conducting certain barter dealings within the jurisdiction of the presidential decree of 18 August 1996, No. 1209, "On state regulation of export trade barter operations," paragraph 3

Date	Reference	Issuing institution	Name of document
31 March 1997	12	High Arbitration Court of the RF	Letter "Review of the practice of implementation of the Arbitration Process Code of the RF in consideration of the cases by cassation instance" (source: "Legal Consultant," No. 7, 1997)
11 April 1997	01-23/6678 Ministry of Justice registration number 1315, from 27 May 1997	State Custom Committee of the RF; Ministry of External Economic Relations and Trade; Federal Service on Foreign Currency and Export Control	Provision "On conducting control and accounting of external trade barter dealings that include the movement of goods across the border of the RF"
17 April 1997	204	Ministry of External Economic Relations	Order on introducing "The Instruction about violations of the requirements of import of goods, work, services, outcome of intellectual activity to be equal to the price of export goods, work, services, outcome of intellectual activity during barter dealings"
28 May 1997	07-26/3226 Ministry of Justice number 1338, from 30 June 1997	Federal Service on Foreign Currency and Export Control	Provision "On conducting control and accounting of external trade barter dealings that include labor, services, and intellectual activities expressed in material or monetary equivalents (*vyrazhennykh v materialnoi forne*) on the territory of the Russian Federation"
1, 3, 9 July 1997	10-83/2508, 01-23/13044, 07-26/3628	Ministry of External Economic Relations; State Custom Committee; Federal Service on Foreign Currency and Export Control	List of documents, regulating works and services, and rights over the outcome of intellectual activity during external trade dealings
14 July 1997	01-15/13368	State Custom Committee	Letter "On implementing provisions of the Customs Code of the RF during violation of the customs rules of export during external trade barter dealings"

Appendix 5. List of Respondents

Below is a list of respondents quoted in the text and identified by a code, in square brackets, containing the number of the chapter in which that respondent is cited most often, followed by the number of the respondent. The fieldtrips are presented in reverse chronological order and subdivided into three groups covering: (1) experts on PR, media, and informational security subjects; (2) experts on the Russian economy and its dependence on informal ways of getting things done; and (3) experts on crime, barter, small business, and present-day tolkachi. The respondents are further identified by occupation, city of residence, gender (M or F), and age.

Interviewed in 2000–2001 (PR, Media, and Informational Security Group)

2.1 Senior technologist of a leading PR firm, Moscow, F, fifty
2.2 PR director of a leading PR firm, Moscow, M, in his fifties (two interviews)
2.3 Founder and technologist of a leading PR firm, M, in his forties (two interviews)
2.4 Technologist of a leading PR firm, Moscow, M, in his forties
2.5 Lawyer and regional campaigner, Novosibirsk, M, in his thirties
2.6 Expert of a think tank, Moscow, M, in his forties
2.7 Founder and technologist of a PR firm, Moscow, M, in his thirties
2.8 Business PR specialist at a transnational firm, Moscow, in thirties
2.9 PR specialist and campaigner of a center-left political party, Moscow, M, in his thirties
2.10 PR specialist and regional campaigner, Novosibirsk, M, thirty
3.11 Sportsman and a head of a private security firm, sportsman, St. Petersburg, M, in his thirties
3.12 Head of agency of investigative journalism, St. Petersburg, M, forty
3.13 Security officer and former policemen, St. Petersburg, M, forty
3.14 Security officer in an oil company, St. Petersburg, M, in his forties

Interviewed in 1999–2000 (Davos Group and Legal Experts)

3.15 Political lobbyist, a Kremlin insider, Moscow, M, in his forties
3.16 Former diplomat, PR representative of a media empire, Moscow, M, fifty
3.17 Successful industrialist, Moscow, M, thirty
3.18 Founder of a British security firm working in Moscow for U.S. and U.K. companies, M, in his fifties
3.19 Owner of a big bank, Moscow, M, fifty (two interviews)
3.20 Owner of one of the biggest industrial groups, Moscow, Urals, M, in his forties
2.21 Top journalist, Moscow, F, mid-thirties
3.22 One of the leaders of a rightist political party, Moscow, F, forty-five
3.23 Financial expert working as consultant in an intermediary firm, well connected in political and business circles, M, forty

3.24 Owner of a medium-sized bank, Moscow, M, in his fifties

3.25 Official in a state-owned precious stones company, Moscow, M, in his sixties

3.21 One of the leaders of a populist political party, Moscow, M, in his sixties

3.26 Deputy of State Duma, Committee of Natural Resources, Moscow, M, forty-five

6.27 One of the leaders of a center-left political party, Moscow, M, in his late forties

6.28 Owner of a medium-sized bank, Moscow, M, in his fifties (two interviews)

6.29 Director of a federal audit firm, Moscow, M, fifty

5.30 Businessman who made his fortune on barter deals, Moscow, M, in his late fifties

7.31 Officer of the Ministry of Finance and tax expert, F, in her forties (two interviews)

6.32 Auditor of a regional audit firm, F, in her fifties (three interviews)

6.33 Lawyer and consultant at a legal firm, F, in her fifties (three interviews)

6.34 Accountant of a multinational firm, Moscow, F, in her forties

6.35 Judge, Tomsk, F, in her forties

Interviewed in 1997–1998 (Crime, Barter, Small Business, Regions)

7.36 General, regional department of the fight against organized crime, St. Petersburg, M, in his sixties

7.37 Deputy head of a regional department of the fight against organized crime, St. Petersburg, M, in his fifties

7.38 Head of the corruption and bribery branch at a regional department of the fight against organized crime, St. Petersburg, M, in his forties

7.39 Businessmen, Moscow, M, in his late forties

5.40 General, fund of support for former military and security officers, Urals, M, in his sixties

5.41 Co-owner and chief executive of a large privatized enterprise, Urals, M, in his fifties

5.42 Manager in charge of economic development of a large enterprise, Urals, M, in his forties

5.43 Tolkach, specialist on making barter schemes work, Urals, M, fifties

5.44 Director of a spin-off firm, Urals, M, fifties (two interviews)

5.45 Manager for supplies and deliveries department at a large enterprise, M, in his sixties

5.46 Accountant of a spin-off firm, Novosibirsk, F, in her forties

5.47 Entrepreneur, running small industrial business in Urals, M, in his fifties (2 interviews)

5.48 Entrepreneur, running small business in services in Moscow and Far East, F, in her forties (two interviews)

5.49 Small business entrepreneur, Siberian border with Kazakhstan, F, forty-five

5.50 Ministerial official, coal industry, Moscow, Kuzbass, M, in his sixties

Appendix 6. List of Questions

Questions about PR

What is black PR and why is it so widespread in the 1990s?

Which functions does PR have in electoral campaigns?

Who is behind black PR?

What do PR companies do?

How significant are sociological polls or so-called marketing research for the PR specialists? What does "knowing the electorate" involve?

Use of images is an important constituent of PR campaigns. What are the Russian specifics of working with images, especially in the context of party formation?

Which legal restrictions enable PR practices?

Which loopholes are particularly often used?

What are the main problems in the legal side of the elections?

How would you prioritize these problems?

Black finances for elections seem to be commonplace in the 1990s, but how widespread is the direct bribery of the electorate? Are there rural/urban specifics?

Which forms of "administrative resource" are used in the election campaigns? Rank their significance.

How common is the instrumental use of law enforcement agencies in the regional elections?

What are the practical channels of exerting administrative pressure on the media?

Could you assess the capacity of electoral commissions in sustaining/undermining the legality of elections? Please give examples.

What are the functions of lawyers working for PR companies during the election campaigns?

How open is competition between PR firms working, say, in regional elections?

Questions about Kompromat

Is it relevant to speak about kompromat as a phenomenon? How would you define it?

Why is kompromat so prominent in Russia?

Why has kompromat been so omnipresent in the 1990s? Who is responsible?

What are the sources of kompromat?

Who are the collectors of kompromat?

What are the rarest and the most common types/cases of kompromat?

What are the functions of kompromat? Give examples.

What happens behind the scenes, before the kompromat gets leaked to the press?

Which channels are used for obtaining kompromat?

Who are the intermediaries/guarantors in kompromat transactions?

How do the mechanisms of mutual restraint and prevention of the release of kompromat work?

How can kompromat be used? What are its powers and limitations? Instructions for use?

There are a few big stories, like the Shkuratov story, but how widespread is the "making" of kompromat?

Which discrediting information does not constitute kompromat?

Are there any legal loopholes that are specifically associated with kompromat?

Are there ownership or property rights in relation to kompromat?

Is there a link between kompromat and violence?

Please give examples of kompromat that is available but not used; used and effective; used but inefficient and not published; used, inefficient, and published; or used, inefficient, published, and unnoticed.

How reliable are websites? Which ones are better?

How reliable is the information about the costs of kompromat in the media?

Are there any general trends in kompromat's past and present?

Have you heard of lustration? What are the prospects for lustration in Russia?

Does kompromat really work?

Questions about the Russian Economy and Its Dependence on Informal Ways of Getting Things Done

Questions about Russia and the World Economic Forum (WEF)

Have you attended the WEF before? How many times? Do you notice any tendencies in the interest of the Forum toward Russia?

Did you feel that you/your company attracted the interest of foreign colleagues/companies? Did you make any business contacts at the Forum?

Did you have the impression that Russians circulate only among themselves at the Forum?

Primakov has emphasized that it is essential to make "the rules of the game transparent." How would you define the nontransparency of the rules of the game?

Questions on the Russian Economy and Globalization

What difficulties do you see in the integration of the Russian economy into the international business community?

How would you define openness and closeness in the Russian economy?

Are you working under the pressure of competition with overseas firms?

What are the specifics of the Russian market? In your sector?

Do you think that the thesis about the "virtual economy" in Russia describes the situation adequately? In your sector?

The roots of the virtual economy are associated with the Soviet legacy. But is such a legacy fully negative for the current developments? Could it also be protecting people and companies from the exigencies of the market? Could you think of some examples to this effect?

Defective economic systems, as a rule, produce some compensatory mechanisms (the more oppressive the systems are, the more safety valves they need). For example, the workings of the planned economy were provided for by the informal networks and personalized ties widespread in managerial structures. To mention just a few widely known phenomena: tolkachi, telephone justice (*telefonnoe pravo*), personal ties (*svoi liudi*), party pressure, and other forms of informal leverage. Do analogous practices exist today? What has changed?

How have the relationships between the center and the regions changed in the market context?

In which sense do the economic methods (the market) not work? What are the reasons for that? What would you consider to be antimarket forces in the Russian economy in the 1990s?

Questions about Unwritten Rules, Blat, and the Shadow Economy

One hears a lot about the *bespredel* in Russia today. On the other hand, many of these developments are predictable. If they cannot be explained rationally from an economic point of view, it does not mean that we cannot understand them. It is just that this sort of order is more difficult to describe in market terms as it is run by what we call "unwritten rules." Do you think you could try to formulate some of these unwritten rules? (Sometimes it's easier to think about rules through the examples of how they are broken.)

The Soviet economy was coupled with fairly ubiquitous practices of blat. What is happening to blat in the 1990s?

How did the blat networks change?

Can one say that the scale of the shadow economy today is understandable? What makes the shadow economy so pervasive?

Final Questions

How would you define your top three problems in business/work?

Where can I find published interviews with you and press releases in association with your company?

Thank you!

Questions about Barter, Financial Scheming, and Post-Soviet Tolkachi

What percentage of the business transactions in your region are barter transactions? In your sector? At your enterprise? How unique is your situation?

Is it possible to operate without money?

Which function does barter perform?

Do you use barter for paying wages to employees?

What kind of barter goods are in demand of your employees? What would they take instead of money?

Do you feel compelled to engage in this practice?

Which money surrogates are used in your region?

What are the most common barter schemes?

Does barter work in transactions with foreign partners?

Do barter schemes involve cash?

What are the sources of cash at your enterprise?

How do you work out the prices used in barter transactions?

How complicated or clever are these schemes? Who designs them?

Which promissory notes do you trust to include in your schemes?

Which goods are most liquid if you need money surrogates for your purposes?

Does liquidity depend on demand, or are there other factors defining it?

How long does it normally take to complete a barter scheme?

Please give some examples of quick and slow barter transactions.

What is the role of trust in barter transactions?

What are the risks involved? How often do partners let each other down?

Who are your partners? Do you work with firms specializing in intermediary functions?

Who runs these intermediary firms?

Do you know all your partners personally? Do you employ anybody to follow up these contacts?

How do you establish and maintain relationships with barter partners?

Do you use courts and other law enforcement agencies to pressure your partners?

What does personalization of relationships involve: flowers, chocolates, drinking tea?

Do you still support social services for the employees of your enterprise (kindergarten, health resorts, etc.?) Has the role of the collective changed in the 1990s?

Does your relationship with the town authorities help to deal with arrears and to conduct barter transactions?

Are there any parallels between dependence upon partners in a barter scheme and krugovaia poruka?

Do criminalized schemes work in a similar way?

Do you use tolling schemes and *daval'cheskoe syr'e?*

Are these barter schemes conducive to krugovaia poruka?

(See also the questions in the interview with Tatiana in chapter 7.)

Notes

Introduction

1. As Vera Dunham put it in her *In Stalin's Time*, "backscratching is the least sinister and most functional aspect of Stalinist bureaucracy, its most human feature without which the economy could not survive. It is, in fact, a second, albeit illicit, national economy: the Soviet name for it is *blat*" (1976/1990, 15). Joseph Berliner (1957) and Klaus Mehnert (1958/1962, 87–89) emphasized the indispensability of *tolkachi* for the workings of planned economy.

2. See Ledeneva 1998, 175. Blat can generally be associated with pulling strings and using connections, with influence peddling and fixing, with networking or the "old-boy" network phenomenon. Most Russian language dictionaries contain the prerevolutionary meaning of blat, which refers to criminal activity, although it was generally used to mean less serious kinds of crime, such as minor theft. In the vernacular, "by blat" (*po blatu*) means "by acquaintance" (*po znakomstvu*) and would be used to mean ways of obtaining (*dostat'*) or arranging (*ustroit'*) something using connections.

3. These have been referred to as "social bribes," to include bribes in health and education. See "Spor o vziatkakh," http://www.vedomosti.ru, June 18, 2003 (accessed April 2003).

4. See http://www.indem.ru and INDEM data in "$38 mlrd na lapu," *Vedomosti*, May 22, 2002, http://dlib.eastview.com/sources/article.jsp?id=4142985 (accessed March 22, 2005).

5. Ibid.

6. Needless to say, not every frequently used idiom was helpful, and I will address this point in more detail in a theoretical discussion in Chapter 1. The opposite was also

sometimes true: the word *tolkachi* is not used much but is very useful for grasping the range of practices described in Chapter 7.

7. See Eva Busse, "The Formal and Informal Workings of Russian Taxation: The Case of Small and Medium Sized Enterprises in Western Russia 1999–2000" (PhD diss., Cambridge University, 2002); and Yuko Adachi, "Informal Corporate Governance Practices in Russia in the 1990s: The Cases of Yukos Oil, Siberian (Russian) Aluminium, and Norilsk Nickel" (PhD diss., University College London, 2005).

8. Igor Malashenko interviewed by Tatiana Koshkareva and Rustam Narzikulov, "SShA vse eshche vliiaiut na vybory presidenta Rossii," *Nezavisimaia Gazeta*, November 4, 1998, 8.

9. T. I. Kutkovets, A. I. Grazhdankin, I. M. Kliamkin, and I. I. Iakovenko, "Samoin-defikatsiia rossiian v nachale XXI veka" (project presented by the consulting firm Nikkolo M for the "*Klub-2015*"), http://www.club2015.ru; A. Kabakov, A. Gelman, and D. Dragunskii, *Stsenarii dlia Rossii: Tri povestvovaniia o budushchem* (Moscow, 1999); and many others.

10. See the discussion of the "system" in Karklins 2005.

11. For a brief history of the emergence of the independent press in Russia see "Komu prinadlezhit Rossiia: Sredstva massovoi informatsii. Istoriia: 1991–2000" in *Kommersant" Vlast'*, December 18, 2001, 62–66.

Chapter 1. Why Are Informal Practices Still Prevalent in Russia?

1. Andrei Shleifer and Daniel Treisman sum up the debates about whether Russia is a normal country and state their affirmative position in "A Normal Country?" *Foreign Affairs*, March–April 2004.

2. According to the Business Environment and Enterprise Performance Survey (BEEPS), developed jointly by the World Bank and the European Bank for Reconstruction and Development (EBRD), conditions in Russia improved significantly between 1999 and 2002. BEEPS is a survey of managers and owners of firms across the countries of Central and Eastern Europe (CEE), the former Soviet Union (FSU) and Turkey designed to generate comparative measurements of the quality of governance, the investment climate and the competitive environment, which can then be related to different characteristics of enterprises and enterprise performance. Russia is ahead of other FSU countries but behind all CEE economies. While the "bribe tax as percent of total sales" has gone down in both Russia (from 4.1 percent in 1999) and CEE (from 2 percent) to 1.6 percent in 2002, the percentage of "firms paying bribes frequently" in Russia has gone up from 29 percent to 39 percent (in CEE it fell from 32 percent to 26 percent) over the same period. See http://info.worldbank.org/governance/beeps2002/ (accessed July 2003).

3. The sale of the Tiumen Oil Company (TNK) to British Petroleum for $6.75 billion is arguably the most significant foreign purchase in Russia. British Petroleum Press Release, February 11, 2003.

4. The Non-Cooperating Countries and Territories (NCCT) list includes fifteen countries. See FATF website, www.oecd.org/fatf/, and the 2002 NCCT Report, http://

www.fatf-gafi.org/pdf/NCCT2002_en.pdf (accessed April 2004). See also Putin's commentary on the FATF decision in "Russia to Become FATF Member," October 14, 2002, http://www.pravda.ru.

5. "Commission Officially Recognizes Russia as a Market Economy Country," European Union Press Release, August 20, 2002. See also "Relations with the Countries of Eastern Europe, the Caucasus and Central Asia, and with Mongolia" Bulletin EU 5–2002, June 6, 1990, http://www.europa.eu.int/abc/doc/off/bull/en/200205/p106090 .htm (accessed April 2004).

6. For reflection on the investment climate in Russia see Pavlenko 2002, 48; "World Bank Gives Estimate of Capital Flight from Russia," October 29, 2002, http://www.pravda.ru; Chrystia Freeland, Andrew Jack, and Arkady Ostrovsky, "Russia For Sale," *Financial Times*, October 6, 2003, 17.

7. Chernomyrdin was the longest-serving Prime Minister of Russia in the 1990s and one of the most experienced practitioners of the system.

8. The volume of Cypriot investments in Russia accumulated as of October 1999 was $3,214 million, while the volume of French investments was $3,350 million and that of Great Britain was $3,584 million. In view of its accession to the EU, Cyprus is changing its policies (Aleksashenko et al. 2000, 362).

9. For facts and figures see, for example, Maria Kakturskaia, "Nalogoviki sobiraiut kompromat," *Argumenty i Fakty*, July 19, 2000, 8.

10. Oxbridge unwritten rules are spelled out in Cornford (1908).

11. Analysis of networks has contributed to the conceptualization of informal practices that are both supportive and subversive of the institutional framework. Networks used for blat purposes are not exclusively blat networks. Although one might choose to study blat networks and the ways they operate, what one studies in this case is but one aspect of personal networks, the origins and functions of which go beyond their blat applications. Study of networks and their functionality contributed to my understanding of the ambiguity of networks (Ledeneva 2004a). Networks provide channels for and are conducive to practices that both support and subvert the institutional framework.

12. On difficulties of articulation of the implicit rules see Alexandra Daugavet "Neformal'nye praktiki rossiiskoi elity (Aprobatsiia kognitivnogo podkhoda)." Quoted in Yaroslav Starkov, see note 13.

13. See the discussion on unwritten rules in Yaroslav Starkov, "Informal Institutions and Practices: Objects to Explore and Methods to Use for Comparative Research. *Perspectives on European Politics and Society* 6, no. 2 (2004): 337.

14. I fully support the idea of comparative research of informal institutions presented by Helmke and Levitsky (2004) and find their typology of informal institutions useful, but I also have a few reservations about associating blat with an informal institution of the accommodating type. It is arguable whether one can assume that the formal rules were mostly enforced under the Soviet regime (a type-creating criterion in Helmke and Levitsky typology). According to my research, the Soviet system in its late years operated on the basis of a "system of suspended punishment," and *blat* practices served in multiple capacities, some of which would fall into competing and substitutive types in the Helmke and Levitsky typology, although not necessarily in a political field.

15. North avoids using the term "informal rules" in his book; the term does not ap-

pear in the index and only rarely in the text. He refers instead to informal constraints as opposed to formal rules.

16. North introduces another important distinction: between institutions and organizations (1990, 5). His own focus is on the interaction between institutions, which are the underlying rules of the game, and organizations.

17. It should be mentioned that some scholars successfully integrate rules and players into one category. For example, Guillermo O'Donnell defines institutions not as rules but as the actors' perception of the rules and their regularized practices: "By an institution I mean a regularized pattern of interaction that is known, practiced, and accepted (even if not approved) by actors who expect to continue interacting under the rules sanctioned and backed by that pattern" (1996, 34).

18. Hans-Joachim Lauth (2000) introduces three types of interactions between formal and informal institutions: complementary, substitutive, and conflicting (when the two systems of rules are incompatible). Helmke and Levitsky's typology (2004) includes complementary, accommodating, competing, and substitutive informal institutions. It attempts to remedy the asymmetry of Lauth's typology but by introducing a criterion of effectiveness of formal rules in distinguishing their types, they also prioritize formal rules and define informal institutions through them. Essentially, their types are construed on the basis of assumptions that formal rules are legal and useful and that it is normal and possible to follow them. This is not how it appears from the participants' perspective in the context of Russian transition.

19. Hans-Joachim Lauth defines "parasitic institutions" as informal institutions that live at the expense of formal institutions, "by exploiting them for their own purposes, by either partially occupying or penetrating them. In this sense they are parasitic institutions which, for example, find their expression in corruption. Such institutions, which should be understood, so to speak, as 'penetrating' environments, evade to a considerable degree any quantitatively oriented empirical analysis. This is because they do not change the form of formal institutions and 'shy away from publicity' themselves. At the same time, however, their relevance is not to be underestimated, as they are capable of exerting quite considerable pressure upon the way in which formal institutions function" (2000, 29).

20. North (1990) shows that when people perceive the structure of the rules of the system to be fair and just, transaction costs are low and enforcement costs are negligible, promoting economic efficiency. But when a system is perceived as unjust, transaction costs rise.

21. See Petr Aven "Ekonomika torga: O krakhe liberal'nykh reform v Rossii," *Kommersant-Daily*, January 27, 1999, 1, 4, 5.

22. As I am most concerned with practices relevant to the existing legal framework, I do not consider issues related to lobbying, or the elaboration or adoption of legislation that reflects various international and domestic pressures. The weakest areas of legislation in the 1990s are associated with property rights, minority shareholders' rights, creditors' rights, intellectual property rights, and the land code.

23. Iurii Biriukov, "Prokuratura bystrogo reagirovaniia," *Nezavisimaia Gazeta*, February 28, 2001, 8. Some measures to counteract these tendencies are starting to take place under Putin's administration. According to First Deputy Prosecutor-General Iurii

Biriukov, approximately 18,000 officials were charged with economic crimes last year, including more than 1,000 Interior Ministry officials, 120 customs officials, more than 20 tax police officials, 30 judges, and 10 prosecutors. ITAR-TASS, quoted from *RFE/RL Newsline*, February 13, 2001.

24. See "A Number of Regions Accused of Slacking in Bring [sic.] Local Laws in Line with Federal," *RFL/RL Newsline*, February 15, 2001, http://www.rferl.org/news line/2001/02/150201.asp (accessed July 2003).

25. See also "Chaika stroit diktaturu s novymi polnomochiiami," *Kommersant*, February 8, 2000, 3.

26. As a result of laws' being used as ammunition, there is uncertainty about the hierarchy of laws, a war of laws not won by legal means, and laws regarded as purchasable and dispensable (just like any other ammunition).

27. At the top level, the cases of oligarchs Gusinskii, Berezovskii and later on, Khodorkovskii are the best known.

28. For other institutions the division between those who have either full or some confidence and those who have not much or none is as follows: government, 31 vs. 65; parliament, 16 vs. 75; political parties, 11 vs. 79. For the media the numbers are a bit more balanced: 57 vs. 39 for state television; 53 vs. 33 for radio; 47 vs. 42 for the printed press; 38 vs. 40 for independent television; 7 vs. 10 for the Internet (Wyman 2002, 40). It should be mentioned, however, that trust in political institutions is generally low. According to a worldwide survey, politicians are least trusted (13 percent), whereas religious leaders are the most trusted (33 percent), followed by military/police leaders (26 percent), journalists (26 percent), and business leaders (19 percent). Only 4 percent of Ukrainians and 8 percent of Russians said they trusted military and police leaders (1 percent in Japan). See Brian Whitaker, "Politicians Are Voted the World's Least Trusted People," *Guardian*, September 15, 2005.

29. Respondents have mentioned (1) managerial accounts, (2) financial accounts according to Russian standards, (3) financial accounts according to international standards (where necessary), and (4) accounts for the purposes of taxation [6.29].

30. "*Pravda* subsumes not only correspondence with a known, or knowable, state of affairs (like English *truth*, in some of its uses), but also correspondence with norms and standards ('correctness'), and even correspondence with what is considered to be just and proper ('rightness')" (Mondry and Taylor 1992, 134). Berdiaev, in *Filosofskaia istina i intelligentskaia pravda* (1909), worried that "worldly, materialistic ideology, in its attempt to promote *pravda* (with its connotations of social justice), would leave no room for the pursuit of *istina*; that, in fact, *istina* would be reduced to the level of *pravda*." Forty years later he reiterated this fear, saying that the Russian intelligentsia "was always attempting to construct a unified, totalitarian worldview, in which '*pravda-istina*' would be made with '*pravda-spravedlivost'*'" (Mondry and Taylor 1992, 136).

31. For detailed data on state capture, see http://www.worldbank.org/wbi/governance.

32. Another example illustrates how in the run to the 2003 parliamentary elections, a new law was introduced in July 2003 prohibiting all illegal campaigning. Journalists were forbidden to report on information that would reflect candidates in a "positive or negative" light. Three months later the constitutional court ruled the law unconstitutional.

Chapter 2. *Chernyi Piar*

1. In the Yeltsin era the possibility of enacting major legal reforms was critically halted by the fierce political struggle between the president and the parliament.

2. Carothers (2002) describes consolidation as a slow but purposeful process in which democratic forms are transformed into democratic substance through the reform of state institutions, the regularization of elections, the strengthening of civil society, and the overall habituation of the society to the new "rules of the game." He concedes that many scholars offer caveats about the illusory tidiness of democratization, especially when elections do not equal democracy: transitional countries can go backward or stagnate, as well as make progress; sometimes the breakthrough process is drawn out, and sometimes it is rapid. According to Carothers, these caveats miss the central point: the problem is that even acknowledged deviations from the paradigm are rationalized in terms of the paradigm itself. As a result, the transition paradigm contains elements of this teleology by assuming that "the establishment of regular, genuine elections will not only give the new government democratic legitimacy, but will also foster a longer-term deepening of democratic participation and accountability" (7). During the Cold War it was commonly held that most Third World countries were not ready for democracy. The transition paradigm marked a break from that way of thinking, as the idea that there was a range of preconditions for democracy (relating to issues of wealth, class, institutional legacy, and political culture) lost ground to the belief that "all that seems to be necessary for democratization [is] a decision by a country's political elites to move towards democracy" (8).

3. Although helpful in identifying the fact that a number of states are not strictly democratic, Carothers (2002) maintains that these terms still implicitly locate states within the rubric of the transition paradigm by granting them the (qualified) label "democracy." The problem is that "by describing countries in the gray zone as types of democracies, analysts are in fact trying to apply the transition paradigm to the very countries whose political evolution is calling the paradigm into question" (10). Carothers suggests that "it is time to recognize that the transition paradigm has outlived its usefulness and look for a better lens" (6).

4. The term *piar*, from the abbreviation PR for public relations, has entered the Russian language without translation.

5. Viktor Shenderovich, "Unfettered Competition," January 28, 2002, at http://www.compromat.ru/main/pricelist/a.htm (accessed April 2005).

6. Russia's most infamous serial killer in the 1990s.

7. In the United States, the first PR company was organized in 1937. Between 1939 and 1955, this company conducted seventy-five political campaigns (Petropavlovskii et al. 1995).

8. Mikhail Kagan recalls: "Before I became a political consultant in 1996, I had a background in history, a master's degree in neuro-linguistic programming, or NLP. I had worked in archaeology, practical psychology, education, marketing, advertising, and public relations. What's surprising is that electoral technology combines all my professional experience. At least, I have never done anything more interesting than that" (Kurtov and Kagan 2002, back cover).

9. For systematic explanation of the role of political consultants in electoral campaigns, see Kurtov and Kagan (2002). Also see the "Kak vyigrat' vybory i mozhno li eto sdelat' chestno?" Film by Aleksei Khaniutin. Parallax Pictures. Russia, 2000, http://www.documentary.msk.ru/resources/movies. I am grateful to Professor Andrei Zorin for sending it to me.

10. Artur Akopov, "Politicheskie konsul'tanty o griaznykh tekhnologiiakh," *Vek*, December 17, 1999, http://www.nns.ru/Elect-99/info_war/stat/st51.html (accessed April 8, 2005).

11. Aleksei Sitnikov, Speech on the roundtable discussion at Central Election Commission, June 4, 1999, http://www.sitnikov.com (accessed July 12, 2003). See also Sitnikov 2000, 9.

12. Gai Khanov in Artur Akopov, "*Politicheskie konsul'tanty o griaznykh tekhnologiiakh*," December 17, 1999, http://www.nns.ru/Elect-99/info_war/stat/st51.html (accessed July 12, 2003).

13. The most expensive service, according to Oleg Tekhmenov, is the blocking of negative information. He claims that one of the most well-known Russian newspapers once agreed to block all negative articles about a certain politician for the duration of the election campaign for $750,000. Fedor Svarovskii, "Informatsionnye voiny ili kak spetsialisty po PR pokupaiut SMI," *Vedomosti*, January 28, 2002, http://www.compromat.ru/main/pricelist/lobbinet.htm (accessed April 8, 2005). See discussion of the costs of electoral campaigns in the film "Kak vyigrat'vybory i mozhno li eto sdelat' chestno?" Film by Aleksei Khaniutin. Parallax Pictures. Russia, 2000, http://www.documentary.msk.ru/resources/movies.

14. Valentina Borodina, "Dymovaia zavesa," *Profil'*, no. 41 (1999): 31.

15. Tat'iana Stepkova, "Imidzh 'po-chernomu,' a reklama 'po-belomu,'" *Sovetnik*, no. 3 (1997).

16. Andrei Grachev, "Nikelirovannaia pravda," *Sovetnik*, no. 11 (2002).

17. Lev Kadik and Gleb P'ianykh, "Rossiiskaia pressa okazalas' prodazhnoi," *Kommersant*, February 24, 2001, p. 1.

18. The numbers 1/8, 1/16, and 1/32 refer to the length of the material, part of a newspaper page.

19. Lev Kadik and Gleb P'ianykh, "Rossiiskaia pressa okazalas' prodazhnoi," *Kommersant*, February 24, 2001.

20. It does not have to be literally the same name. For example, the candidate Volchenko (a phonic association with "wolf" [*volk*]) could find himself competing against Zaichenko (a phonic association with "hare" [*zaiats*]). In a Russian version of the "Tom and Jerry" cartoon, the hare character is cute and smart, and always wins over the wolf.

21. Anna Nikolaeva, "Kandidaty s familiei: V Dumu idut Svetlana i Sergei Kprf." *Vedomosti*, November 6, 2003.

22. Among the most scandalous was the situation on June 19, 1996, three days after the first round of the Russian presidential elections and two weeks before the runoff between Yeltsin and his Communist rival Zyuganov, when the president's security service arrested two men at the exit gate of the Russian White House. Those arrested, Arkadii Evstaf'ev (an assistant to Anatolii Chubais, one of the key players in Yeltsin's election

campaign) and Sergei Lisovskii (who was in show business but also played an important role in Yeltsin's campaign and coauthored a textbook on electoral technologies), were carrying a Xerox-paper box containing $538,000 in cash. The money was to be used for payments to pop stars involved in pro-Yeltsin propaganda. According to their account, Evstaf'ev and Lisovskii had been handed the box by Boris Lavrov, a commercial bank officer, who in turn had received the money personally from the Russian Deputy Minister of Finance. The arrested men were released the following morning. Senior resignations followed, and the press published many controversial accounts of the incident. As Vladimir Gel'man claims, men with Xerox-paper boxes or sports bags full of cash could be found near every candidate's campaign headquarters. During campaigns almost every party and almost every candidate running for office in Russia used extralegal (though not always illegal) payments of cash of either doubtful origin (to put it mildly) or so-called black cash (*chernyi nal*). For details see Gel'man (2002).

23. Dmitrii Pushkin of the Siberian Ekspert Foundation for Political Technology and Prognosis, "Sibirskii Forum," talks about the established amount of the electoral fund as 264,000 rubles. At the same time, he says, it is a known fact that an electoral campaign costs two to three times more. "Ekspertnyi Opros," *Novaia Sibir'*, July 20, 2001. Also see Minchenko (2001, 19, 21, 23, 93) for the details of allocated budgets and the actual costs in the 1995 gubernatorial elections in Sverdlovsk oblast', the 1998 gubernatorial elections in Krasnoiarsk krai, and many others.

24. "Pasha-Discolights" is a nickname of the most popular figure associated with organized crime in the region.

25. Andrei Grachev, "Nikelirovannaia Pravda," *Sovetnik*, no. 11 (2002).

26. Several media cited a Swiss newspaper report that Mabetex president Bedzhet Pacolli admitted giving $300,000 to one of the candidates in Russia's 1996 presidential election. Pacolli did not say precisely to whose campaign he contributed. *Segodnya*, *Tribuna*, March 23, 1996. Each presidential candidate in 1996 was permitted to spend no more than $3 million, but the Yeltsin campaign is believed to have spent as much as one hundred times more than the legal limit. *Jamestown Foundation Monitor* 5, no. 57 (1999).

27. See Freeland (2000, 186–90) for the account of Davos pact.

28. Oleg Ovchinnikov, interview with Aleksandr Ivanchenko, chairman of the Central Election Commission, *Obshchaia Gazeta*, no. 3, January 21–27, 1999.

29. With regard to the 2003 parliamentary election, the OSCE report states that "CEC now plays a large role in deciding which parties get onto the ballot, and ultimately which candidates will be selectively rejected for minor infringements of the new election laws that have been passed since the last parliamentary elections. Although supposedly impartial, the CEC selectively ignored complaints from government opposition and allowed pro-Kremlin candidates to initiate deregistration proceedings as a way to remove rivals." OSCE official report, 18, http://www.osce.org/documents/odihr/2004/01/1947 _en.pdf (accessed July 2004).

30. Examples of candidates being selectively disqualified or prevented from registering are Iurii Shkuratov (Constituency 9, Buriatia), Aleksandr Rutskoi (Constituency 97, Kursk), and Andrei Kliment'ev (Constituency 120, Nizhnii Novgorod).

31. There are records of dialogues with the officials from the CEC who demonstrate both unwillingness and difficulty in dealing with candidates using administrative re-

source, such as Mr. Shoigu flying on the plane of the Ministry for Emergency Situations during his election campaign. See the dialogues at the CEC working group between complainants and advocates of the faction Unity in the speech of Dmitrii Levchik, Coordination Center "Clean Elections," http://www.indem.ru/idd2000/conf/levchik.html (accessed July 2004).

32. "Ekspert Opros," *Novaia Sibir'*, July 20, 2001.

33. See Petr Aven, "Ekonomika torga," *Kommersant-Daily*, January 27, 1999, 1, 4, 5.

34. Anatolii Gusakovskii, "Chernyi PR," undated, http://4p.ru/theory/t_black_pr_riso.html (accessed March 28, 2005).

35. See other arguments of the participants of the PR Congress in Moscow in *Segodnia*, February 23, 2000.

36. On the limitations of spin-doctoring in the context of the mayor of London election in 2000, see Cole Moreton and Jo Dillon, "How Tony's Spin-Doctors Made His Worst Political Nightmare Come True," *Independent on Sunday*, May 7, 2000, 14–15.

37. In his meeting with Valdai Discussion Club experts, President Putin quoted the number of people living below poverty line as 35 million people in 2002 and 25 million in 2004. Ten million Russians were lifted out of poverty in this short period of time. See http://www.valday2005.rian.ru (accessed September 2005).

38. Excerpt from an interview with Andrei Lebedev, "Black piar in Cheliabinsk?" *PR Klub-Rossiia XXI Vek,* a http://www.olersh.chat.ru/pr_noir.html (accessed September 2005).

39. "Administrative resource" is a post-Soviet phrase that was coined in Russia and used widely. For those not exposed to the modi operandi of administrative resource, this term is somewhat misleading. First, it is not strictly speaking a *resource*. It is about abuse of one's power and the *diversion* of resources to some political or economic advantage. Second, it is not strictly *administrative*. The point is to stretch over and control areas beyond the administrative system, such as the courts, media, electorate, etc. Third, the phrase is used in electoral contexts and creates an impression that it applies to politics. But administrative resource is *not exclusively about politics*. It can be associated with every sphere. Finally, the association with elections creates an impression that this is a post-Soviet phenomenon. But in fact, it is about the *continuity* of goverance dependent on the violation of its own rules. Administrative resource relies on unwritten rules understood and shared by players. It is the conversion of the Soviet legacy, power, and nontransparency of the post-Soviet system for newly set purposes.

40. Aleksei Fomin, "Rodina slyshit, Rodina znaet," *Stringer,* June 2000, http://www.compromat.ru/main/pricelist/proslushka.htm (accessed August 8, 2003).

41. See also an interview with a former judge, Sergei Pashin, in chapter 7.

42. On a special project of organizing a "controlled" meeting in support of a candidate, see Kurtov and Kagan (2002, 246–48).

43. Kurtov and Kagan note that even violations of the law can be used manipulatively. The best-known example is Iavlinskii's overt and even televised campaigning in army regiments (banned by law) and presents to the electorate during the 2000 presidential campaign in the hope that he would be disqualified and therefore seen as an unfairly treated opposition leader (2002, 239).

44. What is important for political technologies is not only the final outcome of the

elections but also the tendencies and dynamics of the ratings. See "Besedy s Pavlom Klachkovym, rukovoditelem Krasnoiarskogo otdeleniia Tsentra Geopoliticheskikh Ekspertiz," September 2002, http://www.evrazia.krk.ru/pressa/round.shtm (accessed April 8, 2005).

45. Aleksandr Veshniakov in an interview with Vladislav Vorob'ev and Tamara Shkel', *Rossiiskaia Gazeta*, October 24, 2002, http://www.cikrf.ru/_1_en/int_vesh 211002_en.htm (accessed August 10, 2003).

46. Ibid. Similar optimism was expressed in 1999 by Aleksandr Ivanchenko, chairman of the Central Election Commission who identified the main attraction of the "dirty" technologies for some "experts" as money. "Besides, this money is not paid from the candidates' election funds. I think that future elections will not be able to do without loud scandals as a result of illegal financing." Oleg Ovchinnikov, interview with Aleksandr Ivanchenko, Chairman of the Central Election Commission, *Obshchaia Gazeta*, January 21–27, 1999.

47. Vladimir Pribylovskii, "Election Coverage: Will There Be Any?" *Moscow Times*, April 17, 2003, 2.

48. "Besedy s Pavlom Klachkovym," see note 44.

49. According to my respondent, the 2002 regional elections have shown that the situation in rural areas is changing. The communist electorate has turned pragmatic. Instead of predictable voting for a communist candidate, they start asking them: "What can you do for us? The director of petrol station has organised a free bus service to the town, what can you do?" People indeed have become more pragmatic [2.5].

50. The 2001 law on political parties has reduced their number and eliminated "political movements" from the electoral scene. Parties with fewer than 10,000 members, or branches in fewer than half the electoral regions, will be denied registration in an attempt to drastically reduce the number of parties able to register. Additionally, parties not wishing to register a list were forced to make a payment of 37.5 million rubles, compared with just two million in the previous elections in 1999. The cost of registering a candidate for single member districts was ten times higher than in 1999, which suggests that elections are becoming more exclusive since only the rich or well connected are able to secure registration, in addition to the cost of running media campaigns needed for a victory.

Chapter 3. *Kompromat*

1. Larisa Kislinskaia, "A Ministr-to golyi. Kak bankir Angelevich ministra priruchil," *Sovershenno sekretno*, June 1997, http://www.compromat.ru/main/kovalev/ a.htm.

2. The phrase "compromising materials" refers to evidence (dirt) compiled to damage (compromise) someone's reputation. In this sense it is close to kompromat, but it does not have the same connotations.

3. The *Tolkovyi slovar' sovremennogo russkogo iazyka: Iazykovye izmeneniia kontsa XX stoletiia* provides the following example for kompromat wars: "The loudest and

largest-scale, in terms of kompromat, "duel" of the past year was a fight over the sale of 25 percent of the state-owned AO Sviaz'invest. The desired shares went to Vladimir Potanin and the altruist savior of Russian science, George Soros." See *Profil'*, no. 49–50, 1997, 365–66.

4. Ibid.; see also Vitalii Tsepliaev, "KOMPROMATershchina," *Argumenty i Fakty*, December 27, 2000, http://www.compromat.ru/main/pricelist/vraki.htm compromat .ru (accessed May 10, 2005).

5. Irina Petrovskaia, "Razdrakonit' i zakleimit'," *Izvestia*, March 25, 2000, 8.

6. Michael Gordon, "Russian Mudslinging: State TV Targets Putin's Main Liberal Rival," *International Herald Tribune*, March 25, 2000, 2.

7. *Jamestown Foundation Monitor* 5, no. 30, February 12, 1999.

8. Ibid.

9. Shkuratov's resignation was tied up with a threat of exposure, followed by an outrageous broadcast of kompromat on the RTR TV channel, a videotaped film clip of a sexual scene with a "man who looked like Shkuratov," the phrase that has since become an idiom. The prosecutor general of the Russian Federation, Iurii Shkuratov, offered his resignation to the president on February 2, 1999. Among his reasons was the videotape, a one-and-a-half-year-old kompromat allegedly released by the then executive secretary of the CIS, Boris Berezovskii. The tape was circulated among members of the Federation Council before the March 17 vote, in which 142 out of 151 senators supported Skuratov's decision to withdraw his resignation. The next day, the videotape with its sexually explicit contents was shown on RTR. See Inessa Slavutinskaia and Alexandr Shan'ko, "Malen'kii gigant politicheskogo seksa," *Profil'*, March 22, 1999, 11–12.

10. It has been suggested that President Yeltsin's surprise decision to step down on the eve of the millennium after holding onto the reins of power so tenaciously for many years was due to his fear of kompromat and done in exchange for immunity. "While it is impossible to say with certainty that Yeltsin was made an ultimatum, there are some hints of this. The first is the decree Putin signed on December 31—his first decree as acting head of state—granting Yeltsin and his family full lifelong immunity from criminal prosecution. Not only does this suggest that Yeltsin's resignation was far from the 'impulsive, bold move' conjured up by the *New York Times*' editorial board, but it also strongly suggests that Yeltsin had something to fear. Indeed, Yeltsin may have been presented with two sets of documents—one outlining the immunity deal and the other privileges he would receive upon resignation, the other outlining what he would be prosecuted for if he refused to step down with alacrity." "Did 'Kompromat' Force Yeltsin Out?" *Jamestown Foundation Monitor* 6, no. 3, January 3, 2000.

11. Ibid.

12. Vice Governor Mikhail Manevich was assassinated in August 1997; Dmitrii Filipov (chairman of Menatep bank, St. Petersburg) was killed in October 1998; Galina Starovoitova was killed in November 1998; Pavel Kapysh (chairman of Baltic Financial Industrial Group) was murdered in July 1999; Viktor Novoselov was killed in October 1999.

13. Brian Whitmore, "Media Set Sights on Primakov, Yakovlev," *Moscow Times*, October 26, 1999.

14. Vadim Nesvizhskii, "A Criminal Election in St. Petersburg," *St. Petersburg Times*, November 24, 1998, 1 and 7.

15. Brian Whitmore, "The Strange Investigation of Galina Starovoitova's Murder," *Jamestown Foundation Prism* 5, no. 2, January 29, 1999, http://www.jamestown.org (accessed September 2005).

16. Oksana Iablokova, "Luzhkov Blamed for Death of Paul Tatum," *St. Petersburg Times*, November 9, 1999.

17. Whitmore, "Media Set Sights."

18. *RFE/RL Russian Election Report*, no. 1, November 5, 1999, http://www.rferl .org/specials/russianelection(accessed September 2005).

19. Ibid.

20. Petrovskaia, "Razdrakonit' i zakleimit'," 8.

21. Maria Fedorina, "Nazhivka dlya Nemtsova," *Moskovskii Komsomolets*, March 3, 1998.

22. Mikhail Berger, "Nemtsov's Ills as Warnings for Chubais," *Moscow Times*, August 5, 1997.

23. In February 1999 investigators from the prosecutor general's office raided the offices of Sibneft', where Abramovich was a general director. The raid turned up $8 million in Abramovich's safe, a photo of Abramovich kissing Tat'ana Diachenko, and files of compromising material against Iurii Luzhkov. See *Jamestown Foundation Monitor* 5, no. 34, February 18, 1999.

24. Roman Arshanskii, "Oborona Moskvy," *Moskovskii Komsomolets*, June 8, 1999, 1–2. See also *Jamestown Foundation Prism*, no. 12, June 18, 1999.

25. Arshanskii, "Oborona Moskvy, 1–2.

26. *RFE/RL Russian Election Report*, no. 7, December 17, 1999, http://www.rferl .org/specials/russianelection (accessed September 2005).

27. *AFP*, November 30, 1999.

28. *RFE/RL Russian Election Report*, no. 7.

29. See Russkoe obshchestvo postavshchikov informatsii (ROPI), *Berezovskii: Igra bez pravil* (Moscow: Rossiiskii pisatel', 2002).

30. Ibid.

31. Brian Whitmore, "Agendas Clash on Sunday TV News," *Moscow Times*, October 12, 1999.

32. On October 14 employees of the hospital published a letter in *Segodnia* refuting Pacolli's claims and stating that the reconstruction was in large part due to Luzhkov's efforts and the work of Moscow firms.

33. Whitmore, "Agendas Clash."

34. Iablokova, "Luzhkov Blamed for Death of Paul Tatum."

35. *AFP*, November 30, 1999.

36. Alexander Shashkov, "Luzhkov Demands R450 Million in Compensation from ORT," *TASS*, November 22, 1999.

37. Andrei Zolotov, "Luzhkov Returns Fire in TV Wars," *Moscow Times*, November 27, 1999. Also see RFE/RL Russian Election Report, no. 7. One has to note the comic similarity between these allegations against Luzhkov and those described by Shenderovich in his satirical piece reproduced in chapter 2.

38. Valeria Korchagina, "Luzhkov Faces Battle on All Fronts," *Moscow Times*, December 4, 1999.

39. Andrei Galiev, "Material'nye sekrety," *Ekspert*, December 20, 1999, 14.

40. Quoted by Iurii Skuratov, the then prosecutor general, June 1997.

41. Aleksei Fomin, "Rodina slyshit, Rodina znaet," *Stringer*, June 2000, http://www.compromat.ru/main/pricelist/proslushka.htm (accessed August 8, 2003.

42. See the discussion below on lustration.

43. *RFE/RL Newsline* 5, no. 95, part 1, May 18, 2001.

44. More detail on Internet projects in the 1990s is available in Mukhin (2000).

45. Some respondents quoted Kiselev's case (NTV presenter and director) in 2002 as a demarcation line: a tape analogous to Shkuratov's did not have much impact and was considered a private matter [2.4].

46. See also Darden 2001 on blackmail as a tool of state domination, and Naishul' (2000) on the market of shadow services (*rynok tenevykh uslug*).

47. Andrei Kniazev, "Komu prinadlezhit Rossia: Sredstva massovoi informatsii. Istoriia: 1991–2000," in *Kommersant-Vlast'*, no. 50 (452), December 18, 2001, pp. 61–70.

48. Sergei Pluzhnikov and Sergei Sokolov, "Skol'ko stoit kompromat?" Freelance Bureau, March 15, 2000, http://www.flb.ru/iw0005 (accessed November 2001).

49. Among the high-profile cases of murders of journalists, ORT channel General Director Vladimir List'ev was killed in 1993, and investigative journalist Dmitrii Kholodov was killed in 1994. This trend did not end in the 1990s. The editor of the Russian edition of Forbes, Paul Klebnikov, was shot dead in 2004.

50. Mukhin in his book *Informatsionnaia voina v Rossii* (2000) describes the main players and the use of special services, private security services, and consulting structures as well as Internet technologies and the institution of "media killers."

51. On business wars see Mukhin (2000) and Dinello (1998).

52. See Volkov (2002) on Uralmash.

53. As a result, their main competitor, Boris Govorin, the mayor of Irkutsk, acquired more than 50 percent of the votes as "the only candidate, who is not linked to Moscow financial circles and who can therefore defend the region in the center" (Minchenko 2001, 88–91).

54. See the classic literature on blackmail plus derivatives (Forward and Frazier 1998).

55. This comment refers to the period before the 1999 parliamentary election campaign and before the 1999–2000 memorable confrontation between the RTR and ORT television channels. The ORT campaign against Fatherland—All Russia became an unprecedented case of kompromat spillover onto public television. It was compared to "necrophilia," and according to Mukhin (2000, 45), the organization Doctors for Human Rights accused the ORT anchorman Sergei Dorenko of using technologies of neurolinguistic programming and "zombie-ing" the audience. As one political consultant described it, "It was not an information war—but rather an information rape of the whole country" [2.2]. In such circumstances, kompromat is best seen as a weapon of war and a means of symbolic violence.

56. "Material'nye sekrety," *Ekspert*, December 20, 1999.

57. According to some sources, the site was originally based on Media-MOST/flb.ru files. More detail on the Internet projects of the 1990s is available in Mukhin (2000).

58. The use of kompromat seems to be narrowing down under Putin, but it will take a detailed study to determine the trends of this process.

59. In June 2002, the website http://www.compromat.ru (accessed June 17, 2002) published a list of 216 deputies of the Duma against whom criminal investigations could be launched at any time if needed and an assessment of attitudes toward the abolition of deputies' immunity.

60. Vladimir Semago, "Lobbit' po-russki-2," *Novaia Gazeta*, July 17, 2000.

61. Vladimir Razuvaev, "A Compromising War," *Moscow Times*, January 9, 1997.

62. Similarly, no regional election campaign passes without the theme of at least some candidate's private wealth (cottage, apartment, and car) (Minchenko 2001, 21).

63. It certainly took courage to say it from the tribune of an academic conference at the time.

64. The term "lustration" is derived from the Latin word *lustrum*, which refers to expiatory sacrifices (or a purificatory rite).

65. For the detailed summary of the debate see Hornem and Levi (2004).

66. Stanley Cohen (1995) outlines the following phases through which transitional societies generally absolve themselves of the past: (1) establishing truth about the regime, (2) rendering justice for past abuses, (3) determining who is given impunity, (4) granting expiation, and (5) reconciling and reconstructing.

67. Moving to stabilize Russia's shaky business climate and to soothe fearful investors, President Putin told members of the Russian Union of Industrialists and Entrepreneurs in March 2005 that he favors a new law limiting investigations into 1990s-era privatizations. The law would reduce the statute of limitations on such inquiries to three years from ten. Erin E. Arvedlund, "Putin Sends Signal to Russian Oligarchs" *International Herald Tribune*, March 25, 2005, 1.

Chapter 4. *Krugovaia Poruka*

1. In Muscovite Rus' "surety bonds" (*poruchnye zapisi*) were drawn up "to cover debts and contractual obligations, military and administrative service, payment of fiscal levies, obligatory labor, trial procedure, personal conduct, public safety, political allegiance—and even matters of conscience and orthodoxy ('spiritual surety')" (Dewey 1988, 249).

2. For example, if payments to the treasury on customs and tavern income fell short, the difference could be exacted from local inhabitants. If a *poriadchik*, or local arm of the law, incurred any losses for the state treasury, the amount owed would sometimes be collected from the people living in the area in which the *poriadchik* lived. Similarly, when local *strel'tsy* divisions were formed from among free men in the region, their loyalty and service were ensured through krugovaia poruka; each *strelets* was responsible for making sure that the others fulfilled their obligations and would be forced to pay for any losses to the treasury incurred in the event that a *strelets* evaded military service (Brokgauz and Efron 1895). Krugovaia poruka was used to fulfill one's military requirement. A village was given a quota and decided who was to be sent into the twenty-five years of military service (Hosking 2001).

3. For more detail on the nature of peasant communes in relation to krugovaia poruka see Ledeneva (2004b).

4. There are reasons to believe that the communes' internal problem-solving mechanisms were not always conducted in a spirit of mutual cooperation and altruism. There are sources implying that the wealthier peasants may have benefited from the misfortune of their fellow villagers (Tian-Shanskaia 1993, 153–54) by delaying their tax payments until the poorer members of the community had paid (Simonova 1969) or by manipulating the system of krugovaia poruka and essentially becoming debtors themselves. To avoid a situation in which they would be forced to pay twice, they would hold off paying any taxes at all until the poorer residents of the village came up with their payments.

5. The following statistical data provided by authorities in the Tula province was typical: in the ten regions (*uezdy*) of the province, between 1887 and 1892 a total of 5,128 inventories of debtors' property were carried out, and 527 sales were conducted. From these sales, a total of 15,500 rubles was raised—a mere 7 percent of the overall amount of accumulated arrears (Simonova 1969). The arrears had grown to such an extent that no measures could ever possibly be successful in retrieving them, and no steps were taken.

6. The song was first performed in June 1986 and became part of their most popular album, Razluka, recorded in August 1986.

7. A Soviet anecdote depicts a director of an enterprise who interviews applicants for the position of main accountant. His standard question is, "What's two times two?" The "right" answer to get the job is, "How much do you want it to be, comrade director?"

8. Anatolii Kurchatkin, "Russian Thought," no. 4320, June 1 2000, http://www.rusmysl.ru.

9. Some analysts interpret Putin's decision in 2004 to revoke Yeltin's 1996 law on the elections of regional governors as an attempt to reclaim their loyalty to the center and to protect regional governors from the pressures of election campaigns by appointing them. Interview with Olga Kryshtanovskaya, February 2005, http://www.polit.ru.

10. The old Muscovite *druzhina*, held together by personal ties centered around a patron, played a dual military and political role and competed for favor and influence in Moscow (Easter 2000, 35).

11. Quoted from Ledeneva (2000a, 203). The interview was conducted at the Cambridge Annual Symposium on International Crime, Jesus College, Cambridge, September 1997.

12. See http://www.caricatura.ru/parad/?d=83&w=460.

13. The opposite argument can be found in Lane (1997).

14. See Russian version at http://www.rusglobus.net/meeting/lib/gustafson/6.htm#5.

15. For krugovaia poruka 7,393 pages come up on a yandex.ru search; a search for *blat*, commonly known but also not much spoken about, turned up 13,576 pages.

16. *Pravda* reported that the control of people tied by krugovaia poruka was getting stronger and stronger. *Pravda*, June 3, 1994.

17. Deputy Julia Rybakova argues that civil servants are the worst type of mafia, who have allowed corruption to flourish. The powers of civil servants are too great and they can manipulate the law freely. This is why corruption, violation of the law and human rights, and krugovaia poruka exist in all spheres of society. Krugovaia poruka saves the bureaucrat but undermines the rights of the person in need. A deputy who tries to help a person who has become subject to a civil servants' krugovaia poruka em-

barks on a lengthy battle despite the fact that the actual conflict is petty and could be solved at the lowest level. See *Nevskoe Vremia*, January 27, 2000.

18. See Dmitrii Bugrov, "Komu prinadlezhit Rossiia?" *Ekspert*, September, 2001.

19. The Gazprom management is notoriously known for these practices. See *Neftegazovaia gazeta*, http://www.nefte.ru/events/mart/sob_obz_270300.htm.

20. *Gazeta.Ru*, September 25, 2000, http://www.gazeta.ru/komprocherna.shtml.

21. *RFE/RL Newsline*, March 7, 2002.

22. *RFE/RL Newsline*, March 15, 2002.

23. See "Borodin Made a Mistake When He Transferred Millions of Dollars into His Accounts," http://www.rne.org/vopd/rusnews/rnew_32.htm (accessed July 2002).

24. See Paul Klebnikov's *Godfather of the Kremlin* (2000) and Freeland (2000); on Yeltsin's patriarchalism see Breslauer (2001).

25. "Putin gotovit nary dlia oligarchov po vsemu miru" ("Putin prepares punishment for oligarchs all over the world"), *KM-News*, January 21, http://www.km.ru/mag azin/view_print.asp. (accessed August 2003).

26. *Vedomosti*, December 29, 2001, http://www.vedomosti.ru.

27. See interview with Pavel Burdukov, vice chairman of the State Duma Anti-Corruption Commission, May 10, 2002, http://www.nadsor.vvsu.ru/articles (accessed February 2004).

28. "Du developpement des idees revolutionnaires en Russie," in *Collected Works in Thirty Volumes* (Moscow, 1954–61), 7:121, quoted in Iakovlev (1995, 10).

29. In her economic thrillers, Latynina provides multiple examples of situations where the logic of business is in conflict with the logic of krugovaia poruka and the interests of the local elites, which she defines as "earning a kopek, losing a ruble, but protecting one's power to do so and not letting people with wider interests intervene" (*Sarancha* 2001; *Stal'noi korol'* 2001; *Okhota na iziubria* 1999).

30. This aspect of recruitment is particularly important in the shady financial deals, organized through spin-off companies and trusted accountants [who have been taken out of trouble, employed but kept under control].

31. Although the divide between *svoi* and *chuzhie* (with corresponding moral codes) is characteristic of human societies in general and it is possible to argue that double standards are a fairly ubiquitous (albeit underresearched) phenomenon elsewhere, the Soviet case also suffers from the difference between public and private persona. As a private persona one thinks and does one thing, as a public persona and in public contexts—another. This doublethink has been referred to by many researchers (Levada 2004; Miller 2004; Zinoviev 1978) as significant for understanding both interpersonal and impersonal systems of trust in Russia.

Chapter 5. *Tenevoi Barter*

1. In an interview on a TV news program on the day of his resignation from the Duma. Reported in *Frankfurter Allgemeine Zeitung*, July 18, 2000.

2. *RFE/RL Newsline*, February 9, 2001. The current situation with tax collection has improved. OECD (2004, 36–39) reports the reform in the tax system diminished both incentives and opportunities for tax evasion.

3. "The Slow Flow of Direct Investment," *Euromoney: A Supplement*, Eastern Europe section, April, 1998.

4. Barter has become widespread in the former Soviet Union but not in Eastern Europe, even though value-subtracting enterprises were as common in the latter as the former. See Hare and Hughes (1991).

5. Tat'iana Korostikova, "Zaderzhka zarplaty—orudie v bor'be za vlast'," *Argumenty i Fakty*, no. 27, 1996, 11.

6. V. Nesterovich, "Etot gonimyi spasitel'nyi barter," *Ekonomika i Zhizn'*, no. 14, 1993, 1.

7. V. Butlevich, "Denezhnye surrogaty ne spasaiut biudzhet," *Ekonomika i Zhizn'*, no. 34, 1998.

8. These estimates are confirmed by the 1996 data of Kuznetsova and Butkevich. N. Kuznetsova and V. Butkevich, " 'Biudzhet v plenu neplatezhei," *Ekonomika i Zhizn'*, no. 24, 1996.

9. F. Glisin and A. Iakovlev, "Piataia chast' nalichnogo oborota v promyshlennosti okazyvaetsia nelegal'noi," *Finansovye Izvestiia*, no. 69, 1996.

10. See Jonathan Steele, "Blatting order," *Guardian*, August 8, 1998, 16.

11. T. Alimova and T. Dolgopiatova, "Strategiia predpriiatiia na rynke resursov," *Ekonomika i Zhizn'*, no. 8, 1998.

12. Sources for 1992–99 numbers: Aukutsionek S. et al. *Survey Statistics // Russian Economic Barometer*, no. 4, 1999; 2000 *RIA News*, Russia, December 5, 2000, 13:02 pm; *Segodnia*, January 31, 2001.

13. Barter may be a means whereby fulfillment of contractual terms can be more easily assured in the absence of a credible system of civil law.

14. In cases of capital flight, considered in detail in chapter 6, the payment is diverted by selling the product at a low price to one's intermediary, who then sells it more expensively and transfers the proceeds to offshore companies or private accounts. Some of these funds can then be used to serve the needs of the supplier (for example, to import equipment), or they may simply disappear.

15. See Iu. Latynina, "Surrogate Money: Reform's Illegitimate Child," *Izvestiia*, January 30, 1997, translated in *CDPSP* 49, no. 6 (1997): 8, 23; L. Shabalina, "Surrogaty vmesto deneg," *Ekonomika i Zhizn'*, no. 8, 1998; A. Iakovlev, "Anatomiia bezdenezh'ia," *Ekspert*, January 25, 1999, 27; L. Zhilinskaia, "Dolgi prodaete?" *Ekonomika i Zhizn'*, August 23, 1997.

16. Liubov' Shabalina, "Korporativnye vekslia," *Ekonomika i Zhizn'*, August 2, 1997; Stepan Pavlovskii, "Platit' po vekseliam teper' pridetsia spolna," *Izvestiia*, March 12, 1998, 1; V. Gendlin, "Birzhei bartera ne pereshibesh'," *Kommersant" Den'gi*, November 19, 1997, 34.

17. Andrei Volgin, "The End of the Virtual Economy" (presented at the U.S.-Russia Business Leaders Forum, May 1999), 2.

18. "Here Cash Isn't King: Barter Lines Pockets in Ex-Soviet States," May 1997, http://homeswipnet.se/w-10652/barter.html. See also Viktor Filippov, "Privatization II: No-Holds-Barred Asset Grab," *Izvestiia*, February 25, 1997, 2, in *CDPSP* 49, no. 8 (1997): 5; A. Galiev and T. Lysova, "Ego velichestvo zachet," *Ekspert*, January 25, 1999.

19. *Moscow Times*, May 20, 1997.

20. *Rossiiskie vesti* report on the increasing incidence of fraud with promissory

notes in 1997. By using fake promissory notes, the cheaters received foodstuffs and consumables for further sale. As a result, a number of shareholding companies in the energy sector have suffered severe losses, assessed at 100 billion rubles. It was discovered that cheaters had faked promissory notes exceeding 22 trillion rubles. During the arrest, the police also retrieved 886 faked promissory notes amounting to 11 trillion, 193 billion rubles, documents, faked headed paper and sealing stamps, and a database. Victor Lykov, "Velikie kombinatory popalis'," *Rossiiskie vesti*, October 7, 1997.

21. See the discussion of the nature of necessity in the next chapter.

22. Livshits was deputy prime minister and minister of finance of Russia in 1996–97; in 1997 deputy head of the administration of the president of Russia, the president's personal representative to the G7/G8 Summit; and as of 2004, deputy general director, Russian Aluminum.

23. "The banks were to conduct the operation in three days but often delayed so as to make it a week. So the Ministry of Finance transfers funds to the bank and in a week the bank returns the funds as tax (legally they were not allowed to use those funds). But in reality nobody knows. This is the scheme on a federal level. It is similar but a bit more straightforward on a regional level. That's how we paid all our taxes last year (1997)" [5.42].

24. *Kommersant Daily*, August 28, 1998, quoted in Tompson (1997, 1166).

25. In 1997 the head of the Department for Arrears Collection in the State Tax Service estimated that Gazprom was using 140 different accounts and other companies up to 300 different accounts, transferring money from one to the other as soon as the tax police began to investigate. *Moscow Times*, May 20, 1997.

26. "The government had its own problems to solve, so they pressured Viakhirev, he paid the taxes and ran out of resources. From last year (1997) we knew they went 'on conservation' (no growth). We used to supply for their construction projects twice as much as for their current needs. In 1998 it is in the reverse proportion. This is against the background of the absolute decrease in volume. To sustain our own level of production, we need to explore new possibilities. As the oil prices go down, oil companies start conservation as well. Many of them already sent us a warning that they will be delaying the placement of orders" [5.41].

27. To put it in economic terminology, barter transactions typically give rise to externalities.

28. The lock-in effect has been extensively studied in the literature on the economics of network competition. It refers to the fact that in presence of network externalities, firms may systematically choose intrinsically inferior technologies or production processes because they happen to be part of more developed networks.

Chapter 6. *Dvoinaia Bukhgalteriia*

1. "The Great Pretenders," *Economist*, August 21, 1999, 69.

2. On taxes and regulations as incentives for people to engage in illegal activities, see Benson and Baden (1985).

3. Larry Lambert, "Underground Banking and National Security," *Sapra India Bulletin*, March 1996, http://www.subcontinent.com (accessed in 2000).

4. Ibid.

5. Ibid.

6. Larry Lambert is a California-based specialist on Asian affairs and a consultant on international money-laundering issues. For details, see ibid.

7. Ibid.

8. Ibid.

9. An excellent account of black cash is provided in Iakovlev (1999). For money-laundering schemes, see, for example, the August 1999 Bank of New York scandal as reported in the September 1999 issues of the *Jamestown Foundation Monitor,* especially September 23, 1999, 23.

10. Alexander Solzhenitsyn, *The Gulag Archipelago* (London: Collins, 1976), 2:147–53. Quoted in Shenfield (1983, 243).

11. See the coverage of the Ingosstrakh-Avtobank conflict in which an offshore-based ownership structure was taken over with the help of a fake signature in the autumn 2002 issues of the newspaper *Vedomosti.*

12. See Iakovlev (1999).

13. See Aleksashenko et al. (2000, 364–68).

14. The assets have been reclaimed by the state since Aleksei Miller became chairman of Gazprom in 2001. See Stefan Wagstyl and Arkady Ostrovskii, "Gazprom Recovers 'All Core Assets,'" *Financial Times,* November 28, 2002, 30.

15. See in particular Rozinskii (2002), and also Wolosky (2000).

16. Entrepreneurs widely abuse the freedom to register a business in the name of someone who is not involved with the business. The easy way to shirk any responsibility is to set up a business with a stolen passport or with the borrowed passport of an alcoholic or dead person. Russia's first criminal case for money laundering, prosecuted in a Moscow court in 2001, focused on fictitious marketing contracts and shell companies registered in dead people's names and under lost passports. *Moscow Times,* August 20, 2001.

17. Julia Latynina, "Persecution: The Price of Achievement," *Moscow Times,* November 15, 2000, 8.

18. Ibid.

19. The controversies of tax debtors' accounts are discussed in detail in Tompson (1997).

20. The extraordinary scale of underreporting is facilitated by the collaboration and willingness of the employees to renounce their claim on a pension and social insurance proportionate to their actual salary.

21. Other variations of insurance schemes can be found in Julia Latynina, "Zapiski iz podpol'ia," *Ekspert,* January 25, 1999, 32.

22. With the Adoption of Chapter 25 of the Tax Code, the maximum profit tax has been reduced from 35 percent to 24 percent.

23. *Goskomstat: Finansy v Rossii* (Moscow 2000), 200–201.

24. Some respondents from both the banking and industrial sectors suggested that it might be up to 90 percent if calculated in all strictness, that is, if not just the letter of law but the spirit of it is taken into account.

25. The website http://www.garant.ru is one of several websites dedicated to moni-

toring the "dynamically changing legislative climate" in Russia. It issues a weekly update of legislation adopted by Russian regulatory organs entitled "monitoring izmenenii v zakonodatel'stve s 1 ianvaria 2002 goda" (accessed July 7, 2003).

26. Chapter 25, enacted on January 1, 2002, has resulted in problems of combining conflicting forms of accounting and required "transition phase" documentation.

27. The use of legal means can be illustrated by a more recent fight, the Slavneft' affair, a dominant Russian news story in 2002. Although quieter than in Yeltsin's era, the oligarchs still employed old tricks to gain control of companies and to undermine their rivals. The oligarch battle over Slavneft' contained all the ingredients of the 1990s oligarchic feuds of the "Bankers' War" and earlier "loans-for-shares" battles (Dinello 1998; Freeland 2000). The government aimed to sell 20 percent of state-owned Slavneft', one of the largest remaining state oil companies. The company had been managed by Mikhail Gutseriev, but the government decided that a new CEO was necessary to refresh the company and increase the chance of sale. Besides, Gutseriev's brother had attempted to run for the presidency of Ingushetiia earlier in the year against the Kremlin's wishes. Gutseriev ferociously resisted attempts to remove him. Kompromat was used to discredit the government's choice of replacement, Iuri Sukhanov. Gutseriev declared an ally (Baranovskii) as acting company president while he took a vacation and arranged for a court in Ufa to declare illegal the forthcoming Slavneft' Annual General Meeting (AGM) move to change presidents. He then went into hospital, taking advantage of a law that states that a person cannot be fired if hospitalized. Nonetheless, the AGM elected Sukhanov, who ejected Gutseriev from Slavneft' Moscow headquarters. Gutseriev's hired guns and retook the building before Sukhanov used his government contacts to remove Gutseriev. Incredibly Gutseriev launched another attack on Slavneft' headquarters using antiriot police and private security forces, with the police alleging that they were seeking documents to aid an investigation on Sukhanov. "Russian Wars for Oil," *Pravda*, May 13, 2002, http://www.english.pravda.ru/economics/2002/05/13/28620.html (accessed September 2002). See also R. Cottrell, "Meanwhile, on a Business Page," *Financial Times*, http://www.ft.com, July 3, 2002; A. Uglanov, "Tycoons Are Gathering Their Strength," *Argumenty i Fakty*, June 26, 2002, http://www.cdi.org/russia/johnson/6326–7.cfm (accessed December 2002).

Chapter 7. Post-Soviet *Tolkachi*

1. According to article 4(1) in the Federal Law on State Duties (*Federal'nyi zakon o gosudarstvennoi poshline*), in an arbitration court the claimant must pay a percentage of the claim proportional to its size. Any claim below 10 million rubles, for example, carries a fee of 5 percent of the claim, while claims worth over 1 billion rubles cost 16.6 million rubles plus 0.5 percent of the claim above the first 1 billion rubles (but not more than one thousand of "minimum wages"). The maximum fee is thus just over 17 million rubles. The fact that it has to be paid up front before the trial can proceed, however, can be a greater problem for cash-starved Russian enterprises than the fee itself (Hendley, Murrell, and Ryterman 2000, 639). It seems, though, that the courts have accepted the widespread practice of postponed payment of court fees (Hendley, Murrell, and Ryter-

man 2001, 83). According to Radaev (2002a, 77), the state fee is not comparable to the two-digit percentage figures that legal and illegal private enforcers demand.

2. In January 1999, Evgenii Primakov announced at the World Economic Forum (WEF) that his government had made a decision to grant amnesty to those convicted on minor economic crime charges in order to free the prison space for those involved in serious corruption.

3. In his memoirs *Mrakobesie*, Valerii Streletskii (1998, 116) describes the informal arrangements around such sanctions as *pomirilsia—sanktsii podniali, kakie mezhdu druziami mogut byt' schety?* (they settled—and sanctions were stopped, no problem between friends). According to him, the Kremlin Security Service is not a service of law enforcement but an agency for pressuring and collecting kompromat. These services are not neutral: they were under Korzhakov's control and worked for Yeltsin, who decided how to deploy the collected materials.

4. In the late 1990s a certain pattern emerged in the relationship between large enterprises and state courts. Small provincial courts of ordinary jurisdiction were suddenly deciding a great number of very serious cases involving large enterprises. This was possible in Russia because of the somewhat overlapping distribution of jurisdiction between arbitration courts and ordinary courts. A pensioner holding a single share, for example, could sue the country's largest company for noncompliance in the local district court of ordinary jurisdiction. Such courts were much more vulnerable to external influence than the regional arbitration courts because they were starved financially (Solomon 2002, 12–13). A willing individual, therefore, could be persuaded by a major company to file an absurdly large claim against another large company. For the local judge in the court of ordinary jurisdiction there is little deterrent to keep him or her from letting the wanted decision go through. An appeal is decided by higher courts and the judge will rarely have to account for his actions to anybody else than his immediate supervisor, the senior judge, who might be involved in the affair anyway (Aleksandr Dobrovinskii, "Kleptomaniia. O malen'kikh sudakh i bol'shikh protsessakh," *Novaia Gazeta*, June 3, 2002). This problem seems to have lessened somewhat since the decision in the fall of 2002 to give arbitration courts exclusive jurisdiction in cases of shareholders' disputes and the clarification of the division of jurisdiction with the Code of Arbitration Procedure, CAP 2002 (Tompson 2003).

5. See "Zhizn' dorozhe svobody," *Novaia Gazeta*, April 24–30, 2000, 15.

6. *RFE/RL Newsline*, October 17, 2000, http://www.rferl.org/newsline/.

7. After a number of such scandalous cases, the Supreme Court issued a resolution putting an end to such actions. In accordance with that decision, judges of general jurisdiction cannot ban the conducting of shareholder meetings. Moreover, from October 2001, the judges examine claims by shareholders only after shareholder meetings. However, it is doubtful that this can stop the lawyers. For bringing a suit of private shareholders, they can earn up to $50,000, and for that money you can search for any holes in the law (Golikova 2001, 40).

8. When I met this respondent, he was busy organizing a competition in martial arts and shooting among the private protection agencies. He was concerned about coverage of the event. "Publicity should be different from the last time," he explained. "Last time we invited journalists, they came and then wrote along the lines: 'Security firms are

50/50 percent of cops and criminals.'" Another respondent made a comment on the change in the criminal situation: "Crimes have stopped being chaotic: ninety out of a hundred murders happen for a reason. State law enforcement has infiltrated the private security firms and the criminal structures" [3.11].

9. This is a phrase often quoted by respondents with reference to the Wild West and Marx's "initial accumulation of capital."

10. Originally printed in *Komsomol'skaia Pravda*, July 14, 1998, 3. Quoted in Bennett (2000).

11. According to Varese (2001, 61–64), there were 6,775 private security firms in 1999.

12. In his talk at the Russia Forum 2000 in London, Anatolii Chubais gave an example of informal support for *svoi* regional bosses and of the informal methods of pressure on unsympathetic regional bosses: "First we have our own [*svoi*] bosses attached to the reliable [*k nadelennoi*] energy systems, while the ones we don't like get attached to the Chechen energy system—let them collect energy payments there with all the means they can access [*dostupnymi emu sredstvami*]. . . . And after that we wonder why investors do not come to Russia." He also emphasized that the trends in his company, UES, are representative of the trends of the whole country.

13. The list does not include the Federal Agency of Government Communication and Information (FAPSI). See *Novaia Gazeta*, June 9–15, 1997. The tapping of a telephone line was expensive because six operators were needed for the round-the-clock tapping of one line. The total cost of tapping of one telephone line in the mid-1990s was estimated at 1 million rubles for six months (divide by six for U.S. dollars).

14. The Russian Supreme Court declared unconstitutional a directive of the Communications Ministry that allowed the FSB to eavesdrop on the customers of telecommunications companies without informing them or applying for authorization from the Procurator's Office. Quoted in *RFE/RL Security Watch*, August 28, 2000, http://www.rferl.org/securitywatch/.

15. SORM-2 allows the FSB to monitor electronic mail messages by digitally linking its offices with all Internet service providers throughout Russia. See *RFE/RL Security Watch*, October 9, 2000, http://www.rferl.org/securitywatch/, and Ledeneva (2000b, 174).

16. The World Bank report assessed the efforts required in various countries to register a new business, to achieve a contract enforcement decision in a court, to hire or employ personnel, to receive a loan, or to liquidate the firm. One has to go through twelve procedures to register business in Russia, which can take up to 29 days, and through sixteen procedures to receive a court decision related to contract enforcement, which is likely to take about 160 days. Liquidation of a firm might take one and a half years. See Igor Fediukin and Aleksei Nikolskii, "Den'gi/Vlast'. Arbitrazhnyi proryv," *Vedomosti*, October 9, 2003. See full ranking table of countries at http://www.worldbank.org.

17. To enforce decisions of an arbitration court, a bailiff institution inspired by the U.S. Marshal Service was introduced in 1997 with the Law on Bailiffs (*Federal'nyi zakon o sudebnykh pristavakh*) and Law on Enforcement Procedures (*Federal'nyi zakon o ispolnitel'nom proizvodstve*) (Kononov and Kokarev 1999, 74–76; Kahn 2002, 153–8).

18. When the Soviet state arbitration tribunals were transformed into arbitration

courts, they initially experienced a large fall in cases heard per year, down from 338,162 in 1992 to 208,081 in 1994. After 1994, however, the arbitration courts got steadily rising numbers of cases, and in 1997 their number exceeded the 1992 level. According to the statistics in the *Rezul'taty raboty arbitrazhnykh sudov Rossiiskoi Federatsii v 1992–2002 godakh*, in 2002 arbitration courts decided 697,085 cases, more than twice as many as ten years earlier. Moreover, the same courts heard more appeals per case decided: 5.9 percent of all decided cases in 1992, 8.8 percent in 2002. Statistics collected by Jeppe Hansen.

19. An arbitration trial is initiated by a civil writ in the domain of business, a claim for administrative violation of bankruptcy, a request for appeal, or submission of a protest from the procurator general of the Russian Federation (Sapozhnikov and Ustiuzhaninov 2003, 184). Normally the competent Arbitration court is the court with jurisdiction in the region where the defendant lives, though the plaintiff can choose the court where disputed property is located and the parties can agree on another court (art. 35–37 CAP 2002).

20. Aleksandr Dobrovinskii, "Kleptomaniia. O malen'kikh sudakh i bol'shikh protsessakh," *Novaia Gazeta*, June 3, 2002.

21. The 2002 judicial reform targets some of the judicial tricks mentioned above. This effort, however, can succeed only in the context of respect for the law on the part of the companies. As it stands at the moment, it is inevitable that new loopholes will be found and the law can still be used as ammunition to outwit the competitor.

22. See Wyman (2000); Anna Nikolaeva and Andrei Panov, "Vlast'/Den'gi. Otchet o vziatkakh," *Vedomosti*, February, 19, 2004; Ella Paneiakh, "Pravila igry," *Vedomosti*, October 21, 2003.

23. Putin has started with promoting economic stability and pragmatism (reducing international debts and dependency on oil prices and making attempts at diversification in industry and investment), but his lack of belief that democracy can deliver the desired results has made him strengthen the "vertical of power," introduce restrictions on the media, create paraconstitutional bodies, and eliminate elections for regional governors.

Conclusion

1. For a bibliography on Chinese *guanxi* see Ledeneva (2003). Forms of Russian capitalism are discussed in Janine Wedel, "Who Taught Crony Capitalism to Russia?" *Wall Street Journal Europe,* March 19, 2001; David Hoffman, "Oligarchic Capitalism in Russia: The Past, Present, and Future", February 27, 2002, http://www.ceip.org/files/events/events.asp?pr=2&EventID=463 (accessed April 2005); "Russia: The Making of a Kleptocracy," *Business Week*, October 30, 2000, http://www.businessweek.com/2000/00_44/b3705025.htm (accessed April 2005).

2. An official press story in China in January 2002 claimed that more than four thousand corrupt officials, with $600 million in stolen funds, were on the run (many supposedly abroad). Officials fleeing with stolen assets have become so routine that a vivid term—"evaporation"—has been coined to describe the sudden disappearance of

fugitive officials. Minxin Pei, "The Long March against Graft," *Financial Times*, December 9, 2002, http://www.ft.com (accessed November 2003).

3. One has to note the difference between the "oligarchs" who have made their fortunes more from access than from effort and those who have built their businesses independent of government largess. See Esther Dyson "Making Russian Business Honest," *Washington Post*, July 25, 2000, 13.

4. In 2005, former prime minister Mikhail Kas'ianov, a 2008 presidential hopeful, was accused of signing over to himself a state-owned luxury home. Russian political analysts see the opening of the case against him for alleged fraud as a blatant warning to Kasianov to stay out of politics. Kasianov criticized president Putin's policies and publicly defended Mikhail Khodorkovskii. Arkadii Ostrovskii, "Prosecutor Links Kasyanov to Corruption," *Financial Times*, July 16–17, 2005, 8. One should expect more corruption charges in the run up to the 2008 presidential elections.

Glossary

Beznal, beznalichnye den'gi Literally "noncash," money that serves purposes of financial accounting and bank transfers (no physical money involved)

bezpredel Literally, beyond limits; a colloquial way of referring to breaching of all kind of norms, not just formal rules but also informal norms

blat A colloquial way of referring to the use of personal networks for obtaining goods and services in short supply or for circumventing formal procedures

chernyi nal Abbreviation for *nalichnost'* (black cash), cash that does not appear in the accounting

delit'sia Literally "to divide," meaning to share profits through payouts for various favors and services

dopsoglashenie, dopolnitel'noe soglashenie Literally "additional agreement," a document specifying the terms of the contract but that has no legal status

dvukhkhodovka Literally "a two-step procedure," referring to a simple type of fraud in financial scheming

ekonomika neplatezhei Literally, "an economy of nonpayments," referring to a situation where every economic subject is indebted to everyone else

fizicheskoe litso An individual in legal terminology

iuridicheskoe litso A firm or organization in legal terminology

krutit'sia, also **vykrutit'sia** Literally, "to rotate, to spin," finding ways out of difficult situations, normally associated with hardship

krysha Literally, "roof," protection from above, can be of criminal, military, or security services origins

levye firmy Literally, "left hand firms," referring to scam firms that do not exist as real firms but are used in financial schemes and fake accounting

martyshki Literally, "monkeys," referring to scam firms that do not exist as real firms but are used in financial schemes and fake accounting

naezd A request that often results in *razborka* or *strelka*, originally associated with racketeers but now widely used in vernacular

nagliadka Visual advertising, visual propaganda

nalogovoe osvobozhdenie Literally, "tax liberation," referring to tax allowance given by the government to those entitled to state subsidies that have not been paid

obnulit' Literally, "bring down to zero," referring to asset stripping or minimization of profits in order to avoid financial responsibility

poniatiia Literally "notions," the unofficial code of norms

prikhvatizatsiia A pun from "privatization" and *prikhvatit'*, literally "to take more than was meant," referring to insider dealing, corruption, embezzlement, and theft occurring during the privatization campaign of the 1990s

proslushka Equipment for bugging premises, also referring to a service one purchases for business or other forms of intelligence

prostoi veksel' Literally, "a simple promissory bill," a document that can be exchanged for cash at a certain date

pustyshki Literally, "empties," referring to scam firms that do not exist as real firms but are used in financial schemes and fake accounting

rabotat' po nuliam To work with "zero" profits, accounting for the purposes of tax evasion

razborka Equivalent to *strelka* but is used even more widely, for all kind of disputes including personal rows

raz"iasnit' vopros To clear up an issue, normally during *razborka* or *strelka*

siloviki Literally, "forcers," people of influence associated with the military, police or security forces, and related ministries

spetssluzhby, spetsial'nye sluzhby Literally "special services," meaning security services

strelka Informal dispute settlement taking place at a particular location between "roofs" of the conflicting parties, sometimes resulting in violent shoot-outs

tenevye skhemy Literally, "shadow schemes," referring to schemes that involve hidden operations and do not appear in the books

tolkachi Literally "pushers," engaged in activities of making ends meet in the planned economy by manipulating plan allocations, making up for shortage or nondelivery of supplies, and fiddling with insufficient funds

tolmachi Those who speak and explain

vykolachivanie Literally "beating out," usually associated with debt recovery or extortion

vziat' na poruki To vouch for somebody, to bail someone out, or to take responsibility for somebody's future behavior

zachety, vzaimozachety Offsets or mutual offsets, transactions that result in annulment of mutual obligations, calling it even

zadnim chislom Backdating, used in fake accounting and many kinds of petty fraud

zakaznoi zhurnalism, zakazukha Literally, journalism "produced on order," referring to prepaid, and therefore biased, articles in the press that serve certain political or business clients

Bibliography

Adachi, Yuko. 2005. "Informal Corporate Governance Practices in Russia in the 1990s: The cases of Yukos Oil, Siberian (Russian) Aluminum, and Norilsk Nickel." PhD diss., University of London.

Afanas'ev, Mikhail. 2000. "Issledovanie klientarnykh otnoshenii, ikh roli v evoliutsii i upadke proshlykh form rossiiskoi gosudarstvennosti, ikh vliianiia na politicheskie instituty i deiatel'nost' vlastvuiushchikh grupp v sovremennoi Rossii." In *Klientelizm i Rossiiskaia gosudarstvennost'*, ed. E.B. Abrosimova et al. Moscow: Moscow Social Scientific Foundation.

Ahrend, Rudiger. 2004. "Accounting for Russia's Post-Crisis Growth." OECD Working Paper No. 404. Paris: OECD.

Albats, Yevgenia. 1995. *KGB: State within a State.* Trans. Catherine Fitzpatrick. London: Tauris.

Aleksashenko, Sergei et al. 2000. *Obzor ekonomicheskoi politiki v Rossii za 1999 god.* Moscow: (Biuro ekonomicheskogo analiza) TEIS.

Alexander, James. 1997. "Surveying Attitudes in Russia." *Communist and Post-Communist Studies* 30 (2): 107–27.

Alexeev, Michael. 2002. "The Tax System and the Peculiarities of the Russian Economy." In *Institutional Change in Transition Economies,* ed. Michael Cuddy and Ruvin Gekker, 121–36. Aldershot, U.K.: Ashgate.

Allina-Pisano, Jessica. 2005. "Informal Politics and Challenges to Democracy: Administrative Resource in Kuchma's Ukraine." Paper presented at the Danyliw Research Seminar in Contemporary Ukrainian Studies, University of Ottawa, 29 September–October 1.

Andrle, Vladimir. 1994. *A Social History of Twentieth Century Russia.* London: Edward Arnold.

Arsen'ev, K.K., ed. 1920. *Novyi entsiklopedicheskii slovar'*. Vol. 23. Petrograd: Iz-datel'skoe delo byvshee Brokgauz-Efron.

Aslund, Anders. 2002. *Building Capitalism: The Transformation of the Former Soviet Bloc*. Cambridge: Cambridge University Press.

Backman, Johan. 1998. *The Inflation of Crime in Russia: Social Danger of the Emerging Markets*. Helsinki: National Research Institute of Legal Policy.

Banfield, Edward. 1958. *The Moral Basis of a Backward Society*. Chicago: Free Press.

———. 1975. "Corruption as a Feature of Governmental Organization." Journal of Law and Economics 18: 587–605.

Barabasi, Albert-Laszlo. 2002. *Linked: The New Science of Networks*. Perseus.

Bardhan, Pranab. 1997. "Corruption and Development: A Review of Issues." *Journal of Economic Literature* 35: 1320–46.

Basmannoe pravosudie. Uroki samooborony. Posobie dlia advokatov. 2003. Moscow: Pub-lichnaia reputatsiia. Internet version is available at http://www.ip-centre.ru/books/Basmannoe.pdf (accessed March 2006).

Batalov, Eduard. 1997. "Politicheskaia kul'tura." In *Obshchaia i prikladnaia politologiia*. Moscow: Nauka.

Bauer, R., A. Inkeles, A. Kluckhorn, and C. Kluckhorn. 1959. *How the Soviet System Works*. Cambridge: Cambridge University Press.

Belin, Laura. 2002. "Political Bias and Self-Censorship in the Russian Media." In *Contemporary Russian Politics: A Reader*, ed. Archie Brown. Oxford: Oxford University Press.

Bennett, Gordon. 2000. "The Federal Security Service of the Russian Federation." Working Paper C102. Surrey, U.K.: Conflict Studies Research Centre.

Bennich-Björkman, Li. 2002. "Explaining State Capture in Estonia and Latvia: Identity, International Role Models and Political Formation." In *The Baltics: Culture, Society, Politics*. Poznan.

Benson, Bruce, and John Baden. 1985. "The Political Economy of Governmental Cor-ruption: The Logic of Underground Government." *Journal of Legal Studies* 14: 391–410.

Berliner, J. 1954. "Blat is Higher Than Stalin." *Problems of Communism* 3 (1).

———. 1957. *Factory and Manager in the USSR*. Cambridge Mass.: Harvard University Press.

Birdsall, Karen. 2000. "Everyday Crime in the Workplace: Covert Earnings Schemes in Russia's New Commercial Sector." In *Economic Crime in Russia*, ed. Alena Ledeneva and Marina Kurkchiyan, 145–62. London: Kluwer Law International.

Blundo, G., and Jean-Pierre Olivier de Sardan. 2001. "La Corruption Quotidienne en Afrique de l'Quest." *Politique Africaine* 83: 8–37.

Bourdieu, Pierre. 1986. "The Forms of Capital." In *Handbook of Theory and Research for the Sociology of Education*, ed. John G. Richardson. New York: Greenwood Press.

———. 1989. *The Logic of Practice*. Trans. Richard Nice. Cambridge: Cambridge Univer-sity Press.

———. 1990. *In Other Words*. Trans. Matthew Adamson. Cambridge: Polity Press.

Bourdieu, Pierre, and Loïc Wacquant. 1992. *An Introduction to Reflexive Sociology*. Chi-cago: University of Chicago Press.

Bovenberg, L. 2000. "On the Cutting Edge between Policy and Academia: Challenges for Public Economists." *Economist* 148 (3): 295–329.

Bren, Paulina. 1993. "Lustration in the Czech and Slovak Republics." *RFE/RL Research Report* 2 (29): 16–22.

Breslauer, George W. 2001. "Boris Yeltsin as Patriarch." In *Contemporary Russian Politics. A Reader,* ed. A. Brown, 70–82. New York: Oxford University Press.

Brie, Michael. 1998. "Patterns of Social Order in Transitional Societies: The Russian Case." Paper prepared for the Conference on Formal Institutions and Informal Arrangements in Transformation Societies, Potsdam, Germany: University of Potsdam.

Brokgauz, F., and I. Efron, eds. 1898. *Entsikolopedichsekii slovar'.* Vol. 24a. St. Petersburg.

——. 1895. *Entsikolopedichsekii slovar'.* Vol. 18a. St. Petersburg.

Brown, Archie. 2005. "Cultural Change and Continuity in the Transition from Communism: The Russian Case." In *Cultural Development: Case Studies,* ed. Lawrence E. Harrison and Peter Berger. New York: Routledge.

Bryzgalin, A. et al. 1998. *Vekselia i vzaimozachety. Kniga 2.* Moscow: Analitika Press.

Brzhevskii, N. 1897. *Nedoimochnost' i krugovaia poruka sel'skikh obschestv.* St. Petersburg.

Buchanan, Mark. 2002. *Nexus: The Groundbreaking Science of Networks.* New York: W. W. Norton.

Bunce, Valerie. 1995. "Comparing East and South." *Journal of Democracy* 6 (3): 87–100.

——. 2001. "The Postsocialist Experience and Comparative Politics." *PS: Political Science and Politics* 34 (4): 793–95.

Burawoy, Michael, Pavel Krotov, and Tatyana Lytkina. 2000. "Involution and Destitution in Capitalist Russia." *Ethnography* 1: 43–65.

Burds, Jeffrey. 1991. "The Social Control of Peasant Labor in Russia: The Response of Village Communities to Labor Migration in the Central Industrial Region, 1861–1905." In *Peasant Economy, Culture and Politics of European Russia, 1800–1921,* ed. Esther Kingston-Mann and Timothy Mixter. Princeton: Princeton University Press.

Burt, Ronald. 1997. "The Contingent Value of Social Capital." *Administrative Science Quarterly* 42: 339–65.

Busse, Eva. 2000. "The Embeddedness of Tax Evasion in Russia." In *Economic Crime in Russia,* ed. Alena Ledeneva and Marina Kurkchiyan, 129–44. London: Kluwer Law International.

Butyrskii, Mikhail. 2001. *Bolshaia entsiklopedia Kirilla i Mefodiia.* Moscow: New Media Generation.

CAP, Code of Arbitration Procedure. *Arbitrazhnyi protsesual'nyi kodeks.* Moscow: 2002.

Carothers, Thomas. 2002. "The End of the Transition Paradigm." *Journal of Democracy* 13 (1): 5–21.

Castells, M. 1996. *The Rise of Network Society.* Oxford: Blackwell.

Chabal, Patrick, and Jean-Pascal Daloz. 1999. *Africa Works: Disorder as Political Instrument.* Bloomington: Indiana University Press.

Chorniy, Vladimir. 2000. "Russia: Multiple Financial Systems and Implications for Economic Crime." In *Economic Crime in Russia,* ed. Alena Ledeneva and Marina Kurkchiyan, 223–36. London: Kluwer Law International.

Clarke, Simon. 1999. *New Forms of Employment and Household Survival Strategies in Russia.* Coventry: ISITO/CCL.

Cohen, Stanley. 1995. "State Crimes of Previous Regimes: Knowledge, Accountability, and the Policing of the Past." *Law and Social Inquiry* 20: 7–50.

Coles, N. 2001. "It's Not What You Know—It's Who You Know That Counts." *British Journal of Criminology* 41: 580–94.

Colton, Timothy, and Michael McFaul. 2003. *Popular Choice and Managed Democracy: The Russian Elections of 1999 and 2000.* Washington: Brookings.

Commander, Simon, and Christian Mummsen. 2000. "The Growth of Non-Monetary Transactions in Russia: Causes and Effects." In *The Vanishing Rouble: Barter Networks and Non-Monetary Transactions in Post-Soviet Societies,* ed. Paul Seabright, 114–17. Cambridge: Cambridge University Press.

Cornford, F. M. 1908. *Microcosmographia Academica.* Cambridge: Bowes & Bowes Publishers.

Coulloudon, Virginie. 1999. "The Dichotomy of the Post-Yeltsin Elite." September 30, 1999, http://www.sais-jhu.edu/programs/res/papers/Coulloudon.pdf (accessed on January 19, 2003).

Crankshaw, E. 1956. *Russia without Stalin.* London: Michael Joseph.

Dal', Vladimir. 1996. *Tolkovyi slovar' zhivogo velikoruskogo iazyka.* Vol. 2. St. Petersburg: Diamant. (Orig. publ. 1881).

Dallago, Bruno. 1990. *The Irregular Economy: The "Underground" Economy and the "Black" Labour Market.* Aldershot: Dartmouth.

Dallin, David J. 1951. *The New Soviet Empire.* London: Hollis and Carter.

Dan, S., and A. Valeksa. 1998. *Barter: Tovaroobmennye (barternye) sdelki.* Moscow: Delovoi al'ians.

Darden, Keith A. 2001. "Blackmail as a Tool of State Domination: Ukraine under Kuchma." *East European Constitutional Review* 10, 2/3 (Spring/Summer), 67–71.

Davydova, Irina. 1999. "Moral Traditions of Rural Communities: A Study of Russian Collectivism." PhD diss., University of Manchester.

De Soto, Hernando. 1989. *The Other Path: The Invisible Revolution in the Third World,* London:Tauris.

Dewey, H. W., and A. M. Kleimola. 1970. "Suretyship and Collective Responsibility in Pre-Petrine Russia." *Jahrbucher fur Geschichte Osteuropas* 18: 337–54.

Dewey, Horace W. 1988. "Russia's Debt to the Mongols in Suretyship and Collective Responsibility." *Comparative Studies in Society and History* 30: 249–70.

Dilts, Robert (with John Grinder, Richard Bandler, and Judith Delozier). 1980. *Neuro-Linguistic Programming.* Vol. 1, *The Study of the Structure of Subjective Experience.* Meta Publications.

Dinello, Natalia. 1998. "Bankers' Wars in Russia: Trophies and Wounds," *Post-Soviet Prospects* 6 (1). http://www.csis.org/ruseura/psp/pspvi1.html (accessed February 2001).

Dolgopiatova, Tatiana. 1998. *Small Business in Russia.* Moscow: Conseco.

Dormin, Alexander. 2003. "Ten Years Later: Society, Civil Society, and the Russian State." *Russian Review* 62 (2): 193–211.

Drobizheva, Leokadia. 1996. *Govorit elita respublik Rossiiskoi Federatsii.* Moscow: Institut Etnologii i Antropologii, RAN.

Drobizheva, Leokadia. "Comparison of Elite Groups in Tatarstan, Sakha, Magadan and Orenburg." *Post-Soviet Affairs* 15 (4): 387–406.

Dunham, Vera. 1990. *In Stalin's Time: Middle-class Values in Soviet Fiction.* Durham: Duke University Press. (Orig. pub. 1976.)

Easter, Gerald M. 2000. *Reconstructing the State: Personal Networks and Elite Identity in Soviet Russia.* Cambridge: Cambridge University Press.

——. 2001. "Networks, Bureaucracies, and the Russian State." In *Explaining Post-Soviet Patchworks.* Vol. 2. *Pathways from the Past to the Global,* ed. Klaus Segbers, 39–58. Aldershot: Ashgate.

——. 2002. "The Russian Tax Police." *Post-Soviet Affairs* 18 (4): 332–62.

EBRD (European Bank for Reconstruction and Development. 2002. *Law in Transition. Ten Years of Legal Transition.* London: EBRD.

EIU (Economist Intelligent Unit). 2001. *EIU Country Report Russia 2001.* London: EIU.

Edgerton, Robert. 1985. *Rules, Exceptions and Social Order.* London and Berkeley: University of California Press.

Egorova, Ekaterina. 2003. "Malen'kaia skazka o russkom PR." In *Vybory i zhurnalistskoe rassledovanie,* ed. Dafin Skillen. Moscow: Prava Cheloveka. http://democracy.ru/library/publications/media/jour_inv/ (accessed July 2003).

Egorova-Gantman, E., and K. Pleshakov. 1999. *Politicheskaia Reklama.* Moscow: Nikkolo M.

Eisenstadt, S. N. 1981. "The Growth of Non-Monetary Transactions in Russia: Causes and Effects." In *Political Clientelism, Patronage, and Development,* ed. S. N. Eisenstadt and René Lemarchand. London: Sage.

Ericson, Richard, and Barry Ickes. 2001. "A Model of Russia's 'Virtual Economy.'" *Review of Economic Design* 6 (2): 185–214.

Etzioni-Halevy, Eva. 1990. "Comparing Semi-Corruption among Parliamentarians in Britain and Australia." In *Comparative Methodology: Theory and Practice in International Social Research,* 113–33. London: Sage Publications.

Fainsod, Merle. 1963. *How Russia Is Ruled.* Cambridge, Mass: Harvard University Press.

Fiege, Edgar L. 1997. "Underground Activity and Institutional Change: Productive, Protective and Predatory Behavior in Transition Economies." In *Transforming Post-Communist Political Economies,* ed. Joan M. Nelson, Charles Tilly, and Lee Walker, 21–34. Washington, D.C.: National Academy Press.

——. 1999. "Underground Economies in Transition: Noncompliance and Institutional Change." In *Underground Economies in Transition: Unrecorded Activity, Tax Evasion, Corruption and Organized Crime,* ed. Edgar L. Fiege and Katerina Ott. Aldershot: Ashgate.

Fituni, Leonid. 2000. "Economic Crime in the Context of Transition to a New Market Economy." In *Economic Crime in Russia,* edited by Alena Ledeneva and Marina Kurkchiyan, 17–30. London: Kluwer Law International.

Fitzpatrick, Sheila. 1999. *Everyday Stalinism: Ordinary Life in Extraordinary Times: Soviet Russia in the 1930's.* New York: Oxford University Press.

——. 2000a. "Blat in Stalin's time." In *Bribery and Blat in Russia,* ed. Stephen Lovell, Alena Ledeneva, and Andrei Rogatchevsii, 166–182. London: Macmillan.

——, ed. 2000b. *Stalinism: New Directions.* London: Routledge.

Fitzpatrick, Sheila, and Robert Gellately. 1997. *Accusatory Practices: Denunciation in Modern European History, 1789–1989.* Chicago: University of Chicago Press.

Foley, Michael W., and Bob Edwards. 1998. "Beyond Tocqueville: Civil Society and Social Capital in Comparative Perspective." *American Behavioral Scientist* 42 (1): 5–20.

——. 1996. "The Paradox of Civil Society." *Journal of Democracy* 7 (3): 38–52.

——. 1997. "Escape from Politics? Social Theory and the Social Capital Debate." *American Behavioral Scientist* 40 (6): 550–61.

Forward, Susan, and Donna Frazier. 1998. *Emotional Blackmail: When the People in*

Your Life Use Fear, Obligation, and Guilt to Manipulate You. New York: Harper-Collins.

Foucault, Michel. 1977. *Discipline and Punish: The Birth of the Prison.* New York: Pantheon Books, 1977.

Frantsev, Iu.P., ed. 1955. *Vsemirnaia istoriia.* Vol. 1. Moscow: Politicheskaia Literatura.

Freeland, Chrystia. 2000. *Sale of the Century.* London: Crown.

Frisby, Tania. 1998. "The Rise of Organized Crime in Russia: Its Roots and Social Significance," *Europe-Asia Studies* 50 (1): 27–49.

Frye, Timothy. 2002a. "Capture or Exchange? Business Lobbying in Russia." *Europe-Asia Studies* 54 (7): 1017–36.

———. 2002b. "The Two Faces of Russian Courts." *East European Constitutional Review* 11 (1–2): 125–29.

Fukuyama, Francis. 1995a. "Social Capital and the Global Economy." *Foreign Affairs,* September/October, 89–103.

———. 1995b. *Trust: The Social Virtues and the Creation of Prosperity.* New York: Free Press.

Gaddy, Clifford G., and Barry W. Ickes. 2002. *Russia's Virtual Economy.* Washington, D.C.: Brookings Institution.

Galeotti, Mark. 2000. "The Russian Mafia: Economic Penetration at Home and Abroad." In *Economic Crime in Russia,* ed. Alena Ledeneva and Marina Kurkchiyan, 31–42. London: Kluwer Law International.

Galiev, Andrei. 1999. "Material'nye sekrety" (Material Secrets), *Ekspert,* December 20.

Galligan, Denis J., and Marina Kurkchiyan, eds. 2003. *Law and Informal Practices. The Post-Communist Experience.* Oxford: Oxford University Press.

Gambetta, Diego. 2002. "Displaying One's Skeleton's in One's Cupboard: Why Norms Breed Corruption." In "Symposium—Dirty Politics," ed. Daniel Treisman. *APSA-CP* 13 (1): 6–18.

Gelman, Vladimir. 2002. "The Iceberg of Political Finance." In *The Contemporary Russian Politics: A Reader,* ed. Archie Brown. Oxford: Oxford University Press.

———. 2003. *Making and Breaking Democratic Transitions: The Comparative Politics of Russia's Regions.* Lanham, Md.: Rowman and Littlefield.

Gel'man, Vladimir, Grigorii Golosov, and Elena Meleshkina. 2000. *Pervyi Elektoral'nyi Tsikl v Rossii, 1993–1996gg.* Moscow: Ves' Mir.

———. 2002. *Vtoroi elektoral'nyi tsikl v Rossii, 1999–2000gg.* Moscow: Vek.

Gel'man, Vladimir, Sergei Ryzhekov, and Michael Brie, eds. 2002. *Rossiia regionov: Transformatsiia politicheskikh rezhimov.* Moscow: Ves' Mir.

Gel'man, Vladimir, and Grigorii Golosov, eds. 1999. *Elections in Russia, 1993–1996.* Berlin: Die Deutsche Bibliotek.

Gerasimova, Ekaterina. 1998. "Sovetskaia kommunal'naia kvartira." *Sociologicheskii Zhurnal* 1–2: 224–44.

Gerber, Theodore. 2002. "Joining the Winners: Self-Employment and Stratification in Post-Soviet Russia." In *The New Entrepreneurs of Europe and Asia,* ed. Victoria Bonnell and Thomas Gold, 3–38. Armonk: M. E. Sharpe.

Gerber, Theodore, and Michael Hout. 1998. "More Shock Than Therapy: Market Transition, Employment, and Income in Russia, 1991–1995." *American Journal of Sociology* 104: 1–50.

Getty, J. Arch. 1986. *Origins of the Great Purge: The Soviet Communist Party Reconsidered, 1933–1938.* New York: Cambridge University Press.

Gill, Graeme. 1990. *The Origins of the Stalinist Political System.* New York: Cambridge University Press.

Goldman, Marshall. 2003. *The Piratization of Russia: Russian Reform Goes Awry.* New York: Routledge.

Golikova, Liza. 2001. "Oruzhie v zakone." *Kommersant-Dengi* 50: 39–41.

Gouldner, Alvin. 1977. "The Norm of Reciprocity: A Preliminary Statement." In *Friends, Followers and Factions: A Reader in Political Clientelism,* ed. S. Schmidt. London: University of California Press.

Graham, Thomas. 1999. "From Oligarchy to Oligarchy: The Structure of Russia's Ruling Elite," *Demokratizatsiia* 7 (3).

Granovetter, Mark. 1973. "The Strength of Weak Ties." *American Journal of Sociology* 78: 1360–80.

——. 1985. "Economic Action and Social Structure: The Problem of Embeddedness." *American Journal of Sociology* 91: 481–510.

Grossman, Gregory. 1977. "Economy of the USSR." *Problems of Communism* 5 (26): 25–40.

——. 1990. "The Second Economy in the USSR and Eastern Europe: A Bibliography." Berkeley-Duke Occasional Papers on the Second Economy in the USSR. Paper No. 21.

Gudkov, Fedor A. 1998. *Veksel': Defekty formy.* Moscow: Bankovskii Delovoi Tsentr.

Gudkov, Lev, and Boris Dubin. 2002. " 'Nuzhnye znakomstva': Osobennosti sotsial'noi organizatsii v usloviiakh institutsional'nykh defitsitov." Polit.ru, http://www.polit.ru/documents/490769.html (accessed October 2005).

Gustafson, Thane. 1999. *Capitalism Russian-Style.* Cambridge: Cambridge University Press.

Guthrie, Doug. 1998. "The Declining Significance of Guanxi in China's Economic Transition." *China Quarterly* 154: 254–82.

——. 1999. *Dragon in a Three-Piece Suit.* Princeton, N.J.: Princeton University Press.

——. 2002. "Information Asymmetries and the Problem of Perception: The Significance of Structural Position in Assessing the Importance of *Guanxi* in China." In *Social Connections in China,* ed. Thomas Gold, Doug Guthrie, and David Wank. Cambridge: Cambridge University Press.

Hahn, Gordon M. 2001. "Putin's 'Federal Revolution': The Administrative and Judicial Reform of Russian Federalism." *East European Constitutional Review* (Winter): 60–67.

Hahn, Jeffrey. 1991. "Continuity and Change in Russian Political Culture," *British Journal of Political Science* 21: 393–421.

Halevy, Etzioni. 1979. *Political Manipulation and Administrative Power.* London: Routledge.

Halmai, Garbor, and Kim Lane Scheppele. 1997. "Living Well Is the Best Revenge: The Hungarian Approach to Judging the Past." In *Transitional Justice and the Rule of Law in New Democracies,* ed. A. J. McAdams. Notre Dame, Ind.: University of Notre Dame.

Hanson, Philip. 2003. "The Russian Economic Recovery: Do Four Years of Growth Tell Us That the Fundamentals Have Changed?" *Europe-Asia Studies* 55 (3): 365–82.

Hare, P., and G. Hughes. 1991. "Competitiveness and Industrial Restructuring in Czechoslovakia, Hungary and Poland." *European Economy.* Special edition, no. 2, 83–110.

Harter, Stefanie, and Gerald Easter. 2000. *Shaping the Economic Space in Russia.* Aldershot: Ashgate.

Hellman, Joel, and Daniel Kaufmann. 2001. "Confronting the Challenge of State Capture in Transition Economies." *Finance and Development* 38 (3): 40–44.

Helmke, Gretchen, and Steven Levitsky. 2004. "Informal Institutions and Comparative Politics: A Research Agenda." *Perspectives on Politics* 2 (4): 725–40.

Hendley, Kathryn. 2001. "Rewriting the Rules of the Game." In *Contemporary Russian Politics: A Reader,* ed. Archie Brown. Oxford: Oxford University Press.

Hendley, Kathryn, Barry W. Ickes, and Randi Ryterman. 1998. "Remonetizing the Russian Economy." In *Russian Enterprise Reform: Policies to Further the Transition,* ed. H. G. Broadman. Washington, D.C.: World Bank.

Hendley, Kathryn, Peter Murrell, and Randi Ryterman. 2000. "Law, Relationships and Private Enforcement: Transactional Strategies of Russian Enterprises." *Europe-Asia Studies* 52 (4): 627–56.

———. 2001. "Law Works in Russia: The Role of Legal Institutions in the Transactions of Russian Enterprises." In *Assessing the Value of Law in Transition Economies,* ed. Peter Murrell, 56–93. Ann Arbor: University of Michigan Press.

Hoffman, David. 2002. *The Oligarchs: Wealth and Power in the New Russia.* Oxford: Public Affairs.

Hopkin, Jonathan. 2002. "Comparative Methods." In *Theory and Methods in Political Science,* 2d ed., ed. David Marsh and Gerry Stoker, 249–67. New York: Palgrave.

Horne, Cynthia M., and Margaret Levi. 2004. "Does Lustration Promote Trustworthy Governance? An Exploration of the Experience of Central and Eastern Europe." In *Trust in Post-Socialist Economies,* ed. Janos Kornai, Susan Rose-Ackerman, and Bo Rothstein. New York: Macmillan.

Hosking, Geoffrey. 2000. "Patronage and the Russian State." *Slavonic and East European Review* 78 (2): 301–20.

———. 2001. *Russia and the Russians: A History.* Allen Lane: Penguin Press.

———. 2004. "Forms of Social Solidarity in Russia and the Soviet Union." In *Trust and Democratic Transition in Post-Communist Europe,* ed. I. Markova. Oxford: British Academy and Oxford University Press.

Howard, Marc Morje. 2003. *The Weakness of Civil Society in Post-Communist Europe.* Cambridge: Cambridge University Press.

Hughes, James. 1999. "Transition Models and Democratization in Russia." In *Russia after the Soviet Union,* ed. C. Ross and M. Bowker, 7–19. London: Longman.

Humphrey, Caroline. 2000a. "An Anthropological View of Barter in Russia." In *The Vanishing Rouble: Barter Networks and Non-Monetary Transactions in Post-Soviet Societies,* ed. Paul Seabright, 71–90. Cambridge: Cambridge University Press.

———. 2000b. "Dirty Business, 'Normal Life,' and the Dream of Law." In *Economic Crime in Russia,* ed. Alena Ledeneva and Marina Kurkchiyan, 177–90. London: Kluwer Law International.

———. 2002. *The Unmaking of Soviet Life: Everyday Economies after Socialism.* Ithaca: Cornell University Press.

Hyde, Matthew. 2001. "Putin's Federal Reforms and Their Implications for Presidential Power in Russia." *Europe-Asia Studies* 53 (5): 719–43.

Iakovlev, Aleksandr M. 1995. *Striving for Law in a Lawless Land: Memoirs of a Russian Reformer.* London: M. E. Sharpe.

Iakovlev, Andrei. 1999. "Black Cash Tax Evasion in Russia: Its Forms, Incentives and Consequences at the Firm Level." BOFIT Discussion Paper No. 3. Helsinki: Bank of Finland.

———. 2000a. "Kriterii klassifikatsii nedenezhnykh transaktsii v rynochnoi i perekhodnoi ekonomike." In *Diskussionnye materially*. 2d ed. Moscow: Vysshaia Shkola Ekonomiki.

———. 2000b. "Pochemu v Rossii vozmozhen bezriskovyi ukhod ot nalogov?" *Voprosy ekonomiki* 11: 134–52.

Iasin, Evgenii. ed. 2002. *Modernizatsiia Rossiiskoi ekonomiki*. Vols. 1–2. Moscow: Vysshaia Shkola Ekonomiki.

Ikels, Charlotte. 1996. *The Return of the God of Wealth: The Transition to a Market Economy in Urban China*. Stanford: Stanford University Press.

Il'in, Mikhail V. 1994. "Slova i smysly." *Politicheskie Issledovaniia* 6.

INDEM (Information for Democracy). 2001. "Diagnostika rossiiskoi korruptsii. Sotsiologicheskii analiz." Moscow. http://www.anti-corr.ru/awbreport/index.htm (accessed July 2003).

———. 2002. "Regional'nye indeksy korruptsii." Moscow. http://www.anti-corr.ru/rating_regions/index.htm (accessed July 2003).

Inglehart, R., and W. Baker. 2000. "Modernization, Cultural Change and the Persistence of Traditional Values." *American Sociological Review* 65: 19–51.

Inoguchi, Takashi, and Paul Bacon. 2003. "Governance, Democracy, Consolidation and the 'End of Transition.'" *Japanese Journal of Political Science* 4(2): 169–90.

Jensen, Donald N. 1998. "Rumors of Oligarchs' Demise Greatly Exaggerated: A December 1998 Update to 'How Russia is Ruled—1998.'" *RFE/RL*, December. http://www.rferl.org/nca/special/ruwhorules/oligarchs.html (accessed January 2001).

———. 1999. "How Russia Is Ruled—1998." *Demokratizatsiia* 7 (3).

———. 2000. "The Boss: How Yuri Luzhkov Runs Moscow." *Demokratizatsiia* 8 (1).

Johnson, Simon, Daniel Kauffman, and Andrei Shleifer. 1997. "The Unofficial Economy in Transition." *Brookings Papers on Economic Activity* 2.

Johnson, Simon, John McMillan, and Christopher Woodruff. 2002. "Courts and Relational Contracts." *Journal of Law, Economics and Organization* 18: 221–77.

Jowitt, K. 1983. "Soviet Neotraditionalism: The Political Corruption of a Leninist Regime." *Soviet Studies* 35 (3): 275–97.

Kahn, Jeffrey. 2002. *Federalism, Democratization, and the Rule of Law in Russia*. Oxford: Oxford University Press.

Kahn, Peter L. 2002. "The Russian Bailiff Service and the Enforcement of Civil Judgements." *Post-Soviet Affairs* 18 (2): 148–81.

Kandiyoti, Deniz. 1999. "Pol v neformal'noi ekonomike: Problemy i napravleniia analiza." In *Neformal'naia ekonomika: Rossiia i mir*, ed. Teodor Shanin, 356–71. Moscow: Logos.

Kantor, Karl M. 1996. "Sotsio-kul'turnye prichiny rossiiskoi katastrofy." *Politicheskie Issledovaniia* 3.

Kara-Murza, Sergei. 2001. *Manipuliatsiia soznaniem*. Moscow: EKSMO-Press.

Karklins, Rasma. 2005. *The System Made Me Do It: Corruption in Post-Communist Societies*. New York: M. E. Sharpe.

Kasianova, K. 1994. *O Russkom natsional'nom kharaktere*. Moscow: Institut natsional'nykh modelei ekonomiki.

Keenan, Edward. 1986. "Muscovite Political Folkways." *Russian Review* 1 (45): 115–81.

Klebnikov, Paul. 2000. *Godfather of the Kremlin.* New York: Harcourt.

Kliamkin, Igor', and Lev Timofeev. 2000a. *Tenevaia Rossiia: Ekonomiko-sotsiologicheskoe issledovanie.* Moscow: Rossiiskii gosudarstvennyi gumanitarnyi universitet.

———. 2000b. "Tenevoi obraz zhizni (sotsiologicheskii avtoportret postsovetskogo obshchestva)." *Politicheskie Issledovaniia* 4: 19–37.

———. 2000c. "Tenevoi obraz zhizni (sotsiologicheskii avtoportret postsovetskogo obshchestva)." *Politicheskie Issledovaniia* 5: 121–32.

Knight, Amy. 1993. "Russian Security Services under Yeltsin." *Post-Soviet Affairs* 9 (1): 40–65.

———. 1996. *Spies without Cloaks: The KGB's Successors.* Princeton: Princeton University Press.

Kommersant 21. 2003. *Komu prinadlezhit Rossiia.* Moscow: Vagrius.

Kononov, O.V., and Iu. G. Kokarev. 1999. "Sudebnye pristavy: Vchera, segodnia, zavtra." *Gosudarstvo i Pravo* 1: 74–78.

Kornai, János, and Susan Rose-Ackerman, eds. 2004. *Building A Trustworthy State in Post-Socialist Transition.* New York: Palgrave Macmillan.

Kornai, János, Bo Rothstein, and Susan Rose-Ackerman, eds. 2004. *Creating Social Trust in Post-Socialist Transition.* New York: Palgrave Macmillan.

Korzhakov, Aleksandr V. 1997. *Boris El'tsin: Ot rassveta do zakata.* Moscow: Interbuk.

Kozlov, Vladimir A. 2000. "Denunciation and Its Functions in Soviet Governance: From the Archive of the Soviet Ministry of Internal Affairs, 1944–53." In *Stalinism: New Directions,* ed. Sheila Fitzpatrick, 117–141. London: Routledge.

Kratkii slovar' sovremennykh poniatii i terminov. 2002. 3d ed. Moscow.

Kryshtanovskaia, Olga, and Stephen White. 1996. "From Soviet Nomenklatura to Russian Elite." *Europe-Asia Studies* 48 (5): 711–33.

Kudinov, O. N. 2000. *Osnovy organizatsii i provedenie izbiratel'nykh kampanii v regionakh Rossii.* Kaliningrad: Iantarnyi Skaz.

Kurtov, Aleksei, and Mikhail Kagan. 2002. *Okhota na drakona: Razmyshleniia o vyborakh i politicheskom konsul'tirovanii.* Moscow: Gosudarstvennyi universitet-Vysshaia shkola ekonomiki.

Lambert, Larry B. 1996. "Underground Banking and National Security." *Sapra India Bulletin,* March http://www.subcontinent.com (accessed July 2001).

Lane, David. 1997. "Transition under Eltsin: The Nomenklatura and Political Elite Circulation." *Political Studies* 45 (5): 855–74.

Latynina, Iuliia. 1999. *Okhota na iziubria.* Moscow: Olma Press.

———. 2001. *Nich'ia.* Moscow: Olma Press.

———. 2001. *Sarancha.* Moscow: Olma Press.

———. 2001. *Stal'noi korol'.* Moscow: Olma Press.

———. 2003. *Promzona.* Moscow: Olma Press.

Lauth, Hans-Joachim. 2000. "Informal Institutions and Democracy." *Democratization* 7 (4): 21–50.

Ledeneva, Alena. 1997. "The Informal Sphere and *Blat*: Civil Society or Post-Soviet Corporatism?" *Pro et Contra* (Fall, special issue on civil society), 113–24.

———. 1998. *Russia's Economy of Favours: Blat, Networking, and Informal Exchange.* Cambridge: Cambridge University Press.

———. 2000a. "Continuity and Change of *Blat* Practices in Soviet and Post-Soviet Russia." In *Bribery and Blat in Russia,* ed. S. Lovell, A. Ledeneva, and A. Rogatchevsii. London: Macmillan.

———. 2000b. "Introduction: Economic Crime in the New Russian Economy." In *Economic Crime in Russia,* ed. Alena Ledeneva and Marina Kurkchiyan, 1–16. London: Kluwer Law International.

———. 2000c. "Russian Hackers and Virtual Crime." In *Economic Crime in Russia,* ed. Alena Ledeneva and Marina Kurkchiyan, 162–76. London: Kluwer Law International.

———. 2000d. "Shadow Barter: Economic Necessity or Economic Crime?" In *The Vanishing Rouble: Barter Networks and Non-Monetary Transactions in Post-Soviet Societies,* ed. Paul Seabright, 298–317. Cambridge: Cambridge University Press.

———. 2001a. "Networks in Russia: Global and Local Implications." In *Explaining Post-Soviet Patchworks.* Vol. 2, *Pathways from the Past to the Global,* ed. Klaus Segbers. Aldershot, U.K.: Ashgate.

———. 2001b. *Unwritten Rules: How Russia Really Works.* London: Center for European Reform, see http://www.cer.org.uk.

———. 2002. "Non-Transparency of the Post-Communist Economies: The Relationship Between the Formal and the Informal." Draft copy. http://www.colbud.hu/honesty-trust/.

———. 2003. "Informal Practices in Changing Societies: Comparing Chinese *Guanxi* and Russian *Blat.*" Working paper no. 45, September. http://www.ssees.ucl.ac.uk/csesce .htm.

———. 2004a. "Ambiguity of Social Networks in Post-Communist Contexts." Working paper no. 48, February. http://www.ssees.ucl.ac.uk/csesce.htm.

———. 2004b. "Genealogy of *Krugovaia Poruka:* Forced Trust as a Feature of Russian Political Culture." In *Trust and Democratic Transition in Post-Communist Europe,* ed. Ivana Markova. Oxford: British Academy and Oxford University Press.

Ledeneva, Alena, and Marina Kurkchiyan. 2000. *Economic Crime in Russia.* London: Kluwer Law International.

Ledeneva, Alena, and Paul Seabright. 2000. "Barter in Post-Soviet Societies: What Does It Look Like and Why Does It Matter?" In *The Vanishing Rouble: Barter Networks and Non-Monetary Transactions in Post-Soviet Societies,* ed. Paul Seabright, 93–113. Cambridge: Cambridge University Press.

Leitzel, James. 1997. "Rule Evasion in Transitional Russia." In *Transforming Post-Communist Political Economies,* ed. Joan M. Nelson, Charles Tilly, and Lee Walker, 118–28. Washington, D.C.: National Academy Press.

Lemarchand, René. 1981. "Comparative Political Clientelism: Structure, Process and Optic." In *Political Clientelism, Patronage, and Development,* ed. S. N. Eisenstadt and René Lemarchand. London: Sage.

Letki, Natalia. 2002. "Lustration and Democratisation in East-Central Europe." *Europe-Asia Studies* 54 (4): 529–52.

Levada, Iurii. 1993. *Sovetskii prostoi chelovek.* Moscow: Mirovoi okean.

Levitsky, Steven. 2001. "An 'Organised Disorganisation': Informal Organisation and the Persistence of Local Party Structures in Argentine Peronism." *Journal of Latin American Studies* 33: 29–65.

Levitsky, Steven, and Lucan A. Way. 2002. "The Rise of Competitive Authoritarianism." *Journal of Democracy* 13 (2): 51–65.

Lewin, M. 1985. *The Making of the Soviet System: Essays in the Social History of Interwar Russia.* New York: Pantheon.

Lin, Y. M. 2000. "Rethinking China's Economic Transformation." *Contemporary Sociology* 29 (4): 608–13.

Lisovskii, Sergei F. 2000. *Politicheskaia reklama.* Moscow: IVTs Marketing.

Lisovskii, Sergei F., and Vladimir A. Evstaf'ev. 2000. *Izbiratel'nye tekhnologii: Istoriia, teoriia, praktika.* Moscow: RAU Universitet.

Litvinenko, A. 2002. *LPG: Lubiankaia prestupnaia gruppirovka: Ofitser FSB daet pokazaniia.* New York: Grani.

Liubarev, A. E. 2001. *Vybory v Moskve: opyt dvenadtsati let 1989–2000.* Moscow: Stol'nyi Grad.

Lloyd, John. 1999. "The Secret Policeman's Plot." *New Statesman.* August 16.

Lonkila, Markku. 1999. *Social Networks in Post-Soviet Russia.* Helsinki: Kikimora Publications.

Lopatin, V. V., and L. E. Lopatina. 1998. *Russkii tolkovyi slovar.* 5th ed. Moscow: Russkii iazyk.

Lukashev, A. V., and A. V. Ponidelko. 2002. *Chernyi PR kak sposob ovladeniia vlast'iu, ili bomba dlia imidzhmeikera.* St. Petersburg: Biznes-Pressa.

Macaulay, Stewart. 1992. "Non-Contractual Relations in Business: A Preliminary Study." In *The Sociology of Economic Life,* ed. Mark Granovetta and Richard Swedberg, 265–83. Boulder, Colo.: Westview Press. (Orig. pub. 1963.)

Maher, K. H. 1997. "The Role of Mass Values." In *Democratic Theory and Post-Communist Change,* ed. R. Grey: 79–105. Englewood Cliffs, N.J.: Prentice Hall.

Makarov, V. L., and G. B. Kleiner, 1996. "Barter in Russian Economy: Characteristics in Transition Period." Working Paper WP96/006. Moscow, CEMI Russian Academy of Sciences.

——. 1997. "Barter in the Economy of Transition: Specifics and Tendencies." *Ekonomika i matematicheskie metody* 33 (2).

Markhinin, V. V., A. N. Nysanbaev, and V. S. Shmakov. 2001. "Modernizatsionnye protsessy v sel'skikh lokal'nykh soobshchestvakh." *Sotsiologicheskie issledovaniia* 1 (12): 53–58.

McAndrew, D. 1999. "The Structural Analysis of Criminal Networks." In *The Social Psychology of Crime,* ed. D. Canter and L. Alison, 52–92. Aldershot, U.K.: Ashgate.

McAuley, Mary. 1997. *Russia's Politics of Uncertainty.* Cambridge: Cambridge University Press.

Mehnert, Klaus. 1962. *Soviet Man and His World.* Trans. Maurice Rosenbaum. New York: Frederick A. Praeger. (Orig. pub. 1958.)

Melnikov, A. 2000. "Sudebnye pristavy—eto ispolnitel'naia vlast'." *Rossiiskaia iustitsiia* 4: 26–27.

Mel'vil, Andrei Iu. 1998. "Politicheskie tsennosti, orientatsii i politicheskie instituty." In *Rossiia Politicheskaia,* ed. Liliia Shevtsova, 139–94. Moscow: Carnegie Endowment for International Peace.

Mendez, J. E., G. O'Donnell, and P. S. Pinheiro, eds. 1999. *The (Un)Rule of Law and the Underprivileged in Latin America.* Notre Dame, Ind.: University of Notre Dame Press.

Merkel, Wolfgang, and Aurel Croissant. 2000. "Formale Institutionen und informale Regeln in defekten Demokratien." *Politische Vierteljahresschrift* 41 (1): 3–30.

Mikul'skii, K.I., ed. 1995. *Elita Rossii: o nastoiashchem i budushchem strany*. Moscow: Vekhi.

Miller A., V. Hesli, and W. Reisinger. 1997. "Conceptions of Democracy among Mass and Elite in Post-Soviet Societies." *British Journal of Political Science* 27 (2): 158–79.

Miller, John. 1998. "Settling Accounts with a Secret Police: The German Law on the Stasi Records." *Europe-Asia Studies* 50 (2): 305–30.

Minchenko, Evgenii N. 2001. *Kak stat' i ostat'sia gubernatorom*. Cheliabinsk: Ural L.T.D.

Mondry, Henrietta, and John R. Taylor. 1992. "On Lying in Russian." *Language and Communication* 12 (2): 133–43.

Mukhin, A. A. 2000. *Informatsionnaia voina v Rossii: Uchastniki, tseli, tekhnologii*. Moscow: Tsentr politicheskoi informatsii.

Mukhin, Aleksei. 2002. *Novye pravila igry dlia bol'shogo biznesa: Prodiktovannye logikoi pravleniia V. V. Putina*. Moscow: GNOM.

Murray, Brian. 2000. "Dollars and Sense: Foreign Investment in Russia and China." *Problems of Post-Communism* 47: 24–33.

Naishul', Vitalii A. 1991. *The Supreme and Late Stage of Socialism: An Essay*. London: Centre for Research into Communist Economies. Russian text is available at http://lib.rin.ru (accessed April 2006).

Nicaso, Antonio. 2000a. "The Code of Honour." *Tandem*. July 9–16.

———. 2000b. "The Fire within Russia's Gang Warfare." *Tandem*. June 25–July 2.

———. 2000c. "The Ruthless Russian Connection." *Tandem*. June 18–25.

———. 2000d. "The Violent Birth of the *Vory v Zakone*." *Tandem*. July 2–9.

Nicholson, Martin. 1999. "Towards a Russia of the Regions." *Adelphi paper* no. 330, International Institute for Strategic Studies, London.

Nomokonov, Vitaly A. 2000. "On Strategies for Combating Corruption in Russia." *Demokratizatsiia* 8 (1).

North, Douglass C. 1990. *Institutions, Institutional Change and Economic Performance*. Cambridge: Cambridge University Press.

———. 1991. "Institutions." *Journal of Economic Perspectives* 5 (1): 97–112.

———. 1997. "Understanding Economic Change." In *Transforming Post-Communist Political Economies*, ed. J. M. Nelson et al., 13–19. Washington, D.C.: National Academy Press.

Nove, Alec. 1993. *An Economic History of the USSR, 1917–1991*. 3d ed. London: Penguin Economics.

Nureev, R. M., ed. 2000. *Transformatsia ekonomicheskikh institutov v postsovetskoi Rossii*. Moscow: Moskovskii obschestvennyi nauchnyi fond.

O'Donnell, Guillermo. 1996. "Illusions about Consolidation." *Journal of Democracy* 7 (2): 34–51.

Oda, Hiroshi 2002. *Russian Commercial Law*. The Hague: Kluwer Law International.

OECD (Organization for Economic Cooperation and Development). 2004. *OECD Economic Surveys: Russian Federation*. Paris: OECD.

Oleinik, A. 2001. "Biznes 'po poniatiiam: Ob institutsional'noi modeli Rossiiskogo kapitalizma." *Voprosy Ekonomiki* 5: 4–25.

———. 2003. *Organized Crime, Prison and Post-Soviet Societies*. Aldershot, U.K.: Ashgate.

Olson, M. 1982. *The Rise and Decline of Nations*. New Haven: Yale University Press.

OSCE (Organization for Security and Cooperation in Europe). 2004. "Russian Federation: Elections to the State Duma 7 December 2003, OSCE/ODIHR Election Observation Mission Report." http://www.osce.org/odihr/ (accessed October 2005).

"Osnovnye pokazateli raboty arbitrazhnykh sudov Rossiiskoi federatsii v 1999–2000 go-dakh." 2001. *Vestnik Vysshego Arbitrazhnogo Suda RF,* no. 4.

"Osnovnye pokazateli raboty arbitrazhnykh sudov Rossiiskoi federatsii v 2001–2002 go-dakh." 2003. *Vestnik Vysshego Arbitrazhnogo Suda RF,* no. 4.

Ozhegov, S. I., and N. Iu. Shvedova, eds. 1999. *Tolkovyi slovar' russkogo iazyka,* Russian Academy of Sciences, Institute of Russian Language. 4th ed.. Moscow: Azbukovnik.

Padgett, John, Philip Bonacich, John Skvoretz, and J. Scott. 2000. *Social Network Analysis.* London: Sage Publications.

Panarin, Igor' N. 2003. *Informatsionnaia voina i vybory.* Moscow: Gorodets.

Pappe, Iakov Sh. 2000. *Oligarkhi: Ekonomicheskaia khronika 1992–2000.* Moscow: Vysshaia shkola ekonomiki.

Pastukhov, Vladimir. 2002. "Law under Administrative Pressure in Post-Soviet Russia." *East European Constitutional Review* 11 (3): 66–74.

Pavlenko, Sergei. 2002. *Nauka oshibok.* Moscow: Tri kvadrata.

Pennings, Paul, Hans Keman, and Jan Kleinnijenuis. 1999. *Doing Research in Political Science.* London: Sage.

Petropavlovskii, Nikolai, Aleksei Sitnikov, Maksim Artem'ev, and Viktor Gaft. 1995. *Samyi korotkii put' k vlasti: Sbornik sovremennykh tekhnologii provedeniia politich-eskikh kampanii.* http://www.sitnikov.com/books/weg.phtml#_Toc506871549 (accessed April 8, 2005).

Pistor, K. 1997. "Company Law and Corporate Governance in Russia." In *The Rule of Law and Economic Reform in Russia,* ed. J. Sachs and K. Pistor. Boulder, Colo.: Westview.

Pleines, H. 2000. "Large-Scale Corruption in the Russian Banking Sector." In *Economic Crime in Russia,* ed. Alena Ledeneva and Marina Kurkchiyan. London: Kluwer Law International.

Pocheptsov, G. 2003. *Informatsionno-politicheskie tekhnologii,* Moscow: Tsentr.

Polanyi, Karl. 1944. *The Great Transformation.* New York: Reinhart.

Polanyi, K. 1957. "The Economy as Instituted Process." In *Trade and Market in the Early Empires,* ed. Karl Polanyi, Conrad Arensberg, and H. Pearson, 243–70. Glencoe, Ill.: Free Press.

Polishcuk, Leonid. 1997. "Missed Markets: Implications for Economic Behavior and Institutional Change." In *Transforming Post-Communist Political Economies,* ed. Joan M. Nelson, Charles Tilly, and Lee Walker, 80–101. Washington, D.C.: National Academy Press.

Portes, Alejandro. 1998. "Social Capital: Its Origins and Applications in Modern Sociology." *Annual Review of Sociology* 24: 1–24.

Povsednevnye praktiki i protsessy institutsional'noi transformatsii v Rossii. 2002. Moscow: ISP RAN.

Preobrazhenskii, A. G. 1959. *Etimologicheskii slovar' russkogo iazyka.* Moscow: State Publisher of Foreign and National Dictionaries.

Pribylovskii, Vladimir. 1999. *Mordodely: nekotorye sekrety tvorchestva politicheskikh imidzhmeikerov.* http://www.deadline.ru/default.asp?wci=clause&d_no=22326 (accessed September 8, 2002).

Putnam, Robert D. 1995a. "Bowling Alone: America's Declining Social Capital." *Journal of Democracy* 6 (1): 65–78.

———. 1995b. "Tuning In, Tuning Out: The Strange Disappearance of Social Capital in America." *PS* 28 (4): 664–83.

———. 1996. "The Strange Disappearance of Civic America." *American Prospect* 24: 34–48.

Putnam, Robert D., R. Leonardi, and R. Y. Nanetti. 1993. *Making Democracy Work: Civic Traditions in Modern Italy.* Princeton: Princeton University Press.

Radaev, Vadim. 1998. *Formirovanie novykh rossiiskikh rynkov: transaktsionnye izderzhki, formy kontrolia i delovaia etika.* Moscow: Tsentr politicheskikh tekhnologii.

———. 2000. "Corruption and Violence in Russian Business in the Late 1990s." In *Economic Crime in Russia,* ed. Alena Ledeneva and Marina Kurkchiyan, 63–82. London: Kluwer Law International.

———. 2001. "Deformalizatsiia pravil i ukhod ot nalogov v rossiiskoi ekonomike." In *Modernizatsiia Rossiiskoi ekonomiki.* Vol. 2, 255–70. Moscow: Vysshaia Shkola Ekonomiki.

———. 2002a. "Entrepreneurial Strategies and the Structure of Transaction Costs in Russian Business." In *The New Entrepreneurs of Europe and Asia,* ed. Victoria Bonnell and Thomas Gold. Armonk, N.Y.: M. E. Sharpe.

———. 2002b. "Informalization of the Rules in the Russian Economy." Draft paper, http://www.colbud.hu/honesty-trust/radaev (accessed September 2003).

Ricker, William. 1986. *The Art of Political Manipulation.* New Haven: Yale University Press.

Ries, Nancy. 1997. *Russian Talk: Culture and Conversation during Perestroika.* Ithaca: Cornell University Press.

———. 1999. "Business, Taxes, and Corruption in Russia." *Anthropology of East Europe Review* 17 (1).

Rigby, T. H. 1981. "Early Provincial Cliques and the Rise of Stalin." *Soviet Studies* 33 (1): 3–28.

———. 1986. "Was Stalin a Disloyal Patron?" *Soviet Studies* 38 (3): 311–24.

Risto, Alapuro. 1996. "Categories, Networks and Civil Society: Teachers' Social Ties in St. Petersburg." In *Civil Society in the European North: Concept and Context.* St. Petersburg: Centre for Independent Social Research.

Rose, Richard. 1983. "Getting by in the Three Economies: The Resources of the Official, Unofficial and Domestic Economies." *Studies in Public Polity* no. 110. Glasgow: University of Strathlyde.

———. 1999. "Living in an Anti-Modern Society." *East European Constitutional Review* 8 (1/2): 68–75.

———. 2002. *A Decade of New Russia Barometer Trends.* Cambridge: Cambridge University Press.

Rose, Richard, and Neil Munro. 2002. *Elections without Order: Russia's Challenge to Vladimir Putin.* Cambridge: Cambridge University Press.

Rose-Ackerman, Susan. 1999. *Corruption and Government: Causes, Consequences and Reform.* Cambridge: Cambridge University Press.

Ross, Cameron. 2002. *Regional Politics in Russia.* Manchester, U.K.: Manchester University Press.

Rozinskii, I. A. 2002. "Mekhanizmy polucheniia dokhodov i korporativnoe upravlenie v rossiiskoi ekonomike." In *Predpriiatiia Rossii: Korporativnoe upravlenie i rynochnye sdelki.* Moscow: GU-VSE.

Ryvkina, R. 1999. "Ot tenevoi economiki k tenevomu obshchestvu" (From a Shadow Economy to a Shadow Society). *Pro et Contra* 4 (1): 25–39.

——. 2001. *Drama peremen.* Moscow: Delo.

Sachs, Jeffrey D., Wing Thye Woo, and Xiaokai Yang. 2000. "Economic Reforms and Constitutional Transition." CID Working paper no. 43. April.

Sakwa, Richard. 2003. "Elections and National Integration in Russia." In *The 1999–2000 Elections in Russia: Their Impact and Legacy,* ed. Vicki L. Hesli and William M. Reisinger. New York: Cambridge University Press.

Salmi, Asta. 1995. *Institutionally Changing Business Networks.* Helsinki: Helsinki School of Economics and Business Administration.

Sampson, S. 1985–86. "Informal Sector in Eastern Europe." *Telos* (66): 44–66.

Sapozhnikov, S. A., and V. A. Ustiuzhaninov, 2003. *Kommentarii k Arbitrazhnomu protsessual'nomu kodeksu Rossiiskoi Federatsii: Sravnitel'nye tablitsy APK RF-1995—Novyi APK RF, Skhemy.* Moscow: Prior-Izdat.

Schelling, Thomas C. 1968. *The Strategy of Conflict,* Oxford: Oxford University Press.

Scheuch, Erwin K. 1990. "Development of Comparative Research." In *Comparative Methodology,* ed. Else Olsen, 19–37. London: Sage.

Schmidt, O. Iu., ed. 1937. *Bolshaia sovetskaia entsiklopedia.* Vol. 35. Moscow: Bolshaia sovietskaia entsiklopedia.

Schneider, Friedrich, and Dominik H. Enste. 2005. *The Shadow Economy: An International Survey.* Cambridge: Cambridge University Press.

Schopflin, George. 2000. *Politics in Eastern Europe.* Oxford: Blackwell.

Schteinberg, I. E. 1996. "Tendentsii transformatsii vlasti v postsovetskom sele." *Sotsis* 7: 21–27.

Scott, J. C. 1972. *Comparative Political Corruption.* Englewood Cliffs, N.J.: Prentice-Hall.

Seabright, Paul, ed. 2000. *The Vanishing Rouble: Barter Networks and Non-Monetary Transactions in Post-Soviet Societies.* Cambridge: Cambridge University Press.

Shanin, Teodor. 1972. *The Awkward Class. Political Sociology of Peasantry in a Developing Society. Russia 1910–1925.* Oxford: Oxford University Press.

Shanin, Teodor. 1986. *Russia as a Developing Society.* Vol. 1, *The Roots of Otherness: Russia's Turn of Century.* New Haven: Yale University Press.

Shanin, Teodor, and Evgenii Kovalev. 1996. *Golosa krest'ian: Sel'skaia Rossiia XX veka v krest'ianskikh memuarakh.* Moscow: Aspekt.

Shanin, Teodor, Aleksandr Nikulin, and Viktor Danilov. 2002. *Refleksivnoe krestianovedenie.* Moscow: MVSSES, Rossiiskaia politicheskaia entsiklopediia (ROSSPEN).

Shanskii, N.M. 1980. *Etimologicheskii slovar' russkogo iazyka.* Moscow: Moscow University Press.

Shapiro, S. P. 1987. "The Social Control of Impersonal Trust." *American Journal of Sociology* 93 (3): 623–58.

Sharlet, Robert. 2001. "Putin and the Politics of Law in Russia." *Post-Soviet Affairs* 17 (3): 195–234.

Shatit'ko, Andrei. 2003. "Anti-Globalization under Transformation: Administrative Barriers in Russian Economy at the Turn of the Millennium." In *Resistance to Globalisation: Political Struggle and Cultural Resilience in the Middle East, Russia, and Latin America,* ed. Harald Barrios, Martin Beck, Andreas Boeckh, and Klaus Segbers, 113–26. New Brunswick: Transaction.

Shcheldnov, V. Ia. et al. 1933. *Entsiklopedicheskii slovar'.* Vol. 26. Moscow: Granat.

Shenderovich, Viktor. 1998. *Kukly.* Moscow: Vagrius.

——. 1998. *Kukly 2.* Moscow: Vagrius.

——. 2002. *Zdes' bylo NTV.* Moscow: Zakharov.

Shenfield, Stephen. 1983. "*Pripiski:* False Statistical Reporting in Soviet-type Economies." In *Corruption: Causes, Consequences and Control,* ed. M. Clarke, 239–58. London: Francis Pinter.

Shlapentokh, Vladimir. 1984. *Love, Marriage, and Friendship in the Soviet Union: Ideals and Practices.* New York: Praeger.

——. 1989. *Public, and Private Life of the Soviet People: Changing Values in Post-Stalin Russia.* Oxford: Oxford University Press.

Shlapentokh, Vladimir. 1999. "Social Inequality in Post-Communist Russia: The Attitudes of the Political Elite and the Masses (1991–1998)." *Europe-Asia Studies* 51 (7): 1167–81.

Shleifer, Andrei. 1998. "State versus Private Ownership." *Journal of Economic Perspectives* 12: 133–50.

Shleifer, Andrei, and Dmitrii Vasiliev. 1996. "Management Ownership and Russian Privatisation." In *Corporate Governance in Eastern Europe and Russia.* Vol. 2, *Insiders and the State,* ed. Roman Frydman, Cheryl W. Gray, and Andrzej Rapaczynski. Oxford: Central European University Press.

Shleifer, Andrei, and R. Vishny. 1992. "Pervasive Shortages under Socialism." *RAND Journal of Economics* 23: 237–46.

——. 1993. "The Politics of Market Socialism." Working paper, Department of Economics, Harvard University.

——. 1998. *The Grabbing Hand: Government Pathologies and Their Cures.* London: Harvard University Press.

Shteinberg, Il'ia. 2002. "K voprosu ob opredelenii seti sotsial'noi podderzhki na sele." In *Refleksivnoe krestianovedenie,* T. Shanin, A. Nikulin, and V. Danilov. Moscow: MVSSES, Rossiiskaia politicheskaia entsiklopediia (ROSSPEN).

Sik, Endre. 1995. "Network Capital in Capitalist, Communist, and Post-Communist Societies." Helen Kellogg Institute for International Studies working paper no. 212. February. http://www.nd.edu/kellogg (accessed March 2001).

Sik, Endre, and Barry Wellman. 1999. "Network Capital in Capitalist, Communist and Post-Communist Countries." In *Networks in the Global Village,* ed. Barry Wellman, 225–55. Boulder, Colo.: Westview Press.

Simonova, M. S. 1969. "Otmena krugovoi poruki." In *Istoricheskie zapiski.* Vol. 83, ed. A. M. Samsonov. Moscow: Nauka.

Sitnikov, Aleksei. 2000. "Kak nas zavtra nazyvat'?" *Sovetnik* 9 (81): 4–6.

——. 2001. *Prikliucheniia nemyslimogo risoval'shchika.* Moscow: Imidzh-Kontakt.

Sitnikov, Aleksei, and M. Gundarin. 2003. *Pobeda bez pobeditelei: Ocherki teorii pragmaticheskoi kommunikatsii.* Moscow: Image-Kontakt.

Sitnikov, Aleksei et al. 2004. *Samye vliiatel'nye liudi Rossii—2003.* Moscow: Institut situatsionnogo analiza i novykh tekhnologii (ISANT).

Skocpol, Theda. 1996. "Unraveling from Above." *American Prospect* 25: 20–25.

Slater, Wendy, and Andrew Wilson. 2004. *The Legacy of the Soviet Union.* New York: Palgrave Macmillan.

Slider, Darrell. 1999. "Pskov under the LDPR: Dysfunctional Federalism in One Oblast." *Europe-Asia Studies* 51: 755–67.

Smart, Alan. 1993. "Gifts, Bribes, and Guanxi: A Reconsideration of Bourdieu's Social Capital." *Cultural Anthropology* 8: 388–408.

Smith, Gordon. 2001. "Russia and the Rule of Law." In *Developments in Russian Politics*, ed. Stephen White, Alex Pravda, and Zvi Gitelman. 5th ed. Basingstoke Hampshire. Duke University Press.

Smith, M. 2003. "Putin: An End to Centrifugalism?" In *Russian Regions and Regionalism: Strength through Weakness*, ed. G. Herd and A. Aldis. London: Routledge Curson.

Sokolov, Veniamin. 1998. "Privatization, Corruption and Reform in Present Day Russia." *Demokratizatsiia* 6 (4).

Solnick, Steven. 1998. *Stealing the State*. Cambridge, Mass.: Harvard University Press.

Solomon, Peter Jr. 2002. "Putin's Judicial Reform: Making Judges Accountable as Well as Independent." *East European Constitutional Review* 11, 1/2 (Winter/Spring): 117–24.

Solomon, Peter Jr., and Todd Foglesong. 2000. *Court and Transition in Russia: The Challenge of Judicial Reform*. Boulder, Colo.: Westview.

Solov'tev, A. I. 1998. "Osobennosti mekhanizma priniatiia gosudarstvennykh reshenii v postsovetskoi Rossii: Sotsiokul'turnye i psikhologicheskie parametry." In *Kuda idet Rossiia? Transformaciia sotsial'noi sfery i social'naia politika*, 155–64. Moscow: Delo.

Sparrow, M. 1991. "The Application of Network Analysis to Criminal Intelligence: An Assessment of the Prospects." *Social Networks* 13: 251–74.

Sreznevskaia, I. I., ed. 1965. *Slovar' drevnerusskogo iasyka*. Vol. 2, pt. 2. Reprint. St. Petersburg: Russian Academy of Sciences.

Staritskii, Dmitrii. 2003. "Chernyi piar v korporativnykh konfliktakh." *Sliianiia i poglashcheniia*, No. 2. http://www.compromat.ru (accessed March 2005).

Stark, David. 1994. "Path Dependence and Privatization Strategies in East Central Europe." In *Transition to Capitalism?* Ed. J. M. Kovacs. London: Transaction.

———. 2002. "Ambiguous Assets for Uncertain Environments: Heterarchy in Post-Socialist Firms." http://www.colbud.hu/honesty-trust (accessed January 2004).

Stark, David, and B. Vedrez. 2003. "The Social Times of Networks Spaces: Sequence Analysis of Network Formation and Foreign Investment." Paper presented at the Workshop on Networks and Markets, Santa Fe Institute.

Stark, David, and Laszlo Bruszt. 1998. *Postsocialist Pathways: Transforming Politics and Property in East Central Europe*. Cambridge: Cambridge University Press.

———. 2001. "One Way or Multiple Paths? For a Comparative Sociology of European Capitalism." *American Journal of Sociology* 106 (4): 1129–37.

State Statistical Bureau, People's Republic of China. 1999. *China Statistical Yearbook*. Beijing: State Statistical Bureau.

Stiglitz, Joseph. 2002. *Globalization and Its Discontents*. New York: W. W. Norton.

Stouffer, S. A., and J. Toby. 1951. "Role Conflict and Personality." *American Journal of Sociology* 56 (5): 395–406.

Streletskii, Valerii. 1998. *Mrakobesie*. Moscow: Detektiv.

Sun, Yan. 1999. "Reform, State, and Corruption: Is Corruption Less Destructive in China Than in Russia?" *Comparative Politics* 32 (1): 1–20.

Szilagyi, Akos. 2000. "A nagy kompromat (I)." *2000* (January–February): 7–24.

Tanzi, Vito. 1998. "Corruption around the World." *IMF Staff Papers* 45 (4).

Tanzi, Vito, and Parthasarathi Shome. 1993. "A Primer on Tax Evasion." *IMF Staff Papers* 40 (4).

Thompson, John. 2000. *Political Scandal: Power and Visibility in the Media Age*. Cambridge: Polity Press.

Tian-Shanskaia, Olga S. 1993. *Village Life in Late Tsarist Russia: An Ethnology*. Bloomington: Indiana University Press.

Tikhomirov, Vladimir. 1997. "Capital Flight from Post-Soviet Russia." *Europe-Asia Studies* 49: 591–615.

Tilly, Charles. 1998. *Durable Inequality*. Berkeley: University of California Press.

———. 2005. *Trust and Rule*. New York: Cambridge University Press.

Tolkovyi slovar' sovremennogo russkogo iazyka: Iazykovye izmeneniia kontsa XX stoletiia. 2001. Moscow.

Tompson, William. 1997. "Old Habits Die Hard: Fiscal Imperatives, State Regulations and the Role of Russia's Banks." *Europe-Asia Studies* 49: 1159–85.

Topil'skaia, Elena V. 1999. *Organizovannaia prestupnost'*. St. Petersburg: Iuridicheskii tsentr.

Tosunian, Garegin. 1995. *Bankovskoe delo i bankovskoe zakonodatel'stvo v Rossii: Opyt, problemy, perspektivy*. Moscow: Delo.

Trompenaars, Fons, and Charles Hampden-Turner. 1998. *Riding the Waves of Culture: Understanding Diversity in Global Business*. 2d ed. New York: McGraw-Hill.

Tsepliaev, Vitalii. 2000. "Analiz. KOMPROMATershchina." *Argymenty i Fakty*. December 12.

Tsyganenko, G. P. 1970. Etimologicheskii slovar' russkogo iazyka. Kiev: Radians'ka shkola.

Uzzi, B. 1996. "The Sources and Consequences of Embeddedness for the Economic Performance of Organizations: The Network Effect." *American Sociological Review* 61 (4): 674–98.

Vainshtein, G. 1998. "Mezhdu polnoi nesvobodoi i polnym khaosom (o prirode politicheskoi sistemy sovremennoi Rossii." *Pro et Contra* 3 (3): 40–56.

Varese, Federico. 2000. "Pervasive Corruption." In *Economic Crime in Russia*, ed. Alena Ledeneva and Marina Kurkchiyan, 99–111. London: Kluwer Law International.

———. 2001. *The Russian Mafia: Private Protection in a New Market Economy*. Oxford: Oxford University Press.

Verdery, Katherine. 2003. *The Vanishing Hectare: Property and Value in Postsocialist Transylvania*. Ithaca: Cornell University Press.

Vinogradova, Elena. 2005. "The Big Issue of Small Businesses: Contract Enforcement in the New Russia." In *Sociology*. College Park: University of Maryland.

Volkov, Vadim. 1999. "Violent Entrepreneurship in Post-Communist Russia." *Europe-Asia Studies* 51: 741–54.

———. 2000a. "Between Economy and the State: Private Security and Rule Enforcement in Russia." *Politics and Society* 28: 483–501.

———, ed. 2000b. *Konkurentsiia za nalogoplatel'shchika*. Moscow: Moskovskii obschestvennyi nauchnyi fond.

———. 2002. *Violent Entrepreneurs: The Use of Force in the Making of Russian Capitalism*. Ithaca: Cornell University Press.

———. 2004. "The Selective Use of State Capacity in Russia's Economy: Property Disputes and Enterprise Takeovers, 1998–2002." In *Trust in Post-Socialist Economies*, ed. Janos Kornai, Susan Rose-Ackerman, and Bo Rothstein. New York: Macmillan.

Vvedenskii, B. A., ed. 1953. *Entsiklopedicheskii slovar'*. Moscow: Bolshaia sovietskaia entsiklopediia.

———. 1957. *Bolshaia sovietskaia entsiklopediia. Ezhegodnik*. Moscow: Bolshaia sovietskaia entsiklopediia.

Waller, J. M. 1994. *Secret Empire: The KGB in Russia Today.* Oxford and Boulder, Colo.: Westview.

Wedel, Janine R. 1998. *Collision and Collusion: The Strange Case of Western Aid to Eastern Europe 1989–1998.* New York: St. Martin's Press.

Weiner, Douglas. 1999. *A Little Corner of Freedom: Russian Nature Protection from Stalin to Gorbachev.* Berkeley: University of California Press.

Wellman, Barry, ed. 1999. *Networks in the Global Village.* Boulder, Colo.: Westview.

Wellman, Barry, and S. D. Berkowitz, 1988. *Social Structures: A Network Approach.* Cambridge: Cambridge University Press.

Wellman, Barry, and Scot Wortley. 1990. "Different Strokes for Different Folks: Community Ties and Social Support." *American Journal of Sociology* 96: 558–88.

Welsh, Helga A. 1996. "Dealing with the Communist Past: Central and East European Experiences after 1990." *Europe-Asia Studies* 48 (3): 413–28.

White, Harrison. 1992. *Identity and Control.* Princeton: Princeton University Press.

White, Stephen, and Olga Kryshtanovskaya. 1993. "Public Attitudes to the KGB: A Research Note." *Europe-Asia Studies* 45 (1): 169–75.

Whitefield, Stephen, ed. 2005. Political Culture and Post-Communism. London: Palgrave.

Williams, Kieran. 2000. "The Rhetoric of Lustration." *Masaryk Journal* 3 (1): 178–84.

Williams, Phil. 1997. *Russian Organized Crime, The New Threat?* London: Frank Cass.

Wilson, Andrew. 2005. *Virtual Politics: Faking Democracy in the Post-Soviet World.* Princeton: Yale University Press.

Wolosky, Lee S. 2000. "Putin's Plutocrat Problem." *Foreign Affairs,* March–April, 79.

Woodruff, David. 1998. "Barter of the Bankrupt: The Politics of Demonetization in Russia's Federal State." In *Uncertain Transition: Ethnographies of Change in a Post-Socialist World,* ed. Michael Burawoy and Katherine Verdery. Lanham, Md.: Rowman and Littlefield.

Woodruff, David. 2000a. *Money Unmade: Barter and the Fate of Russian Capitalism.* Ithaca: Cornell University Press.

——. 2000b. "Rules for Followers: Institutional Theory and the New Politics of Economic Backwardness in Russia." *Politics and Society* 28 (4): 437–82.

Wyman, Matthew. 2000. "Public Opinion and Political Institutions." In *Institutions and Political Change in Russia,* ed. Neil Robinson: 173–192. London: Macmillan.

——. 2002. "Ten Years On, What Do Russians Think?" In *Russia After Communism,* ed. Rick Fawn and Stephen White. Portland: Frank Cass.

Yaney, George L. 1973. *The Systematization of Russian Government: Social Evolution in the Domestic Administration of Imperial Russia,* 1711–1905. Urbana: University of Illinois Press.

Yang, Mayfair Mei-hui. 1994. *Gifts, Favors and Banquets: The Art of Social Relationships in China.* Ithaca: Cornell University Press.

——. 2002. "The Resilience of *Guanxi* and Its New Deployments: A Critique of Some New Guanxi Scholarship." *China Quarterly* 170: 459–76.

Yergin, Daniel, and Thane Gustafson. 1994. *Russia: 2010.* London: Nicholas Brealy.

Yeung, Henry Wai-chung. 2000. "Globalizing Chinese Business Firms." In *Globalization of Chinese Business Firms,* ed. Henry Wai-chung Yeung and Kris Olds. New York: St. Martin's Press.

Yurchak, Alexei. 2005. *Everything Was Forever, Until It Was No More: The Last Soviet Generation (In-formation)*. Princeton: Princeton University Press.

Zheleznov, V. Ia. et al., eds. 1933. *Entsiklopedicheskii slovar'*. 7th ed. Vol. 26. Moscow: Granat.

Zhukov, Ie. M., ed. 1976. *Sovietskaia istoricheskaia entsiklopediia*. Vol. 16. Moscow: Sovetskaia entsiklopediia.

Zinoviev, A. 1978. *The Yawning Heights*. Trans. G. Clough. London: Bodley Head.

Zudin, A. Iu. 1999. "Kul'tura sovetskogo obshchestva: Logika politicheskoi transformatsii." *Obschestvennye nauki i sovremennost'* 3: 59–72.

Index